Human Trafficking

Human Trafficking

SECOND EDITION

Cheryl Taylor Page
DIRECTOR OF EXPERIENTIAL LEARNING AND LAW PROFESSOR
SOUTHERN ILLINOIS UNIVERSITY
SCHOOL OF LAW

Bill Piatt
PROFESSOR OF LAW AND FORMER DEAN
ST. MARY'S UNIVERSITY SCHOOL OF LAW

CAROLINA ACADEMIC PRESS
Durham, North Carolina

Library of Congress Cataloging-in-Publication Data
Names: Page, Cheryl Taylor, author. | Piatt, Bill, author.
Title: Human trafficking / by Cheryl Taylor Page, Robert William Piatt, Jr.
Description: Second edition. | Durham, North Carolina : Carolina Academic Press, LLC, [2022] | Includes bibliographical references and index.
Identifiers: LCCN 2022023501 (print) | LCCN 2022023502 (ebook) | ISBN 9781531023836 (paperback) | ISBN 9781531023843 (ebook)
Subjects: LCSH: Human trafficking--Law and legislation--United States. | Human trafficking--Prevention--United States. | Prostitution--Law and legislation--United States.
Classification: LCC KF9449 .P34 2022 (print) | LCC KF9449 (ebook) | DDC 364.15/510973--dc23/eng/20220729
LC record available at https://lccn.loc.gov/2022023501
LC ebook record available at https://lccn.loc.gov/2022023502

Carolina Academic Press
700 Kent Street
Durham, North Carolina 27701
(919) 489-7486
www.cap-press.com

Printed in the United States of America

Cheryl Taylor Page

I would like to dedicate this book to my awesome husband, James B. Page, III, who loves, supports, and encourages me in all my endeavors, and my two wonderful sons, Nathaniel Hugh George and Gabriel Blair George, who have loved and believed in me from the very beginning.

Bill Piatt

To my mom, Betty

To my wife, Chris

To my children: Seana, Bob, Alicia

To my grandchildren:
Fallyn, Max, Rory, William, Julia, Noah, Caroline, Eva, and Jonah

To my great-great-niece, Kyara

And to my honorary granddaughter, Sophia

Contents

Acknowledgments

We wish to thank Maria Vega (Legal Administrative Assistant, St. Mary's University School of Law) for her line editing and technical assistance in the preparation of our manuscript.

We wish to thank our research assistants, Karen Crawford and Jacob Hernandez.

The following entities and publications granted permission to reprint portions of previously published material included in this book. We wish to thank them for the permission, and for their cooperation and assistance:

Creighton Law Review
Florida Coastal Law Review
Gonzaga Journal of International Law
Illinois Law Enforcement Training and Standards Board Executive Institute
Knoxville Bar Association
Western Journal of Criminal Justice

Finally, Professor Page offers: I'd like to thank my husband, James Page. He allows me to bounce ideas off of him and steers me straight when I've wandered off the path! He has always been my North Star. I'd also like to thank my two incredible sons, Nathaniel and Gabriel George. They've believed in me their entire lives and have supported me from day one. I'd also like to thank my Florida A&M Human Trafficking Law class (Spring 2020 and Spring 2021). These students are amazing and exemplify honor, courage and dignity and I'm looking forward to their contribution to the legal field and the eradication of modern-day slavery. I'd like to recognize my Mentor, Judy Boyle. She is the ROCK upon which I stand for all that involves human exploitation. She has taught me more than she'll ever know and I'm eternally grateful. And finally, I'd like to dedicate this book to my mother, Georgiana G. Taylor and my father, James P. Taylor. They were my first teachers and instilled in me the principle of valuing everyone no matter who they are. My parents lived out the creed, do unto others as you'd have done unto you. Thank you momma and daddy. Thank you!

Human Trafficking

Chapter 1

Introduction

We are about to undertake an examination of a horrible phenomenon: human trafficking. We write from our academic, and importantly, from our personal perspectives, all formed by our personal experiences and life stories. Professor Page, an African-American, is a law professor and former prosecutor. She has published and lectured domestically and internationally on the scourge of trafficking. She has a personal basis for understanding the evils of slavery and her concern with the plight of contemporary slaves will be felt throughout this work. Professor Piatt is a Hispanic/Indigenous (Genízaro) law professor and former law school dean. He has written and lectured extensively in this country and abroad, in Spanish and English, on human rights issues for decades, and now brings his background in immigration law concerns to the discussion of the abolition of trafficking and the protection of its victims. We undertake this examination with the hope that an understanding of the complexities of this human tragedy might ultimately lead to an improvement in efforts to reduce its impact on humankind. Nobody, however, should be led to believe that addressing human trafficking concerns will be an easy task, nor that this will be accomplished in the near future. We begin our study with the brief attempt to understand some basic background of these topics. Subsequent chapters will consider varying aspects of the challenges involved.

A. What Is Human Trafficking?

The informal answer to this inquiry is that human trafficking is slavery. More formal definitions can be found in international and domestic sources. For example, the United Nations Protocol to Prevent, Suppress and Punish Trafficking in Persons, Especially Women and Children[1] provides, in part:

> "Trafficking in persons" shall mean the recruitment, transportation, transfer, harbouring or receipt of persons, by means of the threat or use of force or other forms of coercion, of abduction, of fraud, of deception, of the abuse of power or of a position of vulnerability or of the giving or receiving of payments or benefits to achieve the consent of a person having control over another person, for the purpose of exploitation. Exploitation shall include, at a minimum, the exploitation of the prostitution of others or other forms of sexual exploitation, forced labour or services, slavery or practices similar to slavery, servitude or the removal of organs; (b) The consent of a victim of trafficking in persons to the intended exploitation set forth in subparagraph (a) of this article shall be irrelevant where any of the means set forth in subparagraph (a) have been used...

The United States has adopted the following definition of "severe forms of trafficking in persons" for purposes of immigration relief for trafficking victims, as part of the Victims of Trafficking and Violence Protection of 2000[2] discussed in detail in Chapter 4 below:

> Severe forms of trafficking in persons means sex trafficking in which a commercial sex act is induced by force, fraud, or coercion, or in which the person induced to perform such act has

1. United Nations Office of the High Commissioner for Human Rights, *Protocol to Prevent, Suppress and Punish Trafficking in Persons Especially Women and Children, supplementing the United Nations Convention Against Transnational Organized Crime*, General Assembly resolution 55/25 (15 Nov. 2000), http://www.ohchr.org/EN/ProfessionalInterest/Pages/ProtocolTraffickingInPersons.aspx.

2. The Victims of Trafficking: and Violence Protection Act of 2000, Pub. L. No. 106-386, 114 Stat. 1464 (codified as amended in various titles of U.S.C.).

> not attained 18 years of age; or the recruitment, harboring, transportation, provision, or obtaining of a person for labor or services, through the use of force, fraud, or coercion for the purpose of subjection to involuntary servitude, peonage, debt bondage, or slavery.

Sex trafficking means "the recruitment, harboring, transportation, provision, or obtaining of a person for the purpose of a commercial sex act."[3]

Note that both the international and domestic definitions of human trafficking involve two broad components: sex trafficking, and labor trafficking. Both involve elements of coercion, meaning that issues arise where the alleged victim, an adult, has "consented." We will explore the controversial topic of when, if ever, participation in prostitution should be viewed as voluntary in Chapter 5 below. This element surfaces in the immigration context as well, in both sex and labor trafficking matters. (*See* Chapter 4.)

The scope of the problem is staggering. The Polaris Project (discussed in Chapter 7) notes that human trafficking worldwide is a $150 billion industry, involving 20.9 million victims worldwide. Of these victims, 55% are women and children. (*See* the website of the Polaris Project.) Of course, it is impossible to accurately document all illicit trafficking activities. Attempting to locate these victims and help them escape is discussed in Chapter 7.

The Department of State of the United States offers additional background to help the reader grasp the scope of the discussion of what is human trafficking. In its 2021 Trafficking in Persons Report (TIP) the Secretary of State provides this background:

> **Understanding Human Trafficking**
>
> "Trafficking in persons," "human trafficking," and "modern slavery" are umbrella terms — often used interchangeably — to refer to a crime whereby traffickers exploit and profit at the expense of adults or children by compelling them to perform labor or engage in commercial sex. When a person younger than

3. The Victims of Trafficking: and Violence Protection Act of 2000, 22 U.S.C. 7102.

18 is used to perform a commercial sex act, it is a crime regardless of whether there is any force, fraud, or coercion.

The United States recognizes two primary forms of trafficking in persons: forced labor and sex trafficking. The basic meaning of these forms of human trafficking and some unique characteristics of each are set forth below, followed by several key principles and concepts that relate to all forms of human trafficking.

More than 175 nations have ratified or acceded to the UN Protocol to Prevent, Suppress and Punish Trafficking in Persons (the UN TIP Protocol), which defines trafficking in persons and contains obligations to prevent and combat the crime.

The United States' Trafficking Victims Protection Act of 2000, as amended (TVPA), and the UN TIP Protocol contain similar definitions of human trafficking. The elements of both definitions can be described using a three-element framework focused on the trafficker's 1) acts; 2) means; and 3) purpose. All three elements are essential to form a human trafficking violation.

Forced Labor

Forced labor, also referred to as "labor trafficking," encompasses the range of activities involved when a person uses force, fraud, or coercion to obtain the labor or services of another person.

The "**acts**" element of forced labor is met when the trafficker recruits, harbors, transports, provides, or obtains a person for labor or services.

The "**means**" element of forced labor includes a trafficker's use of force, fraud, or coercion. The coercive scheme can include threats of force, debt manipulation, withholding of pay, confiscation of identity documents, psychological coercion, reputational harm, manipulation of the use of addictive substances, threats to other people, or other forms of coercion.

The "**purpose**" element focuses on the perpetrator's goal to secure labor or services. There is no limit on the location or type of industry. Traffickers can commit this crime in any sector or setting, whether legal or illicit, including but not limited to agricultural fields, factories, restaurants, hotels, massage parlors, retail stores, fishing vessels, mines, private homes, or drug trafficking operations.

All three elements are essential to constitute the crime of forced labor.

There are certain types of forced labor that are frequently distinguished for emphasis or because they are widespread:

Domestic Servitude

"Domestic servitude" is a form of forced labor in which the trafficker requires a victim to perform work in a private residence. Such circumstances create unique vulnerabilities. Domestic workers are often isolated and may work alone in a house. Their employer often controls their access to food, transportation, and housing. What happens in a private residence is hidden from the world — including from law enforcement and labor inspectors — resulting in barriers to victim identification. Foreign domestic workers are particularly vulnerable to abuse due to language and cultural barriers, as well as a lack of community ties. Some perpetrators use these types of conditions as part of their coercive schemes to compel the labor of domestic workers with little risk of detection.

Forced Child Labor

The term "forced child labor" describes forced labor schemes in which traffickers compel children to work. Traffickers often target children because they are more vulnerable. Although some children may legally engage in certain forms of work, forcing or coercing children to work remains illegal. Forms of slavery or slavery-like practices — including the sale of children, forced or compulsory child labor, and debt bondage and serfdom of children — continue to exist, despite legal prohibitions and widespread condemnation. Some indicators of forced labor of a child include situations in which the child appears to be in the custody of a non-family member and the child's work financially benefits someone outside the child's family; or the denial of food, rest, or schooling to a child who is working.

Sex Trafficking

Sex trafficking encompasses the range of activities involved when a trafficker uses force, fraud, or coercion to compel another person to engage in a commercial sex act or causes a child to engage in a commercial sex act.

The crime of sex trafficking can also be understood through the "acts," "means," and "purpose" framework. All three elements are required to establish a sex trafficking crime (except in the case of child sex trafficking where the means are irrelevant).

The "**acts**" element of sex trafficking is met when a trafficker recruits, harbors, transports, provides, obtains, patronizes, or solicits another person to engage in commercial sex.

The "**means**" element of sex trafficking occurs when a trafficker uses force, fraud, or coercion. Coercion in the case of sex trafficking includes the broad array of nonviolent means included in the forced labor definition. These can include serious harm, psychosocial harm, reputational harm, threats to others, and debt manipulation.

The "**purpose**" element in every sex trafficking case is the same: to engage in a commercial sex act. Sex trafficking can take place in private homes, massage parlors, hotels, or brothels, among other locations, as well as on the internet.

Child Sex Trafficking

In cases where an individual engages in any of the specified "acts" with a child (under the age of 18), the means element is irrelevant regardless of whether evidence of force, fraud, or coercion exists. The use of children in commercial sex is prohibited by law in the United States and most countries around the world.

Key Principles and Concepts

These key principles and concepts relate to all forms of trafficking in persons, including forced labor and sex trafficking.

Consent

Human trafficking can take place even if the victim initially consented to providing labor, services, or commercial sex acts. The analysis is primarily focused on the trafficker's conduct and not that of the victim. A trafficker can target a victim after a victim applies for a job or migrates to earn a living. The trafficker's coercive scheme is what matters, not a victim's prior consent or ability to meaningfully consent thereafter. Likewise, in a sex trafficking case, an adult victim's initial willingness to engage in commercial sex acts is not relevant where a perpetrator subsequently uses coercion to exploit the victim and cause them to continue engaging in the same acts. In the case of child sex trafficking, the consent of the victim is never relevant as a child cannot legally consent to commercial sex.

Movement

Neither U.S. law nor international law requires that a trafficker or victim move across a border for a human trafficking offense to take place. Trafficking in persons is a crime of exploitation and coercion, and not movement. Traffickers can use schemes that take victims hundreds of miles away from their homes, or exploit them in the same neighborhoods where they were born.

Debt Bondage

"Debt bondage" is focused on human trafficking crimes in which the trafficker's primary means of coercion is debt manipulation. U.S. law prohibits perpetrators from using debts as part of their scheme, plan, or pattern to compel a person to work or engage in commercial sex. Traffickers target some individuals with an initial debt assumed willingly as a condition of future employment, while in certain countries traffickers tell individuals they "inherited" the debt from relatives. Traffickers can also manipulate debts after the economic relationship begins by withholding earnings or forcing the victim to assume debts for expenses like food, housing, or transportation. They can also manipulate debts a victim owes to other people. When traffickers use debts as a means to compel labor or commercial sex, they have committed a crime.

Non-Penalization

Consistent with the definition of human trafficking, governments should not penalize or prosecute victims of trafficking in persons for the unlawful acts their trafficker compelled them to commit. This principle aims to protect victims from being held legally responsible for conduct that was not their choice, but rather was driven by their trafficker. If a government has penalized or punished a victim in such a way, the government should vacate the conviction and/or expunge the victim's record.

State-Sponsored Human Trafficking

While the TVPA and UN TIP Protocol call on governments to proactively address trafficking crimes, some governments are part of the problem, directly compelling their citizens into sexual slavery or forced labor schemes. From forced labor in local or national public work projects, military operations, and economically important sectors, or as part of government-funded projects or missions abroad, officials use their power to exploit their nationals. To extract this work, governments coerce by threatening the withdrawal of public benefits, withholding salaries, failing to adhere to limits on national service, manipulating the lack of legal status of stateless individuals and other minority groups, threatening to punish family members, or conditioning services or freedom of movement on labor or sex. In 2019, Congress amended the TVPA to acknowledge that governments can also act as traffickers, referring specifically to a "government policy or pattern" of human trafficking, trafficking in government-funded programs, forced labor in government-affiliated medical services or other sectors, sexual slavery in government camps, or the employment or recruitment of child soldiers.

Unlawful Recruitment or Use of Child Soldiers

Another manifestation of human trafficking occurs when a governmental armed group (including police or other security forces), paramilitary organization, rebel group, or other non-state armed group unlawfully recruits or uses children—through force, fraud, or coercion—as combatants or in support roles. Such support roles include children serving as cooks, porters, guards, messengers, medics, servants, or spies. Children are also used as sex slaves. Sexual slavery, as referred to here, occurs when armed groups force or coerce children to "marry" or be raped by commanders or combatants. Both male and female children are often sexually abused or exploited by members of armed groups and suffer the same types of devastating physical and psychological consequences associated with sex trafficking.

Accountability in Supply Chains

Forced labor is well documented in the private economy, particularly in agriculture, fishing, manufacturing, construction, and domestic work; but no sector is immune. Sex trafficking occurs in several industries as well. Most well-known is the hospitality industry, but the crime also occurs in connection with extractive industries where activities are often remote and lack meaningful government presence. Governments should hold all entities, including businesses, accountable for human trafficking. In some countries, the law provides for corporate accountability in both the civil and criminal justice systems. The TVPA provides such liability for any legal person, including a business that benefits financially from its involvement in a human trafficking scheme, provided that the business knew or should have known of the scheme.

B. Is Human Trafficking a Problem Unique to Our Era?

Slavery is probably as old an institution as humankind itself. References to it, and escape from it, are as old as recorded history. For example, the second book of the Old Testament discusses the significance of the slavery imposed by the Egyptian Pharaoh on the Jews, and their escape from bondage under the leadership of Moses.[4] Slavery was a critical feature of Greek[5] and Roman[6] societies. An attempt to soften the institution appears in the writings of the apostle, Paul, where he urges masters to treat their slaves in a decent fashion, and at the same time urges slaves to respect their masters: "Slaves, obey your earthly masters in everything; and do it, not only when their eye is on you and to win their favor, but with sincerity of heart and reverence for the Lord.... Masters, provide your slaves with what is right and fair, because you know that you also have a Master in heaven."[7]

C. What Is the American Experience with Human Trafficking?

Obviously slavery is not an American invention, although its role in the formation of this nation played a critical function in the foundation and expansion of our country, as summarized in Chapter 4, below. Slave labor built the economy of the South, and enabled the development of industry in the North. The history of this tragedy, and its ultimate abolishment, fills many volumes. A system of slavery and peonage was imposed on Native Americans and others. Workers from China were lured to the American West under "agreements" which ultimately resulted in "indentured servitude, kidnapping, forced marriage, and forced prostitution."[8] Concerns regarding contemporary forced labor in this country

---

4. The book of *Exodus*, Zondervan, NIV Study Bible (2002). *See also*, David Meager, *Slavery in Bible Times*, Church Society, Autumn 2006, http://archive.churchsociety.org/crossway/documents/Cway_102_Slavery1.pdf.

5. *Slavery in Ancient Greece*, Crystal Links, http://www.crystalinks.com/greekslavery.html.

6. *Slavery in Ancient Rome*, Crystal Links, http://www.crystalinks.com/romeslavery.html.

7. *Colossians* 3:22 and 4:1, Zondervan, NIV Study Bible (2002). The notes accompanying this text at p. 1857 indicate that Paul's letter to the Colossians might have been delivered by Tychicus, to Philemon in Colosse, with Philemon's slave, Onesimus, accompanying Tychicus. *See also*, *The Apostle Paul, Freeing the Slaves, and Gender Equality*, JusticeBeforeCharity.org, http://justicebeforecharity.org/paul.php.

8. Ivy C. Lee & Mie Lewis, *Human Trafficking from A Legal Advocate's Perspective: History, Legal Framework and Current Anti-Trafficking Efforts*, 10 U.C. Davis J. Int'l L. & Pol'y 169, 175 (2003).

led to the inclusion of protection in an immigration context as we explore in Chapter 4.

At the same time, prostitution also played a role in the history of this country. In her article, *Nevada Sex Trade: A Gamble for the Workers*, Nicole Bingham provides a history of prostitution in the United States.[9] She notes that because men outnumbered women in the early history of the colonies, a market for prostitution was created. With increased industrialization and the arrivals of immigrant men who often had left their families behind, prostitution thrived, even though it was illegal. Some women, she observed, turned to prostitution to earn a living, while others viewed it as a means of "affection or escape," or as a means of finding a husband.[10] The expansion westward also produced imbalances in the number of men and women. That fact, coupled with the limited employment opportunities for women led to women working as prostitutes. Bingham notes that while illegal, prostitution was tolerated. It was viewed as a "necessary evil," because it kept "... virtuous women, married women in particular, safe from the sexual desires of men."[11] However, concern about the influx of foreign prostitutes led the U.S. Congress to enact an exclusion ground prohibiting those seeking to participate in prostitution to enter the United States. That prohibition continues today:

> **§ 40.24 Prostitution and Commercialized Vice**
>
> (a) Activities within ten years preceding visa application. An alien shall be ineligible under INA 12(a)(2)(D) only if—
> (1) The alien is coming to the United States solely, principally, or incidentally to engage in prostitution, or has engaged in prostitution, or the alien directly or indirectly procures or attempts to procure, or procured or attempted to procure or to import prostitutes or persons for the purposes of prostitution, or receives or received, in whole or in part, the proceeds of prostitution; and

---

9. Nicole Bingham, *Nevada Sex Trade: A Gamble for the Workers*, 10 Yale L.J. & Feminism 69 (1988); *see also* Vern Bullough & Bonnie Bullough, *Women and Prostitution: A Social History* 210–11 (1987).

10. *Id.* at 72.

11. *Id.* at 73.

(2) The alien has performed one of the activities listed in §40.24(a)(1) within the last ten years.[12]

Not all female immigrants who became prostitutes entered for that purpose. In the article by Lee and Lewis, the authors note that some immigrant girls from China were kidnapped and sold into prostitution. "Some were sold by their families who believed that their children would become indentured domestic servants or brides."[13] "Others were deceived by promises of honest, gainful employment opportunities in America and found themselves subsequently forced into prostitution or other exploitative labor upon arrival."[14] Unfortunately, that same type of deception and trafficking still exists.

However, there are a few areas in this country where prostitution is legal. Ten counties out of 16 in Nevada have active brothels.[15] Any county with population under 700,000 as of the last census is allowed to license a brothel.[16] Nevada Revised Statute (NRS) §201.354 1. "It is unlawful for any person to engage in prostitution or solicitation therefor, except in a licensed house of prostitution."[17] Proposed legislation in 2015, NV A.B. 354 (NS), "[r]evises provisions relating to human trafficking," but keeps the previous language regarding legal prostitution.[18] The debate as to whether sex workers should be allowed to engage in their work, and whether the U.S. government can withhold funds from groups advocating the legalization of prostitution, is discussed below in Chapter 5.

Currently the Polaris Project has determined that the top venues for forced labor trafficking in this country involve domestic work, traveling sales, restaurant and food services, agriculture, and health and beauty.

---

12. 22 C.F.R. §40.24 (2014).

13. Lee & Lewis, *supra* note 8, at 175; *see also* Robert G. Lee, *The Origins of Chinese Immigration to the United States 1848–1882*, *in* The Life, Influence And The Role Of The Chinese In The United States, 1776–1960, at 183 (Chinese Historical Society of America ed., 1976).

14. *Id.* at 176.

15. The Indy Explains: How legal prostitution works in Nevada - Nevada Brothel Association.

16. N.R.S. §244.345.

17. N.R.S. §201.354 1 *available at* www.westlawnext.com.

18. NV A.B. 354 (NS) (2015) *available at* www.westlawnext.com.

In the sex trafficking context, commercial brothels, hotel/motels, online ads, and escort services serve as the primary locations. While prostitution is the most recognizable form of human trafficking, it is critical to realize that forced labor issues exist throughout much of our economy. While we discuss both forms of trafficking throughout, and devote an entire chapter specifically to the issue of prostitution (Chapter 5), perhaps from the outset we should be aware of the very real possibility that we might actually be indirectly benefiting from labor trafficking.

D. Who Participates in, or Benefits from, Human Trafficking?

Let us assume that nobody reading this book owns slaves or participates in prostitution. Does that mean that we are not at least indirectly impacted by human trafficking? Do people inadvertently "use" slaves today? Consider some examples from the fishing, gold mining, clothing and agriculture industries.

1. Slavery at Sea

Working conditions aboard many commercial fishing vessels are among the worst in the world. At sea, vessels can operate without scrutiny, depending upon their flag and nationality and whether they operate in areas with limited monitoring, control, surveillance, and enforcement such as the high seas. Workers can encounter a whole spectrum of issues ranging from extremely low wages, inadequate sanitation, lack of safety equipment, lack of personal space and long working hours. Beyond these difficult conditions, there are documented cases of forced labor, human trafficking and even murder at sea. While the issue of labor abuse in the fisheries sector has been known for years it is only recently getting attention from mass media and news organizations and consequently from some buyers of seafood associated with documented slavery at sea.[19]

19. Greenpeace, *Slavery and Labor Abuse in the Fishing Sector* 2 (2014), *available at* http://www.greenpeace.org/international/Global/international/briefings/oceans/2014/Slavery-and-Labour-Abuse-in-the-Fishing-Sector.pdf.

Lack of control and enforcement, at time coupled with low profitability and the resulting race to catch and sell fish, often result in poor labor standards. The poor state of fish stocks, the fact that many fleets are operating in a state of excess fishing capacity (*i.e.*, overcapacity) and an increasing demand for cheap seafood, motivates companies to keep vessels at sea for longer periods of time and in more dangerous and inhumane conditions.[20]

With increased overheads and diminished yields, the incentives to employ cheap or forced laborers and to break fishing and environmental rules increase. The resulting human misery and environmental destruction often are hidden, with little or no opportunity for the crew to seek help or escape. These men are slaves on the high seas and have no way to get help or be rescued from a grueling life of bondage.[21]

It is important to ask, how does slavery continue to exist in such an open industry and in the 21st century? One reason could be the cooperation between local fishermen and the police force who turn a "blind eye" and a "deaf ear" to the illegal activities of which they were aware.

Recurring problems involve the country of Thailand. Many natives fall victim to such harsh fishing practices in return for a hopeful profit. A hope that rarely, if ever comes true. Those that are lured or coerced into this lifestyle come from an impoverished background. Many, if not all, see this as a means to feed their families. They see it as an opportunity to survive and have a better life. Unfortunately, it very rarely turns out the way they imagine.[22]

Thailand is the third largest seafood exporter in the world. The sector was worth some $7.3 billion dollars in 2011, and around a fifth of the catch ends up on American dinner tables—particularly tuna, sardines, shrimp and squid. But the industry heavily relies on trafficked and forced labor on unlicensed vessels. Victims typically hail from Cambodia, Laos and, most commonly, Burma. Beatings and starvation are commonplace.[23]

---

20. *Id.* at 2.

21. *Id.*

22. Charlie Campbell, *Child Slaves May Have Caught the Fish in Your Freezer* (Mar. 5, 2014), http://time.com/12628/human-trafficking-rife-in-thai-fishing-industry.

23. *Id.*

Most of the fifty-five million population subsists on less than a dollar a day, and three quarters do not have electricity. Promises of well-paid jobs in neighboring nations continue to entice victims of this industry. Around three million Burmese migrants currently live in Thailand. Many would-be migrants, not possessing valid documentation, pay brokers several hundred dollars to arrange their passage over the border, with the promise of well-paying jobs upon arrival.[24]

Three factors combine in a perfect storm to drive extreme exploitation in the Thai fishing industry.

- First is the demand for cheap labor. Fishing is a marginal economic activity because there are too many boats and not enough fish. To boost profits they pay next to nothing for labor, which would otherwise be the biggest operational cost.
- Second is the presence of vulnerable populations — large migrant communities in neighboring Myanmar and Cambodia that can easily be exploited.
- Third is the weak rule of law. It's illegal to engage in human trafficking and forced labor but the boats are not inspected rigorously. It's not a priority for the Thai authorities because most victims are not Thai and there are powerful vested interests that benefit from the trade.

Unfortunately, it is extremely hard to prove that those who fall victim to the industry are in fact being mistreated and it is hard to convict the industry leaders guilty of a crime. And even if a crime were committed, it is more difficult to find a crime worthy of sufficient punishment.[25]

Thai immigration and law enforcement officials are often complicit in these deals. Prosecution of perpetrators is unlikely and is very rare. Many migrants get sold from boat to boat and do not see land for years, sleeping in the open and forced to take bizarre amphetamine cocktails to stay awake for days on end. Due to dangerous conditions and tortuously long hours, work-related injuries are commonplace, and many throw themselves overboard to their deaths as their only means of escape.[26]

---

24. *Id*
25. *Id.*
26. *Id.*

Overfishing has compounded the problem. Back in 1961, fishermen in the Gulf of Thailand caught 300 kg (661 lb.) of fish an hour. Fast-forward half a century, and they now pull in a measly 25 kg, says Greenpeace. Falling profits leads to a demand for cheaper labor. According to the International Labor Organization, last year the Thai fishing industry had a 50,000-worker shortfall, "both a cause and an effect of the abusive labor practices that are seen in the fishing sector."[27]

2. Slavery and Gold Mining

Mining is a dangerous physical labor, and often those who perform this work are coerced into it in countries in South America and Africa. Here are a couple of examples:

a. Peru

Peru is one of the world's top producers of gold, and research shows more than 20% of the precious metal is mined illegally, under slave conditions, by children and others who receive no pay.[28]

Often, workers receive no form of payment or any form of compensation. Most must toil for free for a certain amount of time, and then they are allowed to mine for themselves. Whatever gold they can find constitutes their payment, the report said.[29]

Peru is the world's fourth-largest producer of gold, and there is little attention paid to the exploitation of miners from international companies and jewelers. The Madre de Dios region is home to the country's biggest illegal operations. Gold is a $3 billion annual business in this South American country.[30]

Besides sub-standard pay, or no pay at all, miners also face myriad health issues in the isolated jungle mines including industrial accidents that cause severe injuries, malaria and mercury poisoning. Liquid mercury is used during mining operations because it adheres to gold in

---

27. *Id.*

28. Deborah Hastings, *Held as Slaves, Children in Peru Forced to Work in Mines that Produce Much of World's Gold* New York Daily News (Feb. 11, 2014), http://www.nydailynews.com/news/world/child-labor-sex-slaves-peru-gold-mines-article-1.1610110.

29. *Id.*

30. *Id.*

chunks of ore, making it easy to spot. Mercury also is a highly dangerous, toxic chemical.[31]

While boys are forced to labor in mining operations hauling ore, girls from neighboring areas are sometimes forced into the sex trade, which services the miners. These girls can be as young as pre-teens. They are forced to have sex with multiple men two and three times their age.

Peru's human rights ombudsman estimated last year that informal and illegal mines directly employ 100,000 people and indirectly employ another 400,000. According to estimates by experts cited by Verité, such mines produce 15% to 22% of all the country's gold, valued at $3 billion annually.[32]

A 2012 newspaper investigation found that "the majority of this illegally produced gold was exported by formal businesses that helped to launder it"—a process explored in *In Sight Crime*'s *Breaking Down the Chain of Illegal Gold in Peru.* A network of family clans and illegal criminal groups control much of the extraction of the gold via forced labor that some would say is akin to slavery.[33]

Poor Peruvians travel to mining regions with hopes of escaping poverty. Many of these are "indocumentados," people who lack a National Identity Document (DNI), meaning they cannot work in any formal sector of employment in Peru.[34]

Many of those that are targeted for this type of work are extremely poor, geographically isolated, or are indigenous Peruvians who never obtained a birth certificate and have thus been unable to acquire a DNI. Research has shown that these targeted individuals are generally very vulnerable due to their lack of alternative employment and their low levels of education and socio-economic status.[35]

---

31. *Id.*

32. Miriam Wells, *How the Global Gold Trade Fuels Modern Day Slavery in Peru,* In Sight Crime (Feb. 9, 2014), http://www.insightcrime.org/news-analysis/how-the-global-gold-trade-fuels-modern-day-slavery-in-peru; *see also*, Anne Holmes, *Risk Analysis of Indicators of Forced Labor and Human Trafficking in Illegal Gold Mining in Peru,* Verité (Mar. 12, 2014), http://www.verite.org/sites/default/files/images/Indicators%20of%20Forced%20Labor%20in%20Gold%20Mining%20in%20Peru_0.pdf.

33. Wells, *supra* note 32.

34. *Id.*

35. *Id.*

Typically recruited in their local communities by middle men paid by the mine owners, the workers are tricked when it comes to pay and employment conditions, and "told stories about miners striking it rich."[36]

Having to work a ninety-day contract unpaid, purportedly to pay off recruitment fees or travel expenses, is common. But workers often fall ill to tropical diseases, animal bites or mercury exposure; they get injured in workplace accidents, and time off sick does not count towards the ninety days. They also accrue debts for food and lodging during that time, so the ninety-day period only increases.[37]

b. Africa

Mining for precious metals and rocks such as gold and diamonds tops the list of the industry's most likely to employ child labor in Africa. A recent PBS report stated that there are almost one million children currently working in the gold mines in Africa. For less than $2 a day, children as young as five spend 12–15 hours a day mining gold in Burkina Faso, Mali and the Democratic Republic of Congo. Many times the children are orphaned from various wars.[38]

"Ghana is the tenth biggest producer of gold in the world. A 2003 report found that the exportation of gold garners 'approximately 50%' of the country's GDP. But much of the mining industry is made up of galamsey operators—artisanal miners who often operate in unregulated, illegal mines. It is estimated that between 30,000 and 50,000 people work as galamsey operators. And of these, 10,000 are children who are forced to work in hazardous conditions." These children have no child labor laws that govern the fact that they are working as children. They have no rights or say in how they are treated or what conditions they work in. Slavery in the form of debt bondage and forced prostitution also occur in these communities, and children are subjected to these as well.[39]

---

36. *Id.*

37. *Id.*

38. Michelle Lillie, *Child Forced Labor Part I: The Mining Industry*, Human Trafficking Search (July 18, 2013), http://humantraffickingsearch.net/wp/forced-child-labor-in-the-mining-industry.

39. *A Program in Ghana Works to End Slavery in Mining Industry*, Huffington Post (Dec. 21, 2010), http://www.huffingtonpost.com/free-the-slaves/a-program-in-ghana-works-_b_79356.html (last updated May 25, 2011).

In these unregulated, small-scale mines, fatal accidents occur with alarming regularity. In 2009, a landslide at a galamsey site killed about twenty miners—fourteen of whom were women. Last year, many galamsey operators were buried alive when the gold mine in which they were working, caved in. Many of the workers experience serious health complications as a result of working in these toxic, hazardous conditions. One of the dangers is exposure to mercury and other toxic chemicals, which seriously threaten the miners' health.[40]

Another negative offshoot from this industry is the pollution and deforestation damage that is being done to the environment.[41]

For all the dangers, illegal mining is a source of valuable income for these communities. Many can find no alternative livelihood. But in 2009, "Free the Slaves" began a partnership with Ghanaian human rights "NGO Social Support Foundation" to launch a program to combat slavery in Ghana's illegal mining communities. The project, entitled "Community Resistance to Slavery and Forced Slavery (CRSFL)," helps vulnerable communities organize and create community-based action plans to eradicate slavery.[42]

Both fishing and the gold mining industry have considerable impact on the world. Due to the demand of these commodities, businesses have taken extremely risky and deadly steps to ensure that profit margins are large. Although consumers are interested in receiving a good price on commodities sold, it should never be at the hand of a human who is unwillingly risking his or her life.[43]

3. Slavery in the Clothing Industry

The clothing industry is one of the main industries that uses slave labor in product manufacturing.[44] Countries like Cambodia are hubs for companies like "Gap," "H&M," and "Adidas" and have been implicated in

---

40. *Id.*

41. *Id.*

42. *Id.*

43. *Id.*

44. *The Slave Labor Behind Your Favorite Clothing Brands: Gap, H&M and more exposed*, SALON (22 Mar. 2015), http://www.salon.com/2015/03/22/the_slave_labor_behind_your_favorite_clothing_brands_gap_hm_and_more_exposed_partner/ (last accessed Sept.1, 2015).

cases involving slave labor.[45] Many of the workers are females and earn less than 60¢ an hour.[46] Wages like that enable manufacturers to sell hooded sweatshirts for rates Americans will pay.[47]

These people are forced to work in the "sweat shops" under poor working conditions.[48] The air is so hot and toxic; workers have fainted and been threatened with beatings or actually beaten if they do not work for long inhumane hours.[49] For many, these working conditions are tolerated because the alternative, the rice paddies, are worse.[50] Workers have complained (many anonymously for fear of reprisal) and told of horrible abuse being done to them for not working or not working quickly enough under intolerable conditions.[51]

4. U.S. Farms and Slavery

So far we have considered acts of slavery abroad. However, the agricultural industry in the United States remains an area plagued with the problems of involuntary servitude. It is estimated that over two million people are employed on farms throughout the country.[52] Agricultural work is consistently among the most hazardous industrial work; in 2012, fatal injury accidents were 21.2 per 100,000, ranking it the highest fatality rate of any industry that year.[53] Agricultural workers experience "increased rates of respiratory diseases, noise-induced hearing loss, skin disorders, certain cancers, exposure to toxic chemicals and heat related illnesses."[54] Most agricultural work is seasonal, as crops vary by harvest

---

45. *Id.*

46. *Id.*

47. *Id.*

48. *Id.*

49. *Id.*

50. *Id.*

51. *Id.*

52. *NIOSH Pesticide Poisoning Program Protects Farmworkers*, Centers for Disease Control and Prevention (Dec. 2011), www.cdc.gov/niosh/docs/2012-108/.

53. *Agriculture, Forestry, and Fishing*, Centers for Disease Control and Prevention, www.cdc.gov/niosh/agforfish/ (last visited Aug. 8, 2015).

54. *Produce Workers*, www.foodispower.org/produce-workers/ (last visited Aug. 8, 2015).

time and geographic location. Thus, many farms are dependent on migrant workers. *Id.* Between 2001 and 2002, only 23% of hired farm workers were born in the United States and 75% were of Mexican descent.[55]

Immigrant workers are most susceptible to unscrupulous land owners or labor brokers who entice workers "by falsely promising steady work and good wages."[56] In 2008, a slavery ring in Florida was exposed and led to the subsequent indictment of six people.[57] Prosecutors alleged that over a dozen people were hired to work in citrus groves in Florida, but were held as slaves and "made to sleep in box trucks and shacks, charged for food and showers, [denied pay] for picking produce, and beat [if they] tried to leave."[58] In a separate case in Florida, over 100 Haitian laborers in pea and bean fields were being held as slaves after being recruited by labor contractors who promised them "high steady wages and free room and board for three years."[59] Upon the workers' arrival, their visas and passports were confiscated by the farm owners.[60] Additionally, the federal indictment stated that "the defendants supplied substandard housing and few beds, and denied necessary medical care, causing the workers to suffer chronic hunger, weight loss, illnesses, and fatigue."[61]

5. Slavery in the International Food Market

Even if human trafficking concerns were eliminated in the U.S. agricultural industry, the fact that much of our food is imported means that other concerns would remain. In 2008, an estimated 25,000 to 40,000 laborers were victims of working conditions considered slavery in Brazil

---

55. U.S. Dep't of Labor, *A Demographic and Employment Profile of U.S. Farm Workers, Research Report No. 9* (2005).

56. *Slavery in the U.S.*, www.foodispower.org/slavery-in-the-us/ (last visited Aug. 9, 2015).

57. Pat Gillespie, *Sixth Immokalee Slavery Case Suspect Arrested: Group Accused of Keeping, Beating, Stealing from Immokalee Laborers*, Fort Myers News-Press, Jan. 18, 2008, *available at* ciw-online.org/blog/2008/01/slavery_plain_and_simple/.

58. *Id.*

59. *Produce Workers*, *supra* note 54.

60. *Id.*

61. *Id.*

alone.[62] It is the world's largest agricultural exporter of "sugar, coffee, orange juice, tobacco, beef, and poultry meat."[63] Brazil has long employed tactics such as "forced labor" and "debt bondage."[64] Debt bondage occurs when a person's "labor is demanded as the means of repayment for a loan or an advance."[65] A common tactic used by labor recruiters in Brazil is to visit the slums or poor, rural areas to find people willing to work.[66] The laborers agree to relocate to a distant job; however, once they are separated from their homes, they become susceptible to abuse.[67] Often times they are told that they owe money for "transportation, food, housing, and other services."[68] Thus, they are forced to work to pay off their "debt," and "once in debt, they lose all control over their conditions of work and what, if anything, they are paid... often making it impossible to repay and trapping them in a cycle of debt."[69] Moreover, workers are infrequently paid small sums, with the promise of receiving their full pay at the end of the contract.[70] However, when the contract has ended, "the workers find many expenses were unknowingly deducted from their wages."[71]

Although forced labor remains prevalent in Brazil, the government is being proactive at eradicating the problem. Their "Special Mobile Inspection Group" is a group that consists of "labor inspectors, federal police, and [federal prosecutors]... that raids workplaces, looking for

62. *Forced Labour in Brazil: 120 Years After the Abolition of Slavery, the Fight Goes On*, International Labour Organization, (May 13, 2008), http://www.ilo.org/global/about-the-ilo/newsroom/features/WCMS_092663/lang—en/index.htm (last visited Aug. 12, 2015).

63. *Trade*, http://www.ers.usda.gov/topics/international-markets-trade/countries-regions/brazil/trade.aspx#.VCyAvufZV3W (last accessed Aug. 12, 2015).

64. *Importing Slavery*, www.foodispower.org/importing-slavery/ (last visited Aug. 12, 2015).

65. Arthur Brice, *Government fights slave labor in Brazil*, (Jan. 9, 2009, update 4:38 AM) edition.cnn.com/2009/WORLD/americas/01/09/brazil.slavery/index.html.

66. *Id.*

67. *Id.*

68. *Id.*

69. *Id.*

70. *Importing Slavery*, *supra* note 64.

71. *Id.*

abuses and laborers held against their will."[72] The group has freed 33,000 people since its inception in 1995.[73] While the numbers sound impressive, the country remains plagued with the issue of slavery. Brazil's agriculture industry is large and powerful.[74] Thus, the government faces numerous obstacles in attempting to enact harsher laws. For example, a proposed law that calls for the confiscation of land "on which slave labor is used" has sat dormant for years.[75] Many officials object to labeling the forced working conditions as "slavery," claiming it "mischaracterizes the situation," as what occurs in modern-day practice cannot be compared to the typical definition of slavery.[76]

Cocoa farming is also gaining the attention of anti-slavery activists across the world. Chocolate is derived from the cacao bean, which primarily grows in Africa.[77] The Ivory Coast and Ghana are responsible for supplying more than 70% of cocoa worldwide.[78] This billion-dollar industry is saturated with child labor and slavery.[79] The U.S. Department of State estimates that "approximately 109,000 children in the [Ivory Coast's] cocoa industry work under the worst forms of child labor."[80] As the chocolate industry grows, so "has the demand for cheap cocoa."[81]

Children in West Africa grow up in intense poverty, and most begin working at an early age to aid in supporting the family.[82] Traffickers in the region falsely recruit children with the promise of well-paying jobs, while some children are sold into labor by their own family members,

---

72. Brice, *supra* note 65.

73. *Id.*

74. *Id.*

75. *Id.*

76. *Id.*

77. *Child Labor and Slavery in the Chocolate Industry*, www.foodispower.org/slavery-chocolate/ (last accessed Aug. 12, 2015).

78. *Id.*

79. David McKenzie, *Brent Swails, Child slavery and chocolate: All too easy to find*, The CNN Freedom Project (Jan. 19, 2012), http://thecnnfreedomproject.blogs.cnn.com/2012/01/19/child-slavery-and-chocolate-all-too-easy-to-find/.

80. Kemi Mustapha, *Taste of Child Labor Not So Sweet: A Critique of Regulatory Approaches to Combating Child Labor Abuses by the U.S. Chocolate Industry*, 87 Wash. U. L. Rev. 1163, 1164 (2010).

81. *Child Labor and Slavery in the Chocolate Industry, supra* note 77.

82. *Id.*

and some are even abducted from their villages.[83] Children as young as five have been found on cocoa farms, although most are between the ages of twelve and sixteen.[84] Child laborers are required to use chainsaws to clear forests, climb the cocoa trees to cut the bean pods down with machetes, and haul sacks of pods that can weigh more than 100 pounds.[85] Most children have scars from where they have cut their hands, arms, or legs with machetes when attempting to crack the bean pods open.[86] Younger children must spray pesticides on the crop, without wearing protective clothing.[87] Their diet consists of corn paste and bananas.[88]

Accusations of complicity were initially denied by U.S. chocolate manufacturers, as they stated they "neither owned the cocoa farms nor controlled he labor practices of local farmers."[89] Added to the burden are the long and complex methods that chocolate reaches consumers.[90] Exporters, international traders and manufacturers are only a few of the people involved, as well as the fact the "cocoa beans from various farms are combined before being exported, making it impossible to discern their source; cocoa beans originating from farms that use child labor are indistinguishable from the cocoa beans originating from farms that do not."[91]

The U.S. Congress has struggled in finding successful ways to regulate the U.S. chocolate industry. Representative Eliot Engel "proposed and amendment to the 2002 Agriculture Appropriations Bill that would have earmarked $250,000 for the [FDA] to develop a 'slave free' label for chocolate products."[92] After intense lobbying by the Chocolate Manufacturers Association, the amendment failed.[93] The Harkin-Engel Protocol, enacted in September 2001, is a compromise between chocolate manu-

83. *Id.*
84. *Id.*
85. *Id.*
86. *Id.*
87. *Id.*
88. *Id.*
89. Mustapha, *supra* note 80, at 1166.
90. *Id.*
91. *Id.*
92. *Id.* at 1166–67.
93. *Id.* at 1167.

facturers and lawmakers. It is a "voluntary, nonbinding, and nonlegislative document that outlines six steps for the chocolate industry to take in order to eliminate the worst forms of child labor in its supply chain in compliance with international labor standards."[94] However, since it is voluntary, little progress has been made in eradicating child labor.[95]

Since consumers have no way of knowing whether the chocolate they purchase involves child labor, it is largely up to the chocolate companies to fully support the efforts to eliminate the child labor epidemic in West Africa.[96] While some manufacturers label their candy with fair trade certifications, it is not a guarantee that no child labor was involved.[97] Consumers can contribute to the efforts of both government and non-government organizations by researching and boycotting companies who refuse to reveal their cocoa sources, or refusing to buy chocolate that came from West Africa. Chapter 7 contains a listing of additional areas where labor trafficking might be involved, as well as a mechanism for determining and reporting such activity.

E. Are We Helpless to Prevent and Eliminate Trafficking?

The simple answer is that while trafficking has existed from the time of recorded history, and while the problem persists in the face of attempts to eradicate it, there is room for hope. Increasing awareness of the scourge of trafficking is leading to efforts to address the problem through legislation, the activities of churches and non-governmental organizations, and individuals. The authors hope that this book will add to both awareness and these efforts.

Finally, before concluding this chapter, it is important to note that one of the best sources for information on trafficking is the Polaris Project. An examination of their website provides access to many important articles and data compilations. The reader is encouraged to pause before

94. *Id.* at 1168.

95. *Id.*

96. *Child Labor and Slavery in the Chocolate Industry*, *supra* note 77.

97. *Id.*

continuing on to Chapter Two, and examine the extensive information available on the Polaris Project website at polarisproject.org.

F. For Further Thought

1. Has your view of what might constitute human trafficking been altered by your reading of this chapter? In what ways?
2. The listing in this chapter of industries employing the victims of human trafficking is not exhaustive. What other areas of commerce might you suspect involve trafficking? Why? How would you identify whether your suspicions are correct?
3. What can be done to alleviate the instances of trafficking identified so far? Reconsider your thoughts after concluding this book, including the last segment on approaches to minimize, if not eliminate, these tragedies.

Chapter 2

What Domestic Efforts Seek to Eradicate Trafficking?

While it is emotionally difficult to examine the horror of human trafficking, it is important to note that our domestic and international legal systems recognize the evil and continue to make efforts to address it. Before considering how our country and others are attempting to work together on an international basis, we first examine how the United States and individual states continue to create and implement legal mechanisms to prevent trafficking. In some instances these are overlapping. Obviously and unfortunately, they have not yet succeeded in eradicating trafficking.

A. Federal Authority

For well over a century, legislative efforts aimed at eradicating human trafficking have been adopted by United States Congress and by the various states. The cornerstone, of course, of the effort to eradicate slavery is the Thirteenth Amendment to the Constitution of the United States. That amendment was ratified in 1865, following the Civil War. The amendment reads:

> Section 1. Neither slavery nor involuntary servitude, except as a punishment for crime whereof the party shall have been duly convicted, shall exist within the United States, or any place subject to their jurisdiction.

> Section 2. Congress shall have power to enforce this article by appropriate legislation.[1]

A series of statutes, and case decisions, have sought to eradicate not only the practice of slavery, but the remaining effects of it. Among these are 42 U.S.C. section 1981:[2]

> (a) Statement of equal rights
> All persons within the jurisdiction of the United States shall have the same right in every State and Territory to make and enforce contracts, to sue, be parties, give evidence, and to the full and equal benefit of all laws and proceedings for the security of persons and property as is enjoyed by white citizens, and shall be subject to like punishment, pains, penalties, taxes, licenses, and exactions of every kind, and to no other.
> (b) "Make and enforce contracts" defined
> For purposes of this section, the term "make and enforce contracts" includes the making, performance, modification, and termination of contracts, and the enjoyment of all benefits, privileges, terms, and conditions of the contractual relationship.
> (c) Protection against impairment

The rights protected by this section are protected against impairment by nongovernmental discrimination and impairment under color of State law.[3]

Also, 42 U.S.C. section 1983 creates a "civil action for deprivation of rights."[4] It provides that:

> Every person who, under color of any statute, ordinance, regulation, custom, or usage, of any State or Territory or the District of Columbia, subjects, or causes to be subjected, any citizen of the United States or other person within the jurisdiction thereof to the deprivation of any rights, privileges, or immunities

---

1. U.S. Const. amend. XIII, § 1–2.
2. 42 U.S.C. § 1981 (2012).
3. *Id.*
4. 42 U.S.C. § 1983 (2012).

> secured by the Constitution and laws, shall be liable to the party injured in an action at law, suit in equity, or other proper proceeding for redress, except that in any action brought against a judicial officer for an act or omission taken in such officer's judicial capacity, injunctive relief shall not be granted unless a declaratory decree was violated or declaratory relief was unavailable. For the purposes of this section, any Act of Congress applicable exclusively to the District of Columbia shall be considered to be a statute of the District of Columbia.[5]

The Constitutional prohibition against slavery and subsequent legislative enactments were originally aimed at redressing the evils of race-based slavery. The post-Civil War amendments and statutes were eventually interpreted by the courts to address broader civil rights issues as well. In addition, Congress began to specifically address problems of human trafficking which were not only race-based.

In 1910 the United States enacted the Mann Act of 1910, which is codified at 18 U.S.C. sections 2421–24. The act has been amended in 1978 and 1986. Essentially, the act made criminal the act of coercing adults in travel across state lines or two other countries for the purpose of participating in commercial sex. This practice was referred to as "white slavery." The transportation of minors is also a crime when that transportation is made for the purpose commercial sex acts. The act provides for a penalty of up to twenty years of incarceration. Transporting minors carries the option for an enhanced sentencing. Consider some of the key provisions of the Mann Act:

18 U.S.C. § 2421

Transportation Generally

> (a) In general.—Whoever knowingly transports any individual in interstate or foreign commerce, or in any Territory or Possession of the United States, with intent that such individual engage in prostitution, or in any sexual activity for which any person can be charged with a criminal offense, or attempts to

---

5. *Id.*

do so, shall be fined under this title or imprisoned not more than 10 years, or both.[6]

18 U.S.C. § 2422
Coercion and Enticement

(a) Whoever knowingly persuades, induces, entices, or coerces any individual to travel in interstate or foreign commerce, or in any Territory or Possession of the United States, to engage in prostitution, or in any sexual activity for which any person can be charged with a criminal offense, or attempts to do so, shall be fined under this title or imprisoned not more than 20 years, or both.

(b) Whoever, using the mail or any facility or means of interstate or foreign commerce, or within the special maritime and territorial jurisdiction of the United States knowingly persuades, induces, entices, or coerces any individual who has not attained the age of 18 years, to engage in prostitution or any sexual activity for which any person can be charged with a criminal offense, or attempts to do so, shall be fined under this title and imprisoned not less than 10 years or for life.[7]

The Mann Act now includes provisions specifically aimed at punishing those engaged in the sex trafficking of minors, and those who travel domestically or abroad as "sex tourists":

18 U.S.C. § 2423
Transportation of Minors

(a) Transportation with intent to engage in criminal sexual activity.— A person who knowingly transports an individual who has not attained the age of 18 years in interstate or foreign commerce, or in any commonwealth, territory or possession of the United States, with intent that the individual engage in prostitution, or in any sexual activity for which any person can be charged with a criminal offense, shall be fined under this title and imprisoned not less than 10 years or for life.

---

6. 18 U.S.C. § 2421 (2012).
7. 18 U.S.C. § 2422 (2012).

> (b) Travel with intent to engage in illicit sexual conduct.—A person who travels in interstate commerce or travels into the United States, or a United States citizen or an alien admitted for permanent residence in the United States who travels in foreign commerce, for the purpose of engaging in any illicit sexual conduct with another person shall be fined under this title or imprisoned not more than 30 years, or both.
> (c) Engaging in illicit sexual conduct in foreign places.—Any United States citizen or alien admitted for permanent residence who travels in foreign commerce or resides, either temporarily or permanently, in a foreign country, and engages in any illicit sexual conduct with another person shall be fined under this title or imprisoned not more than 30 years, or both.[8]

Sex trafficking has not been the only subject of criminal statutes attempting to address the horrors of human trafficking. The Tariff Act of 1930 prohibits importation of materials produced by forced labor.[9]

19 U.S.C. § 1307
Convict-made Goods; Importation Prohibited

> All goods, wares, articles, and merchandise mined, produced, or manufactured wholly or in part in any foreign country by convict labor or/and forced labor or/and indentured labor under penal sanctions shall not be entitled to entry at any of the ports of the United States, and the importation thereof is hereby prohibited, and the Secretary of the Treasury is authorized and directed to prescribe such regulations as may be necessary for the enforcement of this provision. The provisions of this section relating to goods, wares, articles, and merchandise mined, produced, or manufactured by forced labor or/and indentured labor, shall take effect on January 1, 1932; but in no case shall such provisions be applicable to goods, wares, articles, or merchandise so mined, produced, or manufactured which are not mined, produced, or manufactured in such quantities in the

8. 18 U.S.C. § 2423 (2012).
9. 19 U.S.C. § 1304-1683 (2012).

> United States as to meet the consumptive demands of the United States.
>
> "Forced labor," as herein used, shall mean all work or service which is exacted from any person under the menace of any penalty for its nonperformance and for which the worker does not offer himself voluntarily. For purposes of this section, the term "forced labor or/and indentured labor" includes forced or indentured child labor.[10]

In 2009, Congress enacted the Customs and Facilitations and Trade Enforcement Act. These provisions prohibit the importation of goods produced by the victims of human trafficking, or goods produced as a result of coercion.

The federal government is also afforded the opportunity to prosecute traffickers in the Racketeering Influenced Corrupt Organizations Act (RICO). Human trafficking offenses are treated as racketeering offenses:

§ 1961. Definitions
As Used in this Chapter

> (1) racketeering activity means (A) any act or threat involving murder, kidnapping, gambling, arson, robbery, bribery, extortion, dealing in obscene matter, or dealing in a controlled substance or listed chemical (as defined in section 102 of the Controlled Substances Act), which is chargeable under State law and punishable by imprisonment for more than one year; (B) any act which is indictable under any of the following provisions of title 18, United States Code: .... sections 15811592 (relating to peonage, slavery, and trafficking in persons).[11]

Beginning in the year 2000, Congress initiated a legislative effort which continues with amendments through 2013. The Trafficking Victims Protection Act (TVPA) of the year 2000 created additional avenues to address human trafficking. It created a mechanism for protecting victims and survivors of trafficking and requires that victims of human trafficking be afforded restitution. This act is the origin of the T-visa

---

10. 19 U.S.C. § 1307 (2012).
11. 18 U.S.C. § 1961-1968 (2012).

which is available to some victims of trafficking who are brought into the United States from abroad. The particular immigration aspects of trafficking are addressed at greater length in Chapter 4.

In 2003, the Trafficking Victims Protection Reauthorization Act 2003 (TVPRA of 2003) created a civil remedy allowing victims of trafficking to file suit against those who had trafficked them. In 2005, the TVPRA was reauthorized. It created measures that allowed for the combating of trafficking and sheltering of its victims.[12] Specific provisions were included to address the issue of sex tourism.

> (b) Minimum Standards for the Elimination of Trafficking—
> (1) AMENDMENTS—Section 108(b) of the Trafficking Victims Protection Act of 2000 (22 U.S.C. 7106(b)) is amended—
> (A) in paragraph (3), by adding at the end before the period the following: ", measures to reduce the demand for commercial sex acts and for participation in international sex tourism by nationals of the country, measures to ensure that its nationals who are deployed abroad as part of a peacekeeping or other similar mission do not engage in or facilitate severe forms of trafficking in persons or exploit victims of such trafficking, and measures to prevent the use of forced labor or child labor in violation of international standards."[13]

Sex tourism is discussed in Chapter 5 in greater length.

The TVPRA of 2008 included requirements that any alien child entering the United States who is not accompanied by an adult would be evaluated to see whether that child is a victim of human trafficking and to provide safeguards for that child:

> Section 107(a) of Trafficking Victims Protection Act of 2000 (22 U.S.C. 7105(a)) is amended.... (B) by adding at the end the following... "(ii) performance of best interest determinations for unaccompanied and separated children who come to the attention of the United Nations High Commissioner for Ref-

12. Trafficking Victims Protection Reauthorization Act of 2005 (H.R. 972 Sec. 104(b)(1)(A)).

13. *Id.*

> ugees, its partner organizations, or any organization that contracts with the Department of State in order to identify child trafficking victims and to assist their safe integration, reintegration, and resettlement." . . .[14]
>
> SEC. 235. ENHANCING EFFORTS TO COMBAT THE TRAFFICKING OF CHILDREN.
>
> (a) COMBATING CHILD TRAFFICKING AT THE BORDER AND PORTS OF ENTRY OF THE UNITED STATES.—
>
> (1) POLICIES AND PROCEDURES.—In order to enhance the efforts of the United States to prevent trafficking in persons, the Secretary of Homeland Security, in conjunction with the Secretary of State, the Attorney General, and the Secretary of Health and Human Services, shall develop policies and procedures to ensure that unaccompanied alien children in the United States are safely repatriated to their country of nationality or of last habitual residence.[15]

Further, the TVPRA of 2013 included additional provisions to try to prevent US citizens from purchasing goods produced by the trafficking victims.

> (1) United States citizens do not use any item, product, or material produced or extracted with the use and labor from victims of severe forms of trafficking; and
>
> (2) such entities do not contribute to trafficking in persons involving sexual exploitation.[16]
>
> SEC. 1233. INFORMATION SHARING TO COMBAT CHILD LABOR AND SLAVE LABOR.

Section 105(a) of the Trafficking Victims Protection Act of 2005 (22 U.S.C. 7112(a)) is amended by adding at the end the following:

> (3) INFORMATION SHARING.—The Secretary of State shall, on a regular basis, provide information relating to child labor

---

14. William Wilberforce Trafficking Victims Protection Reauthorization Act of 2008, Pub. L. No. 110-457 § 104, 122 Stat. 5044 (2008).

15. 8 U.S.C. § 1232 (2012).

16. 22 U.S.C. § 7103a (2012).

and forced labor in the production of goods in violation of international standards to the Department of Labor to be used in developing the list described in subsection (b)(2)(C)."[17]

Another mechanism introduced by the 2013 amendments is an attempt to prevent child trafficking by restricting child marriage:

> SEC. 1207. PREVENTION OF CHILD MARRIAGE.
> (a) IN GENERAL.—Section 106 of the Trafficking Victims Protection Act of 2000 (22 U.S.C. 7104) is amended by adding at the end the following:
> (j) PREVENTION OF CHILD TRAFFICKING THROUGH CHILD MARRIAGE.—The Secretary of State shall establish and implement a multi-year, multi-sectoral strategy—(1) to prevent child marriage;
> (2) to promote the empowerment of girls at risk of child marriage in developing countries;
> (3) that should address the unique needs, vulnerabilities, and potential of girls younger than 18 years of age in developing countries;
> (4) that targets areas in developing countries with high prevalence of child marriage; and
> (5) that includes diplomatic and programmatic initiatives.
> (b) INCLUSION OF CHILD MARRIAGE STATUS IN REPORTS.—The Foreign Assistance Act of 1961 (22 U.S.C. 2151 et seq.) is amended—
> (1) in section 116 (22 U.S.C. 2151n), by adding at the end the following:
> (g) CHILD MARRIAGE STATUS.—
> (1) IN GENERAL.—The report required under subsection (d) shall include, for each country in which child marriage is prevalent, a description of the status of the practice of child marriage in such country.
> (2) DEFINED TERM.—In this subsection, the term 'child marriage' means the marriage of a girl or boy who is—

17. Violence Against Women Reauthorization Act of 2013, Title XII Trafficking Victims Prevention, Pub. L. No. 113-4 § 1233, 127 Stat. 146 (2013).

(A) younger than the minimum age for marriage under the laws of the country in which such girl or boy is a resident; or
(B) younger than 18 years of age, if no such law exists; and
(2) in section 502B (22 U.S.C. 2304), by adding at the end the following:
(i) CHILD MARRIAGE STATUS—(1) IN GENERAL.—The report required under subsection
(b) shall include, for each country in which child marriage is prevalent, a description of the status of the practice of child marriage in such country.
(2) DEFINED TERM.—In this subsection, the term 'child marriage' means the marriage of a girl or boy who is—
(A) younger than the minimum age for marriage under the laws of the country in which such girl or boy is a resident; or
(B) younger than 18 years of age, if no such law exists.[18]

It also attempts to improve cooperation with state and local law enforcement officials. Note that the presumptive age for consent to marriage, in the absence of other laws, is eighteen. That age is greater than the minimum provided for by many states in this country.

Another important tool in the fight against child trafficking is the statute passed in 2003. Out of a continuing concern for the plight of children, Congress passed the "PROTECT Act": Prosecutorial Remedies and Other Tools to End the Exploitation of Children Today.[19] Those who are convicted of participation in child sex tourism will be subjected to enhanced criminal sanctions under these provisions. The act, in Title III, mandates that the Attorney General of the United States assign a national "Amber Alert" coordinator. It increased funding to the National Center for Missing and Exploited Children. In response to decisions of the Supreme Court of the United States, however, the Act also created, in Title V, some affirmative defenses to a criminal charge regarding "virtual" child pornography. If the alleged pornography only includes actual

18. Violence Against Women Reauthorization Act of 2013, Title XII Trafficking Victims Prevention, Pub. L. No. 113-4 § 1207, 127 Stat. 146.

19. Prosecutorial Remedies and Other Tools to End the Exploitation of Children Today Act of 2003, Pub. L. No. 108-21, 117 Stat. 650.

persons all of whom were adults, or if the alleged pornography does not include any actual minors, no conviction can occur:

> SEC. 502. IMPROVEMENTS TO PROHIBITION ON VIRTUAL CHILD PORNOGRAPHY.
> (a) Section 2256(8) of title 18, United States Code, is amended—
> (1) so that subparagraph (B) reads as follows:
> (B) such visual depiction is a digital image, computer image, or computer-generated image that is, or is indistinguishable from, that of a minor engaging in sexually explicit conduct; or;
> (2) by striking "; or" at the end of subparagraph (C) and inserting a period; and
> (3) by striking subparagraph (D).
> (b) Section 2256(2) of title 18, United States Code, is amended to read as follows:
> (2)(A) Except as provided in subparagraph (B), 'sexually explicit conduct' means actual or simulated—(i) sexual intercourse, including genital-genital, oral-genital, anal-genital, or oral-anal, whether between persons of the same or opposite sex;
> (ii) bestiality;
> (iii) masturbation;
> (iv) sadistic or masochistic abuse; or
> (v) lascivious exhibition of the genitals or pubic area of any person;
> (B) For purposes of subsection 8(B) of this section, 'sexually explicit conduct' means—
> (i) graphic sexual intercourse, including genital-genital, oral-genital, anal-genital, or oral-anal, whether between persons of the same or opposite sex, or lascivious simulated sexual intercourse where the genitals, breast, or pubic area of any person is exhibited;
> (ii) graphic or lascivious simulated;
> (I) bestiality;
> (II) masturbation; or
> (III) sadistic or masochistic abuse; or
> (iii) graphic or simulated lascivious exhibition of the genitals or pubic area of any person;

(c) Section 2256 is amended by inserting at the end the following new paragraphs:

(10) 'graphic', when used with respect to a depiction of sexually explicit conduct, means that a viewer can observe any part of the genitals or pubic area of any depicted person or animal during any part of the time that the sexually explicit conduct is being depicted; and

(11) the term 'indistinguishable' used with respect to a depiction, means virtually indistinguishable, in that the depiction is such that an ordinary person viewing the depiction would conclude that the depiction is of an actual minor engaged in sexually explicit conduct. This definition does not apply to depictions that are drawings, cartoons, sculptures, or paintings depicting minors or adults.

(d) Section 2252A(c) of title 18, United States Code, is amended to read as follows:

(c) It shall be an affirmative defense to a charge of violating paragraph (1), (2), (3)(A), (4), or (5) of subsection (a) that—

(1)(A) the alleged child pornography was produced using an actual person or persons engaging in sexually explicit conduct; and

(B) each such person was an adult at the time the material was produced; or

(2) the alleged child pornography was not produced using any actual minor or minors. No affirmative defense under subsection (c)(2) shall be available in any prosecution that involves child pornography as described in section 2256(8)(C). A defendant may not assert an affirmative defense to a charge of violating paragraph (1), (2), (3)(A), (4), or

(5) of subsection (a) unless, within the time provided for filing pretrial motions or at such time prior to trial as the judge may direct, but in no event later than 10 days before the commencement of the trial, the defendant provides the court and the United States with notice of the intent to assert such defense and the substance of any expert or other specialized testimony or evidence upon which the defendant intends to rely. If the defendant fails to comply with this subsection, the court shall,

absent a finding of extraordinary circumstances that prevented timely compliance, prohibit the defendant from asserting such defense to a charge of violating paragraph (1), (2), (3)(A), (4), or (5) of subsection (a) or presenting any evidence for which the defendant has failed to provide proper and timely notice.[20]

More discussion concerning the possible relationship between pornography and trafficking will be presented in our concluding chapter.

B. State Legislative Efforts

In addition to federal laws, all fifty states are addressing through legislation, the problems associated with human trafficking. (We discuss the international tier system in the next chapter.) Some of the relevant statutes and efforts of the states of Texas and Tennessee, where the authors of this book have lived and taught, are illustrative.

1. Texas

Texas law includes the following:

PENAL CODE

TITLE 5. OFFENSES AGAINST THE PERSON

CHAPTER 20A. TRAFFICKING OF PERSONS

Sec. 20A.01. DEFINITIONS. In this chapter:
(1) "Child" means a person younger than 18 years of age.
(2) "Forced labor or services" means labor or services, other than labor or services that constitute sexual conduct, that are performed or provided by another person and obtained through an actor's use of force, fraud, or coercion.
(3) "Sexual conduct" has the meaning assigned by Section 43.25.
(4) "Traffic" means to transport, entice, recruit, harbor, provide, or otherwise obtain another person by any means....
... Sec. 20A.02. TRAFFICKING OF PERSONS. (a) A person commits an offense if the person knowingly:

20. Prosecutorial Remedies and Other Tools to End the Exploitation of Children Today Act of 2003, Pub. L. No. 108-21 § 502, 117 Stat. 650.

(1) traffics another person with the intent that the trafficked person engage in forced labor or services;
(2) receives a benefit from participating in a venture that involves an activity described by Subdivision (1), including by receiving labor or services the person knows are forced labor or services;
(3) traffics another person and, through force, fraud, or coercion, causes the trafficked person to engage in conduct prohibited by:
(A) Section 43.02 (Prostitution); (B) Section 43.03 (Promotion of Prostitution); (C) Section 43.04 (Aggravated Promotion of Prostitution); or (D) Section 43.05 (Compelling Prostitution);
(4) receives a benefit from participating in a venture that involves an activity described by Subdivision (3) or engages in sexual conduct with a person trafficked in the manner described in Subdivision (3);
(5) traffics a child with the intent that the trafficked child engage in forced labor or services;
(6) receives a benefit from participating in a venture that involves an activity described by Subdivision (5), including by receiving labor or services the person knows are forced labor or services;
(7) traffics a child and by any means causes the trafficked child to engage in, or become the victim of, conduct prohibited by:
(A) Section 21.02 (Continuous Sexual Abuse of Young Child or Children); (B) Section 21.11 (Indecency with a Child); (C) Section 22.011 (Sexual Assault); (D) Section 22.021 (Aggravated Sexual Assault); (E) Section 43.02 (Prostitution); (F) Section 43.03 (Promotion of Prostitution); (G) Section 43.04 (Aggravated Promotion of Prostitution); (H) Section 43.05 (Compelling Prostitution); (I) Section 43.25 (Sexual Performance by a Child); (J) Section 43.251 (Employment Harmful to Children); or (K) Section 43.26 (Possession or Promotion of Child Pornography); or
(8) receives a benefit from participating in a venture that involves an activity described by Subdivision (7) or engages in

sexual conduct with a child trafficked in the manner described in Subdivision (7).

(b) Except as otherwise provided by this subsection, an offense under this section is a felony of the second degree. An offense under this section is a felony of the first degree if:

(1) the applicable conduct constitutes an offense under Subsection (a)(5), (6), (7), or (8), regardless of whether the actor knows the age of the child at the time the actor commits the offense; or

(2) the commission of the offense results in the death of the person who is trafficked.

(c) If conduct constituting an offense under this section also constitutes an offense under another section of this code, the actor may be prosecuted under either section or under both sections.

(d) If the victim of an offense under Subsection (a)(7)(A) is the same victim as a victim of an offense under Section 21.02, a defendant may not be convicted of the offense under Section 21.02 in the same criminal action as the offense under Subsection (a)(7)(A) unless the offense under Section 21.02:

(1) is charged in the alternative;

(2) occurred outside the period in which the offense alleged under Subsection (a)(7)(A) was committed; or

(3) is considered by the trier of fact to be a lesser included offense of the offense alleged under Subsection (a)(7)(A)....

... Sec. 20A.03. CONTINUOUS TRAFFICKING OF PERSONS. (a) A person commits an offense if, during a period that is 30 or more days in duration, the person engages two or more times in conduct that constitutes an offense under Section 20A.02.

(b) If a jury is the trier of fact, members of the jury are not required to agree unanimously on which specific conduct engaged in by the defendant constituted an offense under Section 20A.02 or on which exact date the defendant engaged in that conduct. The jury must agree unanimously that the defendant, during a period that is 30 or more days in duration, engaged in conduct that constituted an offense under Section 20A.02.

(c) If the victim of an offense under Subsection (a) is the same victim as a victim of an offense under Section 20A.02, a defendant may not be convicted of the offense under Section 20A.02 in the same criminal action as the offense under Subsection (a), unless the offense under Section 20A.02:

(1) is charged in the alternative;

(2) occurred outside the period in which the offense alleged under Subsection (a) was committed; or

(3) is considered by the trier of fact to be a lesser included offense of the offense alleged under Subsection (a).

(d) A defendant may not be charged with more than one count under Subsection (a) if all of the conduct that constitutes an offense under Section 20A.02 is alleged to have been committed against the same victim.

(e) An offense under this section is a felony of the first degree, punishable by imprisonment in the Texas Department of Criminal Justice for life or for any term of not more than 99 years or less than 25 years.[21]

As a result, a multi-jurisdictional approach allows law enforcement officials in Texas to pursue state charges, while federal officers utilize the tools available to them under federal statutes.

2. Tennessee

A quick summary of some of the Tennessee provisions are as follows:

39-13-308. Trafficking for Forced Labor or Services

(a) A person commits the offense of trafficking persons for forced labor or services who knowingly: (1) Recruits, entices, harbors, transports, provides, or obtains by any means, or attempts to recruit, entice, harbor, transport, provide, or obtain by any means, another person, intending or knowing that the person will be subjected to involuntary servitude; or

(2) Benefits, financially or by receiving anything of value, from participation in a venture that has engaged in an act described in § 39-13-307.

---

21. Tex. Penal Code Ann. § 20A.01-03.

(b) In addition to any other amount of loss identified or any other punishment imposed, the court shall order restitution to the victim or victims in an amount equal to the greater of: (1) The gross income or value of the benefit received by the defendant as the result of the victim's labor or services; or
(2) The value of the victim's labor as guaranteed under the minimum wage and overtime provisions of the Fair Labor Standards Act (FLSA), compiled in 29 U.S.C. § 201 et seq., or the minimum wage required in this state, whichever is higher.
(c) Trafficking for forced labor or services is a Class C felony.

39-13-309. Trafficking for Commercial Sex Act.

(a) A person commits the offense of trafficking a person for a commercial sex act who: (1) Knowingly subjects, attempts to subject, benefits from or attempts to benefit from another person's provision of a commercial sex act; or
(2) Recruits, entices, harbors, transports, provides, purchases, or obtains by any other means, another person for the purpose of providing a commercial sex act.
(b) For purposes of subdivision (a)(2), such means may include, but are not limited to: (1) Causing or threatening to cause physical harm to the person;
(2) Physically restraining or threatening to physically restrain the person;
(3) Abusing or threatening to abuse the law or legal process;
(4) Knowingly destroying, concealing, removing, confiscating or possessing any actual or purported passport or other immigration document, or any other actual or purported government identification document, of the person;
(5) Using blackmail or using or threatening to cause financial harm for the purpose of exercising financial control over the person; or
(6) Facilitating or controlling a person's access to a controlled substance.
(c) A violation of subsection (a) is a Class B felony, except where the victim of the offense is a child under fifteen (15) years of age, or where the offense occurs on the grounds or facilities or

> within one thousand feet (1,000') of a public or private school, secondary school, preschool, child care agency, public library, recreational center, or public park, a violation of subsection (a) is a Class A felony.[22]

The efforts underway in Tennessee are highlighted by the article by co-author Cheryl Taylor Page, *Sex Trafficking Laws in East Tennessee*:

> There was a time in U.S. history when opponents of the trans-Atlantic slave trade had to convince the watching world that slavery was horrid and against the laws of humanity. Today, modern-day abolitionists are attempting to make a sleeping world aware that slavery still exists. There are approximately 27 million people currently enslaved in the world today. It is a problem that our own community cannot ignore, because slavery exists in East Tennessee and is thriving.
>
> Slavery in East Tennessee takes the form of sex trafficking, in which women and children are bought and sold as property for the sexual pleasure of the "buyer." Those most vulnerable to being caught up in this practice are run-away children. Many, once bought by a pimp, are moved around from location to location and sold daily to strangers. East Tennessee's heavily frequented interstate roadways and highly populated tourist spots make this area a hot bed for this type of criminal activity. Pimps are able to operate in this area and go relatively unnoticed. But their victims are caught in a daily web of systematic abuse, drugs and brutality. Johns are able to "purchase" women and children on Internet websites and remain relatively anonymous.
>
> The only safe house in the state of Tennessee is located in Knoxville and is operated through the non-profit organization "Cry for Justice." The home works as a means to get the victims acclimated and readjusted to society.
>
> Fortunately, in the past few years, the Tennessee General Assembly has enacted numerous laws in an attempt to deal with sex trafficking and protect its victims. In the past, victims of sex

22. Tenn. Code. Ann. § 39-13-308, 39-13-309 (2013).

trafficking, once apprehended, were at risk of being charged with a crime (usually prostitution), despite having been brought into the sex trade via "force, fraud or coercion." In 2011, the General Assembly passed Public Chapter No. 377, which protects minor victims of sex trafficking in two ways: (1) a person suspected to be under 18 years of age shall be immune from prosecution of prostitution as a juvenile or adult, and that person shall be provided with the National Human Trafficking Resource Center hotline, and (2) patronizing prostitution from a person younger than 18 is a Class E felony. In 2012, the legislature passed Public Chapter No. 1075, which made several revisions to Title 39, Chapter 13 of the Tennessee Code Annotated. It strengthened the definition of the offense of "trafficking a person for a commercial sex act," which is committed when a person either "knowingly subjects, attempts to subject, benefits from or attempts to benefit from another person's provision of a commercial sex act" or knowingly recruits, entices, harbors, transports, provides or obtains by any means another person for sexual servitude. Under present law, the offense of trafficking a person for a commercial sex act is generally punished as a Class B felony, except where the victim of the offense is a child under 15 years of age, or where the offense occurs on the grounds or facilities or within 1,000 feet of a public or private school, secondary school, preschool, child care agency, public library, recreational center, or public park, in which case the offense is a Class A felony. Public Chapter No. 1075 also created the offense of "advertising commercial sexual abuse of a minor," a Class C felony, which is committed "if the person knowingly sells or offers to sell and advertisement that would appear to a reasonable person to be for the purpose of engaging in what would be a commercial sex act ... with a minor."

Certain other statutes have been added as of July 2013 that operate to bring better coverage of our state laws to those affected by sex trafficking. They include:

- Public Chapter No. 242, which amends Tennessee Code Annotated section 39-11-118 to require restitution to the victim to be paid by the defendant for the offenses of patronizing prostitution, trafficking for commercial sex acts, solicitation of a minor for sexual purposes, and enlisting or paying a minor to engage in child pornography.

- Public Chapter No. 436, which expands the offense of solicitation of a minor to include solicitations by adults, which, if completed, would constitute trafficking for commercial sex acts, patronizing prostitution, promoting prostitution or aggravated sexual exploitation of a minor.
- Public Chapter No. 465, which creates the offense of "promoting travel for prostitution," a Class D felony, which is committed "if the person sells or offers to sell travel services that the person knows to include travel for the purpose of engaging in what would be prostitution if occurring in the state." The definition of "travel services" includes "transportation by air, sea, road or rail, related ground transportation, hotel accommodations, or package tours, whether offered on a wholesale or retail basis." Public Chapter No. 465 also adds the purchase of another person for the purpose of providing a commercial sex act to the definition of the offense of trafficking a person for a commercial sex act. Finally, the act substitutes the present law definition of "commercial sex act" for the definition of "sexual servitude."
- Public Chapter No. 415, which adds to the definition of criminal gang offenses trafficking for commercial sex acts and receipt, or intended receipt, of income, benefit, property, money or anything of value from the commission of trafficking for commercial sex acts. This recognizes that gangs are now using sex trafficking as another form of income.
- Public Chapter No. 485, which raises the classification of the offense of promoting prostitution of a minor from a Class E felony to a Class A or B felony by making it punishable as trafficking for a commercial sex act under § 39-13-309.
- Public Chapter No. 350, which disallows as a defense to the offenses of solicitation of a minor to observe sexual conduct, sexual exploitation of a minor, aggravated sexual exploitation of a minor, and especially aggravated sexual exploitation of a minor,

the allegation that the victim "consented" to the conduct constituting the offense.

- Public Chapter No. 416, which extends the statutes of limitations for prosecuting a person for trafficking a person for a commercial sex act, soliciting sexual exploitation of a minor, exploitation of a minor by electronic means, prosecuting a person for patronizing prostitution, and promoting prostitution if the offenses were committed against a child on or after July 1, 2013.
- Public Chapter No. 251, which, given the issues with many victims being intimidated by the court system, provides that victims of trafficking for commercial sex act and patronizing prostitution who are under 13 years of age may, under certain circumstances, testify outside the courtroom by closed circuit television.
- Public Chapter No. 337, which removes as a defense ignorance or mistake of fact concerning the age of a minor to the offenses of patronizing prostitution and soliciting sexual exploitation of a minor.

Tennessee has made major strides in passing laws designed to focus on and eradicate sex trafficking. Knowledge of these laws can assist all attorneys in East Tennessee to become a part of the solution in ceasing slavery in our state and region in the twenty-first century.[23]

C. For Further Thought

1. Review the summary of the laws of your state. How do the efforts in your state compare to others? What additional laws, if any, would you want to see enacted in your state? Why? Are there any in effect at the present time that you would eliminate? Why?

23. Cheryl George, *Sex Trafficking Laws in East Tennessee* DICTA (*A Monthly Publication of the Knoxville Bar Association*) 13–14 (2014), *available at* http://works.bepress.com/cheryl_george/12. Reprinted with permission from the Knoxville Bar Association, DICTA, February 2014, Volume 41, Issue 2.

2. As you consider the material that follows in this book, consider whether the laws outlined in this chapter are working. How could we measure their success or lack of it?
3. Would legalizing prostitution eliminate any of the problems associated with sex trafficking? Re-examine your answer after considering the material in Chapter 5 of this book.

Chapter 3

The United States Department of State and the Tier Ranking System

A. Tier Placement

Each year, the U.S. Department of State issues its "Trafficking in Persons (TIP) Report." The 2021 TIP can be found at: https://www.state.gov/reports/2021-trafficking-in-persons-report/. One of the sections of the report identifies four tiers into which various countries are assigned, regarding their efforts to combat human trafficking. The 2021 TIP includes these introductory remarks regarding the placement.

> **TIER PLACEMENT**
>
> The Department places each country in this Report onto one of four tiers, as mandated by the TVPA. This placement is based not on the size of a country's problem but on the extent of government efforts to meet the TVPA's minimum standards for the elimination of human trafficking (see page 56–58), which are generally consistent with the Palermo Protocol.
>
> While Tier 1 is the highest ranking, it does not mean that a country has no human trafficking problem or that it is doing enough to address the crime. Rather, a Tier 1 ranking indicates that a government has made efforts to address the problem that meet the TVPA's minimum standards. To maintain a Tier 1 ranking, governments need to demonstrate appreciable prog-

ress each year in combating trafficking. Tier 1 represents a responsibility rather than a reprieve.

Tier rankings and narratives in the 2021 Trafficking in Persons Report reflect an assessment of the following:

- enactment of laws prohibiting severe forms of trafficking in persons, as defined by the TVPA, and provision of criminal punishments for trafficking crimes;
- criminal penalties prescribed for human trafficking crimes with a maximum of at least four years' deprivation of liberty, or a more severe penalty;
- implementation of human trafficking laws through vigorous prosecution of the prevalent forms of trafficking in the country and sentencing of traffickers;
- proactive victim identification measures with systematic procedures to guide law enforcement and other government-supported front-line responders in the process of victim identification;
- government funding and partnerships with NGOs to provide victims with access to primary health care, counseling, and shelter, allowing them to recount their trafficking experiences to trained counselors and law enforcement in an environment of minimal pressure;
- victim protection efforts that include access to services and shelter without detention and with legal alternatives to removal to countries in which victims would face retribution or hardship;
- the extent to which a government ensures victims are provided with legal and other assistance and that, consistent with domestic law, proceedings are not prejudicial to victims' rights, dignity, or psychological well-being;
- the extent to which a government ensures the safe, humane, and to the extent possible, voluntary repatriation and reintegration of victims;
- governmental measures to prevent human trafficking, including efforts to curb practices identified as contributing factors to human trafficking, such as employers' confiscation of foreign workers' passports and allowing labor recruiters to charge fees to prospective migrants; and

- governmental efforts to reduce the demand for commercial sex acts and international sex tourism.

Tier rankings and narratives are **NOT** affected by the following:

- efforts, however laudable, undertaken exclusively by nongovernmental actors in the country;
- general public awareness events — government-sponsored or otherwise — lacking concrete ties to the prosecution of traffickers, protection of victims, or prevention of trafficking; and
- broad-based law enforcement or developmental initiatives.

A GUIDE TO THE TIERS

Tier 1

Countries whose governments fully meet the TVPA's minimum standards for the elimination of trafficking.

Tier 2

Countries whose governments do not fully meet the TVPA's minimum standards but are making significant efforts to bring themselves into compliance with those standards.

Tier 2 Watch List

Countries whose governments do not fully meet the TVPA's minimum standards but are making significant efforts to bring themselves into compliance with those standards, and for which:

- the estimated number of victims of severe forms of trafficking is very significant or is significantly increasing and the country is not taking proportional concrete actions; or
- there is a failure to provide evidence of increasing efforts to combat severe forms of trafficking in persons from the previous year, including increased investigations, prosecutions, and convictions of trafficking crimes, increased assistance to victims, and decreasing evidence of complicity in severe forms of trafficking by government officials.

Tier 3

Countries whose governments do not fully meet the TVPA's minimum standards and are not making significant efforts to do so.

The TVPA, as amended, lists additional factors to determine whether a country should be on Tier 2 (or Tier 2 Watch List) versus Tier 3:

- the extent to which the country is a country of origin, transit, or destination for severe forms of trafficking;
- the extent to which the country's government does not meet the TVPA's minimum standards and, in particular, the extent to which officials or government employees have been complicit in severe forms of trafficking;
- reasonable measures that the government would need to undertake to be in compliance with the minimum standards in light of the government's resources and capabilities to address and eliminate severe forms of trafficking in persons;
- the extent to which the government is devoting sufficient budgetary resources to investigate and prosecute human trafficking, convict and sentence traffickers; and obtain restitution for victims of human trafficking; and
- the extent to which the government is devoting sufficient budgetary resources to protect victims and prevent the crime from occurring.

In addition, the TVPA directs the Secretary of State to consider, as proof of a country's failure to make significant efforts to fully meet the TVPA's minimum standards, a government policy or pattern of: trafficking; trafficking in government-funded programs; forced labor (in government-affiliated medical services, agriculture, forestry, mining, construction, or other sectors); sexual slavery in government camps, compounds, or outposts; or employing or recruiting child soldiers.

The TVPA also provides that any country that has been ranked Tier 2 Watch List for two consecutive years and that would otherwise be ranked Tier 2 Watch List for the next year will instead be ranked Tier 3 in that third year. The Secretary of State is authorized to waive this automatic downgrade only once, in that third year, based on credible evidence that a waiver is justified because the government has a written plan that, if implemented, would constitute making significant efforts to meet the TVPA's minimum standards for the elimination of trafficking and is devoting sufficient resources to implement the plan. The following year, a country must either go up to Tier 2 or down to Tier 3. Finally, the TVPA limits a country to one year on Tier 2 Watch List after that country received a waiver to stay on the Watch List and was subsequently downgraded to Tier 3.

FUNDING RESTRICTIONS FOR TIER 3 COUNTRIES

Pursuant to the TVPA, governments of countries on Tier 3 may be subject to certain restrictions on foreign assistance, whereby the President may determine not to provide U.S. government nonhumanitarian, nontrade-related foreign assistance as defined in the TVPA.... [There are other sanctions which the President may impose — Ed.]

No tier ranking is permanent. Every country, including the United States, can do more. All countries must continually increase efforts to combat trafficking.

1. Rankings by Country — All Nations

Tier Placements

Tier 1

Argentina
Australia
Austria
Bahamas, The
Bahrain
Belgium
Canada
Chile
Colombia
Estonia
Czech Republic
Finland
France
Georgia
Guyana
Korea, South
Lithuania
Luxembourg
Namibia
Netherlands
Philippines
Singapore
Slovenia
Spain
Sweden
Taiwan
United Kingdom
United States of America

Tier 2

Albania
Angola
Antigua and Barbuda
Armenia
Bangladesh
Benin
Bolivia
Bosnia and Herzegovina
Botswana
Brazil
Bulgaria
Cabo Verde
Central African Republic
Congo, Republic of the
Costa Rica
Cote D'Ivoire
Croatia
Cyprus
Denmark
Dominican Republic
Ecuador
Egypt
El Salvador

Tier 2, continued

Eswatini
Fiji
Gabon
Germany
Ghana
Greece
Guatemala
Honduras
Hungary
Iceland
India
Indonesia
Iraq
Israel
Italy
Japan
Jamaica
Jordan
Kazakhstan
Kyrgyz Republic
Kenya
Kosovo
Kuwait
Laos
Latvia
Lebanon
Madagascar
Malawi
Maldives
Malta
Mauritius
Mexico
Micronesia
Moldova
Mongolia
Montenegro
Morocco
Mozambique
New Zealand
Niger
Nigeria
Nepal
North Macedonia
Norway
Oman
Panama
Paraguay
Peru
Poland
Portugal
Qatar
Rwanda
Saint Lucia
St. Vincent and the Grenadines
Saudi Arabia
Serbia
Seychelles
Sierra Leone
Slovak Republic
Solomon Islands
Sudan
Suriname
Switzerland
Tajikistan
Togo
Tunisia
Turkey
Ukraine
United Arab Emirates
Uruguay
Uzbekistan
Vanuatu

Tier 2 Watch List

Aruba
Azerbaijan
Barbados
Belarus
Belize
Bhutan
Brunei
Burkina Faso
Burundi
Cambodia
Cameroon
Chad
Congo, Democratic Republic of the
Curaçao
Djibouti
Equatorial Guinea
Ethiopia
Gambia, The
Guinea
Haiti
Hong Kong
Ireland
Lesotho
Liberia
Macau
Mali
Marshall Islands
Mauritania
Pakistan
Palau
Papua New Guinea
Romania
Senegal
Sint Maarten
South Africa
Sri Lanka
Tanzania
Thailand
Timor-Leste
Tonga
Trinidad and Tobago
Uganda
Vietnam
Zambia
Zimbabwe

Tier 3

Afghanistan
Algeria
Burma
China
Comoros
Cuba
Eritrea
Guinea-Bissau
Iran
Korea, North
Malaysia
Nicaragua
Russia
South Sudan
Syria
Turkmenistan
Venezuela

Special Case

Libya
Somalia
Yemen

* Auto downgrade from Tier 2 Watch List."

The Trafficking In Persons (TIP) report includes an analysis of the State Department's evaluation of each country. In order to obtain some insight into how the Department compiles its evaluation and ranking, we will consider the analysis of a Tier One country (the United States), a Tier Two country (Mexico) and a Tier Three country (Russia). The significance of each of these countries is obvious. That, and the fact that the respective ranking for each of these three countries has not changed since 2014, makes a case study of these three countries critical in attempting to understand the rankings and the situation in each of these countries. We will start from the bottom ranking, Russia, proceed to Mexico and conclude with the United States.

2. Analysis of Selected Nations

RUSSIA

> The Government of Russia does not fully meet the minimum standards for the elimination of trafficking and is not making significant efforts to do so, even considering the impact of the COVID-19 pandemic, if any, on its anti-trafficking capacity; therefore Russia remained on Tier 3. Despite the lack of significant efforts, the government took some steps to address trafficking, including by facilitating the return of Russian children from Iraq and Syria, identifying some victims, and extending work and residence permits for foreign workers in response to the pandemic. However, during the reporting period there was a government policy or pattern of trafficking. The government was actively complicit in the forced labor of North Korean workers. The government did not screen North Korean workers for trafficking indicators or identify any North Korean trafficking victims, despite credible reports in previous years that the Democratic People's Republic of Korea (DPRK) operated work camps in Russia and exploited thousands of North Korean workers in forced labor. Although the government took steps to repatriate North Korean workers in accordance with UN Security Council resolutions (UNSCRs), citizens from the DPRK continued to arrive throughout the year, many of whom likely engaged in informal labor. While the Russian govern-

ment reported the number of North Korean workers in Russia declined in 2020, the government issued almost 3,000 new tourist and student visas to North Koreans in 2020 in an apparent attempt to circumvent the UNSCRs....

PRIORITIZED RECOMMENDATIONS

Investigate and prosecute trafficking crimes and convict traffickers under the trafficking statutes, including complicit officials and suspected trafficking cases related to North Korean workers in Russia, respecting due process. Implement a formal policy to ensure identified trafficking victims are not punished or deported for unlawful acts traffickers compelled them to commit. Develop and implement formal national procedures to guide law enforcement, labor inspectors, and other government officials in identifying and referring victims to service providers, particularly among labor migrants and individuals in commercial sex, and screen for trafficking indicators among individuals arrested for commercial sex or immigration violations. Given significant concerns that North Korea forces its citizens to work abroad, screen North Korean workers, students, and tourists for trafficking indicators and refer them to appropriate services. Allocate funding to state bodies and anti-trafficking NGOs to provide specialized assistance and care to victims. Create a national anti-trafficking action plan and establish a central coordinator for government efforts. Ensure victim identification and protection measures are not tied to the prosecution of a trafficker and allow all first responders to officially identify potential trafficking victims and refer them to care. Ensure screening of children returned from Iraq and Syria for child soldiering indicators and provide them with rehabilitation and reintegration support. Provide victims access to legal alternatives to removal to countries where they face hardship or retribution. Amend the criminal code to include a definition of human trafficking that is consistent with the definition under international law. Create a central repository for publicly available information on investigation, prosecution, conviction, and sentencing data for trafficking cases. Increase efforts to raise public awareness of both sex and labor trafficking, including among children.

PROSECUTION

The government decreased already minimal law enforcement efforts. Articles 127.1 (trafficking in persons) and 127.2 (use of slave labor) of the criminal code criminalized sex trafficking and labor trafficking. Article 127.1 prescribed penalties of up to five years' prison labor or up to six years' imprisonment for offenses involving an adult victim, and three to 10 years' imprisonment for those involving a child victim. Article 127.2 prescribed penalties of up to five years' prison labor or up to five years' imprisonment for offenses involving an adult victim, and up to five years' prison labor or three to 10 years' imprisonment for those involving a child victim. These penalties were sufficiently stringent and, with respect to sex trafficking, commensurate with punishments prescribed for other serious crimes, such as kidnapping. However, inconsistent with the definition of trafficking under international law, these articles established the use of force, fraud, or coercion as an aggravating factor, rather than an essential element of the crime....

....

PROTECTION

The government maintained negligible efforts to protect victims. The government did not develop or employ a formal system to guide officials in proactive identification of victims or their referral to available services. The law did not specifically define who was a trafficking victim or differentiate trafficking victims from victims of other crimes; experts noted this hindered identification measures and limited access to victim services. The government reported the identification of 52 trafficking victims in 2020, compared with 61 in 2019 and 19 in 2018. According to law enforcement statistics, of these 52 identified victims, 50 were female sex trafficking victims and two were male forced labor victims. Available data did not specify national origin in all cases, but most victims identified were Russian....

....

PREVENTION

The government maintained minimal efforts to prevent trafficking. The government had neither a designated lead agency to coordinate its anti-trafficking efforts nor a body to monitor its anti-trafficking activities or make periodic assessments measuring its performance. Russia did not have a national action plan....

TRAFFICKING PROFILE

As reported over the past five years, human traffickers exploit domestic and foreign victims in Russia, and victims from Russia are exploited abroad. Although labor trafficking remains the predominant form of human trafficking in Russia, sex trafficking also occurs. Traffickers exploit workers from Russia and other countries in Europe, Central Asia, Southeast Asia, China, and DPRK in forced labor in Russia. Instances of labor trafficking have been reported in the construction, manufacturing, logging, textile, transport, and maritime industries, as well as in sawmills, agriculture, sheep farms, grocery and retail stores, restaurants, waste sorting, street sweeping, domestic service, call centers, and begging....

....

MEXICO

The Government of Mexico does not fully meet the minimum standards for the elimination of trafficking but is making significant efforts to do so. The government demonstrated overall increasing efforts compared to the previous reporting period, considering the impact of the COVID-19 pandemic on its anti-trafficking capacity; therefore Mexico remained on Tier 2. These efforts included convicting more traffickers; providing funding to three NGOs that operate trafficking shelters; and increasing efforts of the Secretariat of Finance's Financial Intelligence Unit (UIF) to collect intelligence in support of trafficking investigations and prosecutions....

PRIORITIZED RECOMMENDATIONS

Develop, implement, and fund a national strategic action plan on victim services, in consultation with international organizations and NGOs, to include shelters, comprehensive services, and reintegration support for all victims, including men and boys, LGBTQI+ individuals, and indigenous persons. Develop and implement standardized procedures for front-line officials to proactively identify victims among vulnerable groups in Mexico and overseas — including individuals in commercial sex, children apprehended for illicit gang-related activities, Cuban medical professionals, and migrants, including migrant workers — and refer them to service providers for assistance. Increase efforts to investigate and prosecute trafficking crimes, including forced labor and those involving complicit officials, at both the federal and state levels. Increase and institutionalize anti-trafficking training for police, prosecutors, judges, immigration authorities, and service providers, with a focus on applying trauma-informed, victim-centered procedures. Provide improved security to victims and witnesses testifying against traffickers and ensure victims are not unlawfully detained, coerced into testifying, or otherwise re-traumatized. Allocate funds to a legally required victim assistance fund to cover restitution payments convicted traffickers are unable to pay and develop a mechanism to ensure victims receive court-ordered payments. Strengthen the labor law to adequately criminalize and establish stringent penalties for recruitment practices that facilitate trafficking, and increase enforcement to punish employers and labor recruiters for violations. Enact anti-trafficking legislation and establish specialized anti-trafficking prosecution units in all states. Enact, implement, and allocate sufficient resources toward a new national action plan that is coordinated across federal, state, and local authorities. Conduct culturally relevant awareness campaigns in local languages targeted for rural and indigenous communities. Strengthen data collection efforts.

PROSECUTION

The government maintained law enforcement efforts; while authorities obtained more convictions, the government did not provide complete data on prosecution efforts....

....

Trafficking-related corruption remained a concern. Some government officials colluded with traffickers or participated in trafficking crimes....

PROTECTION

The government maintained protection efforts, identifying more victims; however, it did not provide adequate services to victims. The government reported identifying 673 victims in 2020, compared with 658 victims in 2019 and 706 victims in 2018....

....

PREVENTION

The government maintained prevention efforts. The anti-trafficking commission, led by SEGOB, coordinated efforts among government agencies and civil society organizations. Local experts reported the commission was effective in promoting participation of stakeholders from academia, NGOs, and international organizations, and it encouraged transparency at its regular meetings and in its five permanent working groups. The government lacked a national anti-trafficking action plan for a second year, following the previous plan's expiration in 2018. In December 2020, the government launched its National Program for Human Rights 2020–2024, which included a chapter on prosecution, protection, and prevention efforts to combat trafficking. In November 2020, following the murders of two children who may have been victims of forced criminality, authorities in Mexico City launched a multisectoral strategy to provide opportunities and support for vulnerable children, aimed at preventing their exploitation in criminal activity.

....

TRAFFICKING PROFILE

As reported over the past five years, human traffickers exploit domestic and foreign victims in Mexico, and traffickers exploit victims from Mexico abroad. Groups considered most at risk for trafficking in Mexico include unaccompanied children, indigenous persons, persons with mental and physical disabilities, asylum seekers and migrants, IDPs, LGBTQI+ individuals, informal sector workers, and children in gang-controlled territories. Traffickers recruit and exploit Mexican women and children, and to a lesser extent men, in sex trafficking in Mexico and the United States through false promises of employment, deceptive romantic relationships, or extortion. The majority of trafficking cases occur among family, intimate partners, acquaintances on social media, or through employment-related traps. Transgender persons are particularly vulnerable to sex trafficking. . . ."

UNITED STATES OF AMERICA

The Government of the United States fully meets the minimum standards for the elimination of trafficking. The government continued to demonstrate serious and sustained efforts during the reporting period, considering the impact of the COVID-19 pandemic on its anti-trafficking capacity; therefore the United States remained on Tier 1. These efforts included increasing the number of investigations for the second year in a row; increasing the number of victims served by federal grantees; granting T nonimmigrant status to more victims; increasing enforcement of the prohibition of imports made wholly or in part by forced labor; and issuing its first national action plan to combat human trafficking. Although the government meets the minimum standards, it implemented policies that placed greater limits on access to immigration options for trafficking victims for most of the reporting period prior to repealing them. These policies further increased some foreign national victims' distrust in authorities and caused them to fear for their safety if they came forward to assist law enforcement, pursue these immigration options, or access services. . . .

PRIORITIZED RECOMMENDATIONS

Increase investigation and prosecution of labor trafficking cases, and increase access to protections for labor trafficking victims. Strengthen rules and regulations to ensure immigration enforcement does not hinder human trafficking detection, criminal law enforcement, or victim protections. Screen all individuals in immigration detention or custody for human trafficking indicators. Adopt inclusive policies that address aspects of government-run systems or programs that have disparate negative impact on marginalized communities and increase their vulnerability to human trafficking. Improve access to emergency and long-term housing for all victims. Increase access to and accessibility of specialized victim assistance for men, boys, LGBTQI+ persons, and persons with disabilities. Mitigate vulnerabilities in employment-based or other nonimmigrant U.S. visa programs, including by holding accountable noncompliant employers and their agents, and adopting policies that incentivize workers to report program violations. Increase the number of requests by federal law enforcement officials for Continued Presence. Encourage state and local authorities to implement policies not to prosecute victims for the unlawful acts their traffickers compelled them to commit. Train investigators, prosecutors, and judges to increase the number of forfeiture orders and mandatory restitution orders for trafficking victims, and use all available authorities to ensure restitution is paid. Increase survivor engagement, including by establishing accessible mechanisms for receiving and providing compensation for survivor input when forming policies, programs, and trainings. Increase training for and efforts to pursue financial crime investigations in tandem with human trafficking cases. Conduct agency-level risk assessments for contracts connected to high-risk regions, industries, or sectors. Strengthen efforts to examine the role of demand reduction in preventing human trafficking. As described in the Methodology section of this report, these recommendations were drawn from input solicited from multiple anti-trafficking stakeholders, such as advocates (which includes NGOs and subject matter experts who have survived human trafficking), academia, and government agencies, on how the United States could better meet the minimum standards set forth in the TVPA.

PROSECUTION

The government's prosecution efforts were mixed. The government increased the number of investigations, and law enforcement officials adapted to pandemic-related restrictions by conducting remote forensic interviews. The number of prosecutions decreased for the third year in a row, and the number of convictions decreased for the second year in a row in the midst of pandemic-related court closures and suspension of grand jury proceedings throughout the reporting period. The TVPA, as amended and codified at Title 18 U.S. Code sections 1581, et seq., criminalizes sex and labor trafficking. U.S. law confers extraterritorial jurisdiction for these human trafficking offenses, as long as the defendant (whether individual or entity) is a U.S. national, U.S. lawful permanent resident, or regardless of nationality, present in the United States. The penalties prescribed under these provisions, which can include up to life imprisonment, are sufficiently stringent and, with respect to sex trafficking, commensurate with the penalties prescribed for other serious crimes, such as rape. U.S. law prohibits conspiracy and the attempt to violate these provisions, obstruction of the statutes' enforcement, and benefiting from such acts. Additionally, a criminal statute prohibits the use of fraud to recruit workers abroad to come to the United States to work, or to recruit workers to work on a U.S. government contract performed outside the United States, on U.S. property, or on military installations outside the United States. During the reporting period, the U.S. Congress passed several laws that address human trafficking and related crimes, including a law requiring certain companies—which can be used as fronts for human trafficking and other illicit activities—to disclose their beneficial owners to the government and enable the tracing of human trafficking networks through financial transactions. Congress passed other legislation to extend authorization of the U.S. Advisory Council on Human Trafficking and to allow for compensation of its members.

....

State laws form the basis of most criminal actions in the United States. All U.S. states and territories have anti-trafficking criminal statutes. Forty-six states had laws allowing survivors to seek a court order vacating, expunging, or sealing criminal convictions entered against them that resulted from unlawful acts traffickers compelled them to commit. In three of these states, however, such relief was only available to child trafficking victims. At least 35 states had "safe harbor" laws, which are meant to prevent child sex trafficking victims from being prosecuted for commercial sex.

....

PROTECTION

During the reporting period, the government decreased overall protection efforts. The government increased the number of victims served and the number of federally funded victim assistance programs. The number of victims granted T nonimmigrant status significantly increased, although the median processing time for T nonimmigrant status was longer. Despite these efforts, for the majority of the reporting period until largely being repealed in the final two months, the government implemented policies that increased obstacles for foreign national trafficking victims to secure immigration options, including T and U nonimmigrant status and asylum....

....

The U.S. government continued to provide and fund training to federal, state, local, and tribal officials, as well as to NGO service providers and health and human service providers, to encourage more consistent application of victim-centered, trauma-informed, and culturally responsive approaches in all phases of victim identification, assistance, recovery, and participation in the criminal justice process. In FY 2020, HHS delivered 91 training and technical assistance activities to more than 50,000 federal grantees and health and human service professionals, including more than 46,000 people who completed its online training. In FY 2020, DOJ awarded $3.6 million in funding under two contracts to deliver training and technical assistance to grantees and to organizations building their capacity to respond to human trafficking victims. DOJ's specialized training and technical assistance providers assisted organizations in strengthening their anti-trafficking responses related to housing, employment, legal services, trauma-informed care, courts, and identifying labor trafficking victims.

....

PREVENTION

The U.S. government decreased efforts to prevent trafficking. In October 2020, the government issued and began to implement a comprehensive three-year national action plan to combat human trafficking. Federal agencies conducted numerous educational and training activities for their own personnel, state, local, and tribal officials, and other stakeholders....

....

NGOs noted human trafficking prevention efforts must address the ways systemic exploitation of Black and Brown communities heighten their vulnerability to human trafficking, especially given the disproportionate effect of COVID-19 on their health, economic stability, and safety. For instance, workers in domestic and agricultural sectors, performing duties historically performed by people who were enslaved, people who were formerly enslaved, and their descendants, were and remained specifically excluded from legal worker protections under federal law. Their lack of legal protections combined with the heightened isolation, economic uncertainty, and health risks due to COVID-19 has increased their risk of human trafficking....

....

Advocates asserted that immigration detainee labor and convict labor perpetuate slavery and its legacy of racial injustice. They called for the government to end its use of labor in immigrant detention facilities, whether government-operated or operated through contracts with private entities, as these immigration detainees have not been convicted of a crime. They also called for the government to amend the U.S. Constitution to eliminate the exception to the Thirteenth Amendment that allows for slavery or involuntary servitude as punishment for those convicted of a crime. NGOs and media reported prisons and detention facilities threatened inmates or detainees with disciplinary action if they refused to work due to COVID-19.

. . . .

DOJ published an issue of its journal on federal law and practice dedicated to the topics of missing or murdered American Indians and Alaska Natives, which included discussions on identifying and preventing human trafficking. As part of the task force's work, HHS's operating division released a framework for missing and murdered American Indians and Alaska Natives in October 2020 to guide its programs for those communities. In FY 2020, HHS funded a new grant program in six locations to strengthen the response to victims of human trafficking in American Indian and Alaska Native communities....

. . . .

TRAFFICKING PROFILE

As reported over the past five years, human traffickers exploit domestic and foreign national victims in the United States, and traffickers exploit victims from the United States abroad. Human trafficking cases have been reported in all 50 states, the District of Columbia, and U.S. territories. Traffickers compel victims to engage in commercial sex and to work in both legal and illicit industries and sectors, including in hospitality, traveling sales crews, agriculture, janitorial services, construction, landscaping, restaurants, factories, care for persons with disabilities, salon services, massage parlors, retail, fairs and carnivals, peddling and begging, drug smuggling and distribution, religious institutions, child care, and domestic work. Individuals who entered the United States with and without legal status have been identified as trafficking victims....

B. Political Considerations?

However, while the rankings give the appearance of an objective evaluation, critics have charged that there are political considerations involved in at least some of the decisions. For example, the United States' Voice of America reported on some of the controversy surrounding the 2015 TIP in an article which appeared on July 27, 2015, soon after the 2015 TIP was released. In that report, author Steve Herman noted that members of the U.S. Congress from both parties publicly criticized the Obama administration's decision to move Malaysia into the second tier from the third. They argued that economic and political concerns were overriding legitimate human trafficking concerns. The decision allowed Malaysia to participate in the Trans Pacific Partnership agreement negotiated by the President and his team. The article notes that within Congress, 166 House members, and eighteen Senators had publicly called upon the administration to leave Malaysia on the third tier. Senator Robert Menendez a Democrat from New Jersey charged that the determination "elevated politics over the most basic principles of human rights."[1]

C. For Future Thought

1. What use, if any, should private businesses in the United States take of the ranking system in determinations whether to do business with individuals, or entities within the countries ranked by the U.S. State Department?
2. American universities pride themselves on study abroad programs. Should the State Department rankings regarding human trafficking affect decisions where to locate these programs? Should educational institutions alert their students of the categories before those students travel to participate in such programs, or before those students plan activities on weekends during such programs? What use, if any, should individual students make of the rankings in making their travel plans?

---

1. Steve Herman, *US gives Malaysia Questionable Upgrade in Human Trafficking Ranks* (July 27, 2015), http://www.voanews.com/content/united-states-give-malaysia-questionable-upgrading-human-trafficking-ranks/288104.html.

3. Should private individuals in the United States review these rankings for making vacation plans?
4. Do the ranking systems offer a false sense of security which might cause travelers to lower their guard regarding trafficking issues as they travel into or through a Tier 1 country?
5. What factors account for the differences in the rating classification of Mexico, Russia, and the United States? In view of the U.S. report, how might governments of those other governments classify the U.S.?
6. Is it possible to eliminate all political and economic concerns in assigning countries to one of the tiers? If not, how might those concerns be minimized? Is it likely that such concerns surface in other areas related to trafficking such as asylum and related issues (discussed in Chapter 4 of this book)?
7. If you had the ability to construct such tiers, what information, in addition to the data referred to in the individual country reports in this chapter would you like to examine?

Chapter 4

What Is Being Done to Address Immigration Concerns Related to Trafficking?

Human trafficking obviously involves many aspects of coercion. Some victims experience multiple coercive effects of being moved across borders as well as being forced into labor or prostitution. While human slavery is not a recent phenomenon, neither are the legislative attempts to limit it. In this chapter we will consider historical, international and domestic attempts to reduce trafficking and protect victims through the use of immigration law. While a United Nations Protocol serves as an outline which member states should follow in addressing trafficking concerns, it is up to each individual country to create the mechanisms for protecting the victims of trafficking. We will first examine the international norms. Then we will consider the background of, and the mechanisms for, the protection of victims under the immigration laws of the United States.

However, before examining the technical and complicated legal considerations regarding trafficking and immigration, perhaps it will help focus our attention on these issues and improve our analyses of them, if we consider some hypothetical circumstances, based on composite situations that tragically seem to be recurring. At the end of this chapter, we will be asked to analyze these situations in light of the international and national legal considerations which we are about to study.

Joaquin is married, with three small children. He and his wife live in a rural village in Mexico. The family is impoverished. Joaquin learns of opportunities to work in the United States. He agrees to pay a smuggler $1,000 to bring him into the United States and place him in a job. Joaquin and a number of other residents from his area are smuggled across the southern border of the United States. They are driven to a house in a suburb of Houston. The smugglers demand an additional $3,000 from him. The smugglers force him and the others to work in the home and on day jobs which the smugglers arrange. Joaquin and the others are forced to turn over their wages to pay the smugglers' fees. When one of the workers refuses, he is beaten and taken away, never to be seen again. One day at a jobsite Joaquin escapes and calls police.

Anna is a 20-year-old single woman who lives with her parents in an eastern European country, learns of a dating service that places women in relationships with men in the United States. Eventually she is able to obtain a tourist visa, and using her family's meager savings, pays the dating service and is flown to the United States by a man with whom she has established a friendly relationship over the Internet. Once inside the United States, however, the man with whom she is corresponding demands that she help pay for her living expenses by working as a dancer in a nearby club. He introduces her to other men, and forces her to have sex with them. She is afraid to leave, because he threatens to kill her if she does so.

A family from another country arrives in the United States on a temporary worker visa held by the father. Among the family members is a 14-year-old girl, Sally. The family remains in the United States after their visas expire. Sally becomes increasingly frustrated with her family situation and begins to associate with some older people who use drugs. Sally becomes addicted to heroin, and runs away from home. In order to support her heroin habit, she turns to prostitution. One evening she is arrested, taken to a juvenile detention center, and charged with prostitution.

A group of fishermen in a remote village in Southeast Asia accept employment on a fishing vessel. However, once at sea, the employer refuses to pay them, and instead of returning them to their village, takes them to a detention facility in another country where they are forced to live in locked barracks, and process fish.

A wealthy family who holds permanent resident alien status in the United States arranges to have a 25-year-old woman from their home country live with them and work as a nanny to their two children. After several weeks, however, the nanny is slapped by the children's mother for refusing to do cleaning around the house. On three different occasions the children's father rapes the nanny, threatening to sell her on the streets if she reports the rapes to his wife or to anyone else.

We turn now to a discussion of the international effort to outlaw trafficking and protect its victims.

A. International Approach

It is estimated that worldwide, as many as twenty-one million people are the victims of forced sexual exploitation or labor.[1]

On December 12th, 2000, the United Nations Protocol to Prevent, Suppress and Punish Trafficking and Persons, Especially Women and Children, was adopted.[2] It entered into force on December 25th, 2003, with 117 nations signing it.[3] Under the terms of the Protocol, nations are required to criminalize trafficking (Article 5). They are required to provide for the protection of trafficking victims (Art. 6). Articles 7, 8, and 11 address important immigration issues and encourage nations to provide relief. The Protocol is set forth in its entirety:

PROTOCOL TO PREVENT, SUPPRESS AND PUNISH TRAFFICKING IN PERSONS, ESPECIALLY WOMEN AND CHILDREN, SUPPLEMENTING THE UNITED NATIONS CONVENTION AGAINST TRANSNATIONAL ORGANIZED CRIME

Preamble

> *The States Parties to this Protocol, Declaring* that effective action to prevent and combat trafficking in persons, especially women and children, requires a comprehensive international approach in the countries of origin, transit and destination that includes

---

1. *21 Million People Are Now Victims of Forced Labour*, ILO Says, Int'l Labour Org. (June 1, 2012), http://www.ilo.org/global/about-the-ilo/newsroom/news/WCMS_181961/lang-en/index.htm.

2. 2237 U.N.T.S. 319, Doc. A/55/383.

3. Https://treaties.un.org/doc/Publication/MTDSG/Volume%20II/Chapter%20XVIII/XVIII-12-a.en.pdf.

measures to prevent such trafficking, to punish the traffickers and to protect the victims of such trafficking, including by protecting their internationally recognized human rights, *Taking into account* the fact that, despite the existence of a variety of international instruments containing rules and practical measures to combat the exploitation of persons, especially women and children, there is no universal instrument that addresses all aspects of trafficking in persons, *Concerned* that, in the absence of such an instrument, persons who are vulnerable to trafficking will not be sufficiently protected, *Recalling* General Assembly resolution 53/111 of 9 December 1998, in which the Assembly decided to establish an open-ended intergovernmental ad hoc committee for the purpose of elaborating a comprehensive international convention against transnational organized crime and of discussing the elaboration of, inter alia, an international instrument addressing trafficking in women and children, *Convinced* that supplementing the United Nations Convention against Transnational Organized Crime with an international instrument for the prevention, suppression and punishment of trafficking in persons, especially women and children, will be useful in preventing and combating that crime,

Have agreed as follows:

I. General Provisions

Article 1. Relation with the United Nations Convention against Transnational Organized Crime

1. This Protocol supplements the United Nations Convention against Transnational Organized Crime. It shall be interpreted together with the Convention.

2. The provisions of the Convention shall apply, mutatis mutandis, to this Protocol unless otherwise provided herein.

3. The offences established in accordance with article 5 of this Protocol shall be regarded as offences established in accordance with the Convention.

Article 2. Statement of Purpose

The purposes of this Protocol are:

(a) To prevent and combat trafficking in persons, paying particular attention to women and children;

(b) To protect and assist the victims of such trafficking, with full respect for their human rights; and

(c) To promote cooperation among States Parties in order to meet those objectives.

Article 3. Use of Terms

For the purposes of this Protocol:

(a) "Trafficking in persons" shall mean the recruitment, transportation, transfer, harbouring or receipt of persons, by means of the threat or use of force or other forms of coercion, of abduction, of fraud, of deception, of the abuse of power or of a position of vulnerability or of the giving or receiving of payments or benefits to achieve the consent of a person having control over another person, for the purpose of exploitation. Exploitation shall include, at a minimum, the exploitation of the prostitution of others or other forms of sexual exploitation, forced labour or services, slavery or practices similar to slavery, servitude or the removal of organs;

(b) The consent of a victim of trafficking in persons to the intended exploitation set forth in subparagraph (a) of this article shall be irrelevant where any of the means set forth in subparagraph (a) have been used;

(c) The recruitment, transportation, transfer, harbouring or receipt of a child for the purpose of exploitation shall be considered "trafficking in persons" even if this does not involve any of the means set forth in subparagraph (a) of this article;

(d) "Child" shall mean any person under eighteen years of age.

Article 4. Scope of Application

This Protocol shall apply, except as otherwise stated herein, to the prevention, investigation and prosecution of the offences established in accordance with article 5 of this Protocol, where those offences are transnational in nature and involve an organized criminal group, as well as to the protection of victims of such offences.

Article 5. Criminalization

1. Each State Party shall adopt such legislative and other measures as may be necessary to establish as criminal offences the conduct set forth in article 3 of this Protocol, when committed intentionally.

2. Each State Party shall also adopt such legislative and other measures as may be necessary to establish as criminal offences:

(a) Subject to the basic concepts of its legal system, attempting to commit an offence established in accordance with paragraph 1 of this article;

(b) Participating as an accomplice in an offence established in accordance with paragraph 1 of this article; and

(c) Organizing or directing other persons to commit an offence established in accordance with paragraph 1 of this article.

II. Protection of Victims of Trafficking in Persons

Article 6. Assistance To and Protection of Victims of Trafficking in Persons

1. In appropriate cases and to the extent possible under its domestic law, each State Party shall protect the privacy and identity of victims of trafficking in persons, including, inter alia, by making legal proceedings relating to such trafficking confidential.

2. Each State Party shall ensure that its domestic legal or administrative system contains measures that provide to victims of trafficking in persons, in appropriate cases:

(a) Information on relevant court and administrative proceedings;

(b) Assistance to enable their views and concerns to be presented and considered at appropriate stages of criminal proceedings against offenders, in a manner not prejudicial to the rights of the defence.

3. Each State Party shall consider implementing measures to provide for the physical, psychological and social recovery of victims of trafficking in persons, including, in appropriate cases, in cooperation with non-governmental organizations, other relevant organizations and other elements of civil society, and, in particular, the provision of:

(a) Appropriate housing;

(b) Counselling and information, in particular as regards their legal rights, in a language that the victims of trafficking in persons can understand;

(c) Medical, psychological and material assistance; and

(d) Employment, educational and training opportunities.

4. Each State Party shall take into account, in applying the provisions of this article, the age, gender and special needs of victims of trafficking in persons, in particular the special needs of children, including appropriate housing, education and care.

5. Each State Party shall endeavour to provide for the physical safety of victims of trafficking in persons while they are within its territory.

6. Each State Party shall ensure that its domestic legal system contains measures that offer victims of trafficking in persons the possibility of obtaining compensation for damage suffered.

Article 7. Status of Victims of Trafficking in Persons in Receiving States

1. In addition to taking measures pursuant to article 6 of this Protocol, each State Party shall consider adopting legislative or other appropriate measures that permit victims of trafficking in persons to remain in its territory, temporarily or permanently, in appropriate cases.

2. In implementing the provision contained in paragraph 1 of this article, each State Party shall give appropriate consideration to humanitarian and compassionate factors.

Article 8. Repatriation of Victims of Trafficking in Persons

1. The State Party of which a victim of trafficking in persons is a national or in which the person had the right of permanent

residence at the time of entry into the territory of the receiving State Party shall facilitate and accept, with due regard for the safety of that person, the return of that person without undue or unreasonable delay.

2. When a State Party returns a victim of trafficking in persons to a State Party of which that person is a national or in which he or she had, at the time of entry into the territory of the receiving State Party, the right of permanent residence, such return shall be with due regard for the safety of that person and for the status of any legal proceedings related to the fact that the person is a victim of trafficking and shall preferably be voluntary.

3. At the request of a receiving State Party, a requested State Party shall, without undue or unreasonable delay, verify whether a person who is a victim of trafficking in persons is its national or had the right of permanent residence in its territory at the time of entry into the territory of the receiving State Party.

4. In order to facilitate the return of a victim of trafficking in persons who is without proper documentation, the State Party of which that person is a national or in which he or she had the right of permanent residence at the time of entry into the territory of the receiving State Party shall agree to issue, at the request of the receiving State Party, such travel documents or other authorization as may be necessary to enable the person to travel to and re-enter its territory.

5. This article shall be without prejudice to any right afforded to victims of trafficking in persons by any domestic law of the receiving State Party.

6. This article shall be without prejudice to any applicable bilateral or multilateral agreement or arrangement that governs, in whole or in part, the return of victims of trafficking in persons.

III. Prevention, Cooperation and Other Measures

Article 9. Prevention of Trafficking in Persons

1. States Parties shall establish comprehensive policies, programmes and other measures:

(a) To prevent and combat trafficking in persons; and

(b) To protect victims of trafficking in persons, especially women and children, from revictimization.

2. States Parties shall endeavour to undertake measures such as research, information and mass media campaigns and social and economic initiatives to prevent and combat trafficking in persons.

3. Policies, programmes and other measures established in accordance with this article shall, as appropriate, include cooperation with non-governmental organizations, other relevant organizations and other elements of civil society.

4. States Parties shall take or strengthen measures, including through bilateral or multilateral cooperation, to alleviate the factors that make persons, especially women and children, vulnerable to trafficking, such as poverty, underdevelopment and lack of equal opportunity.

5. States Parties shall adopt or strengthen legislative or other measures, such as educational, social or cultural measures, including through bilateral and multilateral cooperation, to discourage the demand that fosters all forms of exploitation of persons, especially women and children, that leads to trafficking.

Article 10. Information exchange and training

1. Law enforcement, immigration or other relevant authorities of States Parties shall, as appropriate, cooperate with one another by exchanging information, in accordance with their domestic law, to enable them to determine:

(a) Whether individuals crossing or attempting to cross an international border with travel documents belonging to other persons or without travel documents are perpetrators or victims of trafficking in persons;

(b) The types of travel document that individuals have used or attempted to use to cross an international border for the purpose of trafficking in persons; and

(c) The means and methods used by organized criminal groups for the purpose of trafficking in persons, including the recruitment and transportation of victims, routes and links between and among individuals and groups engaged in such trafficking, and possible measures for detecting them.

2. States Parties shall provide or strengthen training for law enforcement, immigration and other relevant officials in the prevention of trafficking in persons. The training should focus on methods used in preventing such trafficking, prosecuting the traffickers and protecting the rights of the victims, including protecting the victims from the traffickers.

The training should also take into account the need to consider human rights and child- and gender-sensitive issues and it should encourage cooperation with non-governmental organizations, other relevant organizations and other elements of civil society.

3. A State Party that receives information shall comply with any request by the State Party that transmitted the information that places restrictions on its use.

Article 11. Border Measures

1. Without prejudice to international commitments in relation to the free movement of people, States Parties shall strengthen, to the extent possible, such border controls as may be necessary to prevent and detect trafficking in persons.

2. Each State Party shall adopt legislative or other appropriate measures to prevent, to the extent possible, means of transport operated by commercial carriers from being used in the commission of offences established in accordance with article 5 of this Protocol.

3. Where appropriate, and without prejudice to applicable international conventions, such measures shall include establishing the obligation of commercial carriers, including any transportation company or the owner or operator of any means of transport, to ascertain that all passengers are in possession of the travel documents required for entry into the receiving State.

4. Each State Party shall take the necessary measures, in accordance with its domestic law, to provide for sanctions in cases of violation of the obligation set forth in paragraph 3 of this article.

5. Each State Party shall consider taking measures that permit, in accordance with its domestic law, the denial of entry or revocation of visas of persons implicated in the commission of offences established in accordance with this Protocol.

6. Without prejudice to article 27 of the Convention, States Parties shall consider strengthening cooperation among border control agencies by, inter alia, establishing and maintaining direct channels of communication.

Article 12. Security and Control of Documents

Each State Party shall take such measures as may be necessary, within available means:

(a) To ensure that travel or identity documents issued by it are of such quality that they cannot easily be misused and cannot readily be falsified or unlawfully altered, replicated or issued; and

(b) To ensure the integrity and security of travel or identity documents issued by or on behalf of the State Party and to prevent their unlawful creation, issuance and use.

Article 13. Legitimacy and Validity of Documents

At the request of another State Party, a State Party shall, in accordance with its domestic law, verify within a reasonable time the legitimacy and validity of travel or identity documents issued or purported to have been issued in its name and suspected of being used for trafficking in persons.

IV. Final Provisions

Article 14. Saving Clause

1. Nothing in this Protocol shall affect the rights, obligations and responsibilities of States and individuals under international law, including international humanitarian law and international human rights law and, in particular, where applicable, the 1951 Convention and the 1967 Protocol relating to the Status of Refugees and the principle of non-refoulement as contained therein.

2. The measures set forth in this Protocol shall be interpreted and applied in a way that is not discriminatory to persons on

the ground that they are victims of trafficking in persons. The interpretation and application of those measures shall be consistent with internationally recognized principles of non-discrimination.

Article 15. Settlement of Disputes

1. States Parties shall endeavour to settle disputes concerning the interpretation or application of this Protocol through negotiation.

2. Any dispute between two or more States Parties concerning the interpretation or application of this Protocol that cannot be settled through negotiation within a reasonable time shall, at the request of one of those States Parties, be submitted to arbitration. If, six months after the date of the request for arbitration, those States Parties are unable to agree on the organization of the arbitration, any one of those States Parties may refer the dispute to the International Court of Justice by request in accordance with the Statute of the Court.

3. Each State Party may, at the time of signature, ratification, acceptance or approval of or accession to this Protocol, declare that it does not consider itself bound by paragraph 2 of this article. The other States Parties shall not be bound by paragraph 2 of this article with respect to any State Party that has made such a reservation.

4. Any State Party that has made a reservation in accordance with paragraph 3 of this article may at any time withdraw that reservation by notification to the Secretary-General of the United Nations.

Article 16. Signature, Ratification, Acceptance, Approval and Accession

1. This Protocol shall be open to all States for signature from 12 to 15 December 2000 in Palermo, Italy, and thereafter at United Nations Headquarters in New York until 12 December 2002.

2. This Protocol shall also be open for signature by regional economic integration organizations provided that at least one member-State of such organization has signed this Protocol in accordance with paragraph 1 of this article.

3. This Protocol is subject to ratification, acceptance or approval. Instruments of ratification, acceptance or approval shall be deposited with the Secretary-General of the United Nations. A regional economic integration organization may deposit its instrument of ratification, acceptance or approval if at least one of its member-States has done likewise. In that instrument of ratification, acceptance or approval, such organization shall declare the extent of its competence with respect to the matters governed by this Protocol. Such organization shall also inform the depositary of any relevant modification in the extent of its competence.

4. This Protocol is open for accession by any State or any regional economic integration organization of which at least one member-State is a Party to this Protocol. Instruments of accession shall be deposited with the Secretary-General of the United Nations. At the time of its accession, a regional economic integration organization shall declare the extent of its competence with respect to matters governed by this Protocol. Such organization shall also inform the depositary of any relevant modification in the extent of its competence.

Article 17. Entry into Force

1. This Protocol shall enter into force on the ninetieth day after the date of deposit of the fortieth instrument of ratification, acceptance, approval or accession, except that it shall not enter into force before the entry into force of the Convention. For the purpose of this paragraph, any instrument deposited by a regional economic integration organization shall not be counted as additional to those deposited by member States of such organization.

2. For each State or regional economic integration organization ratifying, accepting, approving or acceding to this Protocol after the deposit of the fortieth instrument of such action, this Protocol shall enter into force on the thirtieth day after the date of deposit by such State or organization of the relevant instrument or on the date this Protocol enters into force pursuant to paragraph 1 of this article, whichever is the later.

Article 18. Amendment

1. After the expiry of five years from the entry into force of this Protocol, a State Party to the Protocol may propose an amendment and file it with the Secretary-General of the United Nations, who shall thereupon communicate the proposed amendment to the States Parties and to the Conference of the Parties to the Convention for the purpose of considering and deciding on the proposal. The States Parties to this Protocol meeting at the Conference of the Parties shall make every effort to achieve consensus on each amendment. If all efforts at consensus have been exhausted and no agreement has been reached, the amendment shall, as a last resort, require for its adoption a two-thirds majority vote of the States Parties to this Protocol present and voting at the meeting of the Conference of the Parties.

2. Regional economic integration organizations, in matters within their competence, shall exercise their right to vote under this article with a number of votes equal to the number of their member States that are Parties to this Protocol. Such organizations shall not exercise their right to vote if their member States exercise theirs and vice versa.

3. An amendment adopted in accordance with paragraph 1 of this article is subject to ratification, acceptance or approval by States Parties.

4. An amendment adopted in accordance with paragraph 1 of this article shall enter into force in respect of a State Party ninety days after the date of the deposit with the Secretary-General of the United Nations of an instrument of ratification, acceptance or approval of such amendment.

5. When an amendment enters into force, it shall be binding on those States Parties which have expressed their consent to be bound by it. Other States Parties shall still be bound by the provisions of this Protocol and any earlier amendments that they have ratified, accepted or approved.

Article 19. Denunciation

1. A State Party may denounce this Protocol by written notification to the Secretary-General of the United Nations. Such

denunciation shall become effective one year after the date of receipt of the notification by the Secretary-General.

2. A regional economic integration organization shall cease to be a Party to this Protocol when all of its member States have denounced it.

Article 20. Depositary and Languages

1. The Secretary-General of the United Nations is designated depositary of this Protocol.

2. The original of this Protocol, of which the Arabic, Chinese, English, French, Russian and Spanish texts are equally authentic, shall be deposited with the Secretary-General of the United Nations.

IN WITNESS WHEREOF, the undersigned plenipotentiaries, being duly authorized thereto by their respective Governments, have signed this Protocol.

Under the terms of the Protocol, Article 19, state parties may "denounce" it. While the United States signed, it specifically indicated reservations regarding some applications:

> The United States of America reserves the right to assume obligations under this Protocol in a manner consistent with its fundamental principles of federalism, pursuant to which both federal and state criminal laws must be considered in relation to conduct addressed in the Protocol. U.S. federal criminal law, which regulates conduct based on its effect on interstate or foreign commerce, or another federal interest, such as the Thirteen Amendment's prohibition of "slavery" and "involuntary servitude," serves as the principal legal regime within the United States for combating the conduct addressed in this Protocol, and is broadly effective for this purpose. Federal criminal law does not apply in the rare case where such criminal conduct does not so involve interstate or foreign commerce, or otherwise implicate another federal interest, such as the Thirteenth Amendment. There are a small number of conceivable situations involving such rare offenses of a purely local character

> where U.S. federal and state criminal law may not be entirely adequate to satisfy an obligation under the Protocol. The United States of America therefore reserves to the obligations set forth in the Protocol to the extent they address conduct which would fall within this narrow category of highly localized activity. This reservation does not affect in any respect the ability of the United States to provide international cooperation to other Parties as contemplated in the Protocol.[4]

The United States, of course, did not need the prodding of the United Nations to address the evils of trafficking. Unfortunately, however, as noted below, this country *did* require the upheaval and horror of the Civil War before abolishing slavery. In addition to abolishing race-based slavery, the United States had criminalized the interstate trafficking in "white slavery" (prostitution) with the enactment of the Mann Act in 1910.[5] To understand the impact that trafficking has had upon this country, and to try to gain some understanding of the immigration avenues available to trafficking victims brought into this country from abroad, we turn to a discussion of the approach of the United States immigration laws.

B. United States Immigration Approach

One estimate by the United States State Department concludes that each year as many as 17,500 people are brought into this country as trafficking victims.[6] The United States provides several avenues of immigration assistance to trafficking victims. However, U.S. immigration law and policy is complicated and evolving. In order to appreciate the possible areas of immigration relief which might be available to trafficking victims who are brought into this country, we must first examine an

---

4. https://treaties.un.org/doc/Publication/MTDSG/Volume%20II/Chapter%20XVIII/XVIII-12-a.en.pdf.

5. 18 U.S.C. § 2124 (1998).

6. Heather J. Clawson et al., *Human Trafficking Into and Within the United States: A Review of the Literature*, U.S. Dep't of Health & Human Servs. 4 (2009), *available at* http://aspe.hhs.gov/hsp/07/humantrafficking/litrev/index.pdf.

overview of U.S. immigration law in order to determine who is allowed to live and work here.[7]

1. Historical Overview

It is important to begin our discussion of trafficking victims into the United States with some historical perspective. By 1776, new arrivals to the colonies had created a population base of approximately three million people which was sufficiently large to establish a new nation. Most came voluntarily, seeking the freedom and new opportunities promised in the New World. Some were shipped to the colonies because of misconduct or crimes they had committed. And, many of the arrivals were brought here involuntarily as slaves. Continued immigration, both voluntary and otherwise, was viewed as a necessity to continue clearing lands, engaging in agriculture, establishing industries, and protecting against attempts by foreign governments, and Native Americans, to impede the development of the colonies. Far from trying to restrict immigration, the colonists actively encouraged it. In fact, when the colonists rebelled and set forth in the Declaration of Independence a list of the justifications for rebellion, one of those is that the King of England had, "endeavored to prevent the population of these States; for that purpose obstructing the Laws for Naturalization of Foreigners; refusing to pass others to encourage their migrations hither, and raising the conditions of New Appropriations of Lands."[8]

The American Revolution was successful and the new nation was formed. Slavery, which had been an important element of obtaining a labor base, was allowed to continue when the Constitution of the United States was adopted. Article 1, section 9, clause 1 of the United States Constitution provides: "The Migration or Importation of such Persons as any of the States now existing shall think proper to permit, shall not be prohibited by the Congress prior to the year 1808." This clause, which seemed to focus on overall immigration control and strategy, was actu-

---

7. *See generally* Bill Piatt, *Immigration Law: Cases and Materials*, Chapter 4, The Michie Company 1994; *see also* Bill Piatt, Catholic Legal Perspectives (Carolina Academic Press 2d ed. 2015); *see also* Bill Piatt, *Immigration Reform from the Outside In*, 10 The Scholar 269 (2008).

8. The Declaration of Independence para. 2 (U.S. 1776).

ally addressed, however obliquely, to the slavery issue. It was the result of a political compromise. Northern colonies generally opposed slavery and wanted to use the Constitution to prohibit its further practice. Southern colonies sought to have explicit protection written into the Constitution allowing them to continue in trafficking. The compromise set forth above amounted to "kicking the can down the road" to the next generation. Under this compromise, the slave trade would be permitted to continue unimpeded by the new federal government through at least the year 1808. The framers of the Constitution were able to resolve temporarily the issue of trafficking by choosing to permit its existence at least for the time being. Northern and Southern colonies agreed to the compromise, and the Constitution was enacted and ratified.

There obviously was hope that the next generation would somehow be able politically to resolve the issue of slavery. Of course, that proved to be erroneous. It was not until the time of the Civil War and the enactment of the post-Civil War amendments, specifically the Thirteenth Amendment, that slavery was officially banned through the power of the Constitution of the United States.[9] Some erroneously believe that the federal government ended slavery in this country when President Lincoln issued his Emancipation Proclamation in 1863.[10] However, that Proclamation only freed the slaves in those states which were still at war with the United States. That Proclamation read:

> That on the first day of January, in the year of our Lord one thousand eight hundred and sixty-three, all persons held as slaves within any State or designated part of a State, the people whereof shall then be in rebellion against the United States, shall be then, thenceforward, and forever free; and the Executive Government of the United States, including the military and naval authority thereof, will recognize and maintain the freedom of such persons, and will do no act or acts to repress such persons, or any of them, in any efforts they may make for their actual freedom...[11]

---

9. U.S. CONST. amend. XIII.
10. Abraham Lincoln, Emancipation Proclamation (Jan. 1, 1863).
11. *Id.*

There is no mistaking, however, that the Thirteenth Amendment operated to eliminate the legal basis for slavery in this country.[12]

The atrocity of slavery resulted in at least 350,000 Africans arriving in the United States over the course of time when slavery was legally permitted. Many more slaves were trafficked to other areas of the New World. Even more were killed or died in the process of capture and transportation. One scholar, Stannard, estimates that at least thirty million Africans died in this process.[13]

2. Current Immigration Structure

How are modern-day slaves, the victims of human trafficking, treated under current United States immigration law and practice? It is not a simple process, and to understand it, we must first grasp some of the rudiments of U.S. immigration law. It is not simply that any foreign trafficking victim who is discovered and freed in this country is allowed to remain and work in the United States. That victim must qualify to remain under the labyrinth of the U.S. immigration process. In that regard, we will consider citizenship, permanent resident alien ("green card" or "immigrant") status, and non-immigrant (temporary) status. Without intending any disrespect, and in the interest of using precise legal terminology, we will use the language of the Immigration Nationality Act. That Act refers to people who are not citizens of the United States as, "aliens." While popular usage often refers now to anyone who enters this country as an "immigrant," under the Act "immigrants" are only those aliens who obtain permanent resident alien status. (See the discussion of this status below.)

a. Citizenship

First, consider what it means to be a citizen of the United States. A citizen can live here indefinitely, and can work at whatever position that person can acquire. That person can vote, serve on jury duty, and otherwise exercise all the freedoms and responsibilities that come with being a citizen of the United States. A United States citizen cannot be deported. How, then, does one become a United States citizen?

---

12. U.S. CONST. amend. XIII.

13. Stannard, 151, *cited in* Bill Piatt, *Immigration Law and Materials*, *supra* note 7, at 8.

1) Citizenship at Birth

There are two main avenues to obtaining US citizenship. The first is simply by birth. Under the Fourteenth Amendment of the Constitution of the United States, almost everyone who is born in this country is a citizen at birth. That is because the Fourteenth Amendment enacted in 1865, after the Civil War, provides in part, in Section 1: "All persons born or naturalized in the United States, and subject to the jurisdiction thereof, are citizens of the United States and of the State wherein they reside." It is important to understand that this amendment came into existence in order to overturn a decision[14] of the Supreme Court of the United States which had denied citizenship to a victim of trafficking.

In 1857, in that infamous case of *Dred Scott v. Sandford*,[15] the Supreme Court considered a case where a slave had been taken by his "owner" from Missouri to Illinois. Then they moved to what is now Minnesota, in the Louisiana Territory. In 1838, both of them returned to Missouri. Scott was sold as a slave to Sandford. Slavery was legal in Missouri. However, it was prohibited in Illinois and in the Louisiana Territory. Scott argued that he should be considered a free man because he had lived in a free territory. However, the Supreme Court of the United States determined that as a slave, Scott could not be a citizen of Missouri. The court saw the issue as "whether the class of persons described ... compose a portion of this people, and are constituent members of the sovereignty?"[16] The Court concluded, "We think they are not, and that they are not included, and were not intended to be included, under the word 'citizens' in the Constitution, and can therefore claim none of the rights and privileges which that instrument provides for and secures to citizens of the United States. On the contrary, they were at that time considered as a subordinate and inferior class of beings, who had been subjugated by the dominant race, and whether emancipated or not, yet remained subject to their authority, and had no rights or privileges but such as those who held the power and the Government might choose to grant them."[17]

---

14. *See generally* Dred Scott v. Sandford, 60 U.S. 393 (1856).

15. *Id.*

16. *Id.* at 404.

17. *Id.* at 405.

Undoubtedly, the Supreme Court thought that it had laid to rest once and for all the question as to whether slavery and its effects would be allowed to continue. We know that this pronouncement in the *Dred Scott* case did not resolve the slavery issue. Once the issue had been resolved on the battlefields of the Civil War, Congress enacted the Fourteenth Amendment to make clear that the *Dred Scott* decision would no longer be the law of the land. This citizenship by birth which many of us might take for granted, was obviously the result of the struggle to overturn a major impact of trafficking.

Returning to our discussion of citizenship at birth, in addition to the Fourteenth Amendment guarantee that persons born here are citizens, the United States Congress has also enacted complicated provisions that provide that a child born abroad of a US citizen, either mother or father, is also a citizen at birth if the statutory conditions are met. *See* 8 U.S.C. § 1431.

2) Citizenship by Naturalization

The second method of acquiring citizenship is through the process of naturalization. Under this process, a person who has become a permanent resident alien of the United States and who holds that status for the requisite number of years can then become naturalized by applying for citizenship, taking and passing an exam, and otherwise meeting statutory qualifications. *See* 8 U.S.C. § 1445 et seq. Currently, trafficking victims do not automatically qualify for either citizenship or permanent resident status, our next subtopic.

b. Permanent Resident Alien Status

Permanent residency is acquired through a number of complicated means. If we had to attempt to simplify this discussion, we could identify four major categories of people who are eligible to become permanent residents: those who have family sponsors; those who are seeking an employment basis, including investors; those who are seeking to immigrate as diversity immigrants; and finally, the most important are of our discussion, those people who are refugees or asylees. A permanent resident holds a "green card." That person can remain indefinitely, and can live and work anywhere in the United States. That person, however, could still be subject to deportation if that person violates any of the statutes that give rise to deportation. (Note that US citizens cannot be deported.)

Under international treaties and United States domestic law, those people who seek to remain in the United States because they are either persecuted, or have a well-founded fear of persecution on account of race, religion, nationality, membership in a particular social group, or political opinion may remain as permanent residents. Do human trafficking victims in the United States qualify as refugees or asylees? In other words, may a trafficking victim obtain permanent resident alien status based upon the fact that the person has been brought involuntarily into the United States as a trafficking victim? Consider the following cases, reflecting a split among the circuits which has yet to be resolved by the Supreme Court.

420 F.3d 551 (2005)
United States Court of Appeals, Sixth Circuit
Vitore RRESHPJA, Petitioner
v.
Alberto GONZALES, Attorney General of the United States, Respondent

Opinion

GILMAN, Circuit Judge.

Vitore Rreshpja is a citizen of Albania who was born in 1982. She arrived in the United States in November of 2001 with a fraudulently obtained nonimmigrant visa after an unknown man attempted to abduct her in her home country. The Immigration and Naturalization Service (INS) initiated removal proceedings against her several months later. At a hearing before an immigration judge (IJ), Rreshpja requested a grant of asylum or, in the alternative, the withholding of removal and protection under the Convention Against Torture (CAT). She claims that she is at risk of being forced to work as a prostitute if she is returned to Albania. The IJ denied her application. Rreshpja appealed the denial to the Board of Immigration Appeals (BIA), which affirmed the IJ's decision without issuing its own opinion on the matter. She then timely appealed to this court. For the reasons set forth below, we DENY Rreshpja's petition for review of the decision by the BIA.

I. BACKGROUND

Rreshpja grew up in the town of Shkoder in northern Albania. She attended high school in Tirana, the country's capital city, where she lived with her aunt. Her parents and younger brother remained in Shkoder.

In June of 2001, an unknown man attempted to abduct Rreshpja as she was walking home from school. She managed to escape. As she ran away, she heard her attacker say that she should not get too excited because she would end up on her back in Italy, like many other girls. She understood that statement to be a threat that she would be kidnapped and forced to work as a prostitute.

Rreshpja and her aunt reported the incident to the local police, but the police told Rreshpja that the information she had provided was insufficient to identify or arrest the man who had attacked her. Fearful for her safety, Rreshpja's family made arrangements for her to stay with her older brother, who lived in Howell, Michigan. They obtained an F-1 nonimmigrant visa for her to enter the United States. When she attempted to enroll at Michigan State University after arriving in this country, however, she was informed that the documents that had been used to obtain her visa were fraudulent.

The INS (now the Department of Homeland Security) initiated removal proceedings against Rreshpja in June of 2002. At a hearing before an IJ in Detroit, Rreshpja conceded that she had been admitted to the United States without a valid nonimmigrant visa, but she submitted an application for asylum, the withholding of removal, and protection under the CAT, claiming that she risked being forced into prostitution if she were required to return to Albania. The IJ denied Rreshpja's application. Rreshpja appealed the denial to the BIA, which affirmed the IJ's decision without issuing an opinion. She then timely filed a petition for review by this court.

II. ANALYSIS

A. Standard of Review

Because the BIA affirmed the decision of the IJ without issuing an opinion, we review the decision of the IJ directly. See *Denko v. INS*, 351 F.3d 717, 726 (6th Cir.2003) ("When the Board adopts the decision of the IJ in lieu of issuing its own opinion, we review the IJ's decision as the final agency decision."). "[I]n order to reverse the BIA's factual determinations, [we] must find that the evidence not only supports a contrary conclusion, but indeed compels it." *Klawitter v. INS*, 970 F.2d 149, 152 (6th Cir.1992) (emphasis in original).

B. The IJ did not err in denying Rreshpja's application for asylum, the withholding of removal, and protection under the CAT

Rreshpja claims that she is entitled to a grant of asylum or, in the alternative, the withholding of removal and protection under the CAT. She contends that the IJ's opinion contains errors of law and fact regarding her claims.

1. Asylum

Rreshpja argues that she faces persecution because she is an attractive young woman who risks being kidnapped and forced into prostitution if she returns to Albania. The IJ rejected this argument on the grounds that (1) the "social group" as defined by Rreshpja is not cognizable under the Immigration and Nationality Act (INA), 8 U.S.C. § 1101(a)(42)(A), and (2) even assuming that such a social group exists, Rreshpja failed to demonstrate that her attempted kidnapping in June of 2001 or her fear of being forced into prostitution if she is returned to Albania was the result of membership in that social group as opposed to the unfortunate consequences of widespread crime in Albania.

Pursuant to the INA, an applicant for asylum must show that she is a "refugee." 8 U.S.C. § 1158(b). A refugee is an individual who is unable or unwilling to return to her home country "because of persecution or a well-founded fear of persecution on account of race, religion, nationality, membership in a particular social group, or political opinion." 8 U.S.C. § 1101(a)(42)(A).

An applicant claiming to be a refugee must present specific facts demonstrating that she suffered past persecution or that she has a well-founded fear of future persecution. *INS v. Elias-Zacarias*, 502 U.S. 478, 481, 112 S. Ct. 812, 117 L. Ed. 2d 38 (1992) (holding that the "BIA's determination that Elias-Zacarias was not eligible for asylum must be upheld if supported by reasonable, substantial, and probative evidence on the record considered as a whole") [citation and quotation marks omitted]. If the asylum applicant satisfies her burden of establishing past persecution, "she is presumed to have a well-founded fear of [future] persecution." *Mikhailevitch v. INS*, 146 F.3d 384, 389 (6th Cir.1998) (citing 8 C.F.R. § 208.13(b)(1)(i)). The INS may rebut that presumption by establishing, by a preponderance of the evidence, that conditions in the applicant's country have changed since the time of the persecution to such an extent that the applicant no longer has a well-founded fear of being persecuted if she were to return. *Mikhailevitch*, 146 F.3d at 389.

An applicant's fear of persecution must be both subjectively genuine and objectively reasonable. *Perkovic v. INS*, 33 F.3d 615, 620-21 (6th Cir.1994). She must therefore "actually fear that [she] will be persecuted upon return to [her] country," and she must demonstrate "an 'objective situation' under which [her] fear can be deemed reasonable." *Id.* (quoting *INS v. Cardoza-Fonseca*, 480 U.S. 421, 440, 107 S. Ct. 1207, 94 L. Ed. 2d 434 (1987)).

The BIA has defined a "social group" to be "a group of persons all of whom share a common, immutable characteristic." *In re* Acosta, 19 I. & N. Dec. 211, 233 (BIA 1985) (holding that a Salvadoran taxi cooperative did not constitute a particular social group, even though the members were being persecuted for refusing to participate in work stoppages, because the drivers could escape persecution by changing jobs), *overruled on other grounds by In re* Mogharrabi, 19 I. & N. Dec. 439 (BIA 1987). "[W]hatever the common characteristic that defines the group, it must be one that the members of the group either cannot change, or should not be required to change because it is fundamental to their individual identities or consciences." *Acosta*, 19 I. & N. Dec. at 233; see also *Castellano-Chacon v. INS*, 341 F.3d 533, 546, 549 (6th Cir.2003) (adopting the BIA's definition of a "social group," and holding that tattooed youth fall outside of that definition). The BIA, however, has never held that an entire gender can constitute a social group under the INA.

Rreshpja does not explicitly state that she was or will be persecuted on account of her membership in a particular social group, but she suggests that the relevant group is young (or those who appear to be young), attractive Albanian women who are forced into prostitution. This demographic, however, does not constitute a social group under the INA for two reasons. First, almost all of the pertinent decisions have rejected generalized, sweeping classifications for purposes of asylum. See, e.g., *Raffington v. INS*, 340 F.3d 720, 723 (8th Cir.2003) (ruling that mentally ill Jamaicans did not qualify as a particular social group for asylum purposes); *Gomez v. INS*, 947 F.2d 660, 663–64 (2d Cir.1991) (holding that a Salvadoran woman who had been beaten and raped by Salvadoran guerillas during her youth was not for that reason a member of a particular social group for asylum purposes).

Rreshpja, however, cites *Mohammed v. Gonzales*, 400 F.3d 785 (9th Cir.2005), as support for her argument that a social group may in fact be broadly defined. In *Mohammed*, the Ninth Circuit held that female genital mutilation constitutes persecution on account of membership in a particular social group and explained that "the agency could define the social group as that of Somalian females." *Id.* at 796–97. The court noted that "the practice of female genital mutilation in Somalia is ... deeply imbedded [sic] in the culture throughout the nation and performed on approximately 98 percent of all females." *Id.* at 797. We do not necessarily agree with the Ninth Circuit's determination that virtually all of the women in Somalia are entitled to asylum in the United States. Regardless, we find that Mohammed is distinguishable from the present case because Rreshpja did not introduce any evidence to show that the practice of forcing young women into prostitution in Albania is nearly as pervasive as the practice of female genital mutilation in Somalia.

Second, a social group may not be circularly defined by the fact that it suffers persecution. The individuals in the group must share a narrowing characteristic other than their risk of being persecuted. *Castellano-Chacon*, 341 F.3d at 548 ("[S]ociety's reaction to a 'group' may provide evidence in a specific case that a particular group exists, as long as the reaction by persecutors to members of a particular social group is not the touchstone defining the group."). If the group with which Rreshpja is associated is defined noncircularly—i.e., simply as young, attractive Albanian women—then virtually any young Albanian woman who possesses the subjective criterion of being "attractive" would be eligible for asylum in the United States.

Rreshpja also argues that, even in the absence of a well-founded fear of future persecution on account of membership in a particular social group, a "humanitarian grant" of asylum is appropriate in her case. To qualify for such a discretionary grant of asylum, an alien must either demonstrate "compelling reasons for being unwilling or unable to return to the country arising out of the severity of the past persecution" or "establish[ ] that there is a reasonable possibility that he or she may suffer other serious harm upon removal to that country." 8 C.F.R. § 1208.13(b)(1)(iii)(A) & (B); see also *In re* Chen, 20 I. & N. Dec. 16, 21 (BIA 1989) (concluding that, although the respondent did not show a possibility of future persecution because the cultural revolution in China had ended, forcing him to return to China would be inhumane).

Rreshpja contends that requiring her to return to Albania in light of her fears of being abducted and forced into prostitution would be equally inhumane. The BIA's decision in Chen, however, was based upon the fact that the respondent had in fact suffered past persecution, even though the presumption of future persecution had been rebutted. *Chen*, 20 I. & N. Dec. at 20–21. Here, Rreshpja has not proven that she suffered past persecution. See *Mullai v. Ashcroft*, 385 F.3d 635, 638-39 (6th Cir.2004) (holding that the applicant had not demonstrated past persecution and therefore was not eligible for a grant of asylum on humanitarian grounds).

An applicant may also establish eligibility for asylum based solely on a well-founded fear of future persecution, provided that she can demonstrate both a subjective fear of persecution and an objectively reasonable possibility of persecution if forced to return to the country in question. *Recinos De Leon v. Gonzales*, 400 F.3d 1185, 1190 (9th Cir. 2004). Although Rreshpja has established her subjective fear of future persecution, she has not demonstrated an objectively reasonable possibility that she will be persecuted if she is forced to return to Albania. The isolated and apparently random attempt to abduct Rreshpja in 2001 by an unknown assailant is simply not sufficient to establish persecution by the government of Albania. A humanitarian grant of asylum is therefore unwarranted.

Finally, Rreshpja claims that the IJ erred in finding that some aspects of her testimony lacked credibility. We need not determine whether this assertion is correct because, even assuming that all of Rreshpja's testimony was consistent with both her asylum application and the relevant country condition reports, she has not established either past persecution or a well-founded fear of future persecution "on account of … membership in a particular social group." 8 U.S.C. 1101(a)(42)(A); *Castellano-Chacon*, 341 F.3d at 548.

2. Withholding of Removal

To be eligible for the withholding of removal pursuant to the INA, an alien must establish that her life or freedom would be threatened in the proposed country of removal on account of race, religion, nationality, membership in a particular social group, or political opinion. 8 U.S.C. § 1231(b)(3)(A). The petitioner must establish a "clear probability of persecution." *INS v. Stevic*, 467 U.S. 407, 413, 104 S. Ct. 2489, 81 L. Ed. 2d 321 (1984). This burden of proof is more stringent than that required to establish eligibility for asylum. *Cardoza-Fonseca*, 480

U.S. at 431-32, 107 S. Ct. 1207. Because Rreshpja has not established that she is eligible for asylum, she "cannot satisfy the more stringent standard for withholding of deportation." *Koliada v. INS*, 259 F.3d 482, 489 (6th Cir.2001).

3. Protection Under the CAT

To be eligible for protection under the CAT, an alien must establish "that it is more likely than not that he or she would be tortured if removed to the proposed country of removal." 8 C.F.R. § 208.16(c)(2) … (deleted quote defining torture)

The IJ found that Rreshpja was ineligible for relief under the CAT because she had failed to establish that government officials acquiesced in her attempted kidnapping or that they would continue to acquiesce in any future persecution. "According to the regulations, 'the term "acquiescence" requires that the public official, prior to the activity constituting torture, have awareness of such activity and thereafter breach his legal responsibility to intervene to prevent such activity.'" See *Ali*, 237 F.3d at 597 (quoting 8 C.F.R. § 208.18(a)(7)).

The record indicates that the local police in Albania did not ignore Rreshpja's complaint. Rather, they were unable to solve the crime because she could not provide them with adequate information. The record also indicates that the Albanian government is currently taking steps to suppress human trafficking in Albania and to penalize local police officers who are directly or indirectly involved in these activities. Although human trafficking continues to be a serious problem in Albania, Rreshpja did not present evidence that compels a finding that the Albanian government acquiesces in forcing women into prostitution. She is therefore not eligible for protection under the CAT.

C. Rreshpja's due process rights were not violated when the BIA affirmed the IJ's opinion without issuing its own opinion on the matter

Rreshpja next claims that the BIA's use of the summary-affirmance-without-opinion procedure, known as "streamlining," violated her rights under the INA and/or the Due Process Clause of the Fifth Amendment. Because she did not raise her claim for asylum on humanitarian grounds before the IJ, she contends that the BIA was obligated to issue an opinion addressing this claim. Rreshpja also argues that the IJ's opinion contains errors of law and fact that should have been corrected by the BIA.

Pursuant to 8 C.F.R. § 1003.1(e)(4), a single BIA member is authorized to affirm an IJ's decision without stating the basis for the affirmance if the criteria set forth in the regulation are met. Such an affirmance indicates that the IJ decided the case correctly, that any errors committed by the IJ were immaterial or harmless, and either that the issue is squarely controlled by precedent and does not involve a novel factual issue or that the factual and legal issues raised on appeal are too insubstantial to warrant a three-member review. *Id.*

In *Denko v. INS*, 351 F.3d 717 (6th Cir.2003), this court held that the BIA's procedures for issuing an affirmance without opinion comport with due process… [deleted quotation and most of the rest of the next paragraph].

A ruling on the BIA's streamlining procedure is therefore unnecessary.

D. The BIA did not err in denying Rreshpja's motion to reconsider

Finally, Rreshpja contends that the BIA erred in denying her motion to reconsider. The motion, which she filed in June of 2004, was denied by the BIA two months later. In her motion, Rreshpja argued that the BIA improperly issued an affirmance without an opinion. She also claimed that the BIA has granted asylum to rape victims in the past.

We are precluded from considering Rreshpja's arguments regarding the decision of the BIA to deny her motion to reconsider because she did not designate the August 2004 decision in her petition for review. See *Momoh v. BIA*, 75 Fed. Appx. 969, 971 (5th Cir. 2003)… (deleted citations) The only appeal filed by Rreshpja with this court is from the BIA's May 24, 2003 summary affirmance of the IJ's decision. See *Stone v. INS*, 514 U.S. 386, 405, 115 S. Ct. 1537, 131 L. Ed. 2d 465 (1995) (distinguishing between a petition to review the BIA's underlying decision and a petition for review of the denial of reopening or reconsideration).

III. CONCLUSION

For all of the reasons set forth above, we DENY Rreshpja's petition for review of the decision by the BIA.

Conditions in Albania brought another case to the Federal Appellate Courts. Eight years after the *Rreshpja* decision, the Seventh Circuit announced a decision in a similar case:

733 F.3d 662 (2013)
United States Court of Appeals, Seventh Circuit
Johana CECE, Petitioner
v.
Eric H. HOLDER, Jr., Attorney General of the United States, Respondent

ROVNER, Circuit Judge.

United States asylum laws grant refuge to those who have been persecuted in foreign lands because of race, religion, nationality, membership in a particular social group, or political opinion. The complexity surfaces when we try to define terms such as persecution and "social group" — the latter of which has perplexed this court and others, and is in the spotlight once again in this case.

I.

Johana Cece, a native of Albania, arrived in the United States in 2002, and sought asylum within the requisite time allotted. The immigration judge deemed Cece credible, and therefore we use her testimony and the immigration judge's factual findings as a basis to set forth the facts of the case.

Cece lived with her family in Korçë, Albania until her parents left the country in 2001. As a young woman living alone in Albania, Cece caught the attention of a well-known local criminal gang that was notorious for forcing women into prostitution rings. One of the leaders of that gang, a man Cece knew as "Reqi," began following her around town, offering her rides, and inviting her on dates. Cece knew Reqi by reputation — that is, for his membership in a gang known for its participation in prostitution rings, murder of other gang members, and the drug trade. Cece also testified that the gang members appeared to enjoy complete immunity from the law. Cece had long seen Reqi near her high school, where he cruised the area looking for girls and offering drugs to young women. Cece had heard that one of these women had been kidnapped by Reqi and forced into prostitution. Reqi's stalking culminated in a confrontation on June 4, 2001, when Reqi followed Cece into a cosmetics store, cornered her, and pinned her to a wall. There he confronted her and asked her why she would not go out with him. Reqi made it clear to Cece that he could not be stopped and that he would find her and do whatever he wanted to her. She told him to let go, but he merely tightened his grip and held her there. There were several people in the store, but no one came to her aid. Cece surmised that they too were frightened by Reqi. Cece's friend convinced her to report the assault to the police, but the police perfunctorily dismissed her accusation claiming she lacked proof.

A few days later someone threw a rock through Cece's window. She stopped going out, stopped going to school, and made plans to leave Korçë.

Cece moved 120 miles north to Tirana to stay with her sister, who lived in a university dormitory, but her safety there was short-lived. A year later, her sister left the country and, without access to the dormitory or family with whom to live, Cece was once again left alone to fend for herself. As a single woman living alone in Albania, Cece claims she remained a target no matter where she lived.

In 2002, fearing for her safety, Cece fraudulently procured an Italian passport and came to the United States under the Visa Waiver Program. Less than a year later, she applied for asylum and withholding of removal, asserting that she feared returning to Albania because she believed that as a young woman living alone she would be kidnapped and forced to join a prostitution ring.

At Cece's hearing, Dr. Bernd Fischer, a Professor in Balkan History at the Indiana University-Purdue University Fort Wayne and an expert on Albania, testified that Cece's experience was "unfortunately usual." Dr. Fischer described a very serious problem of human trafficking for prostitution in Albania in which gangs, often with the protection, and at times the participation of the police, kidnap women and spirit them out of the country either through Greece, Kosova, or across the Adriatic Sea to Italy. Dr. Fischer described how anomalous it is for a single woman to live by herself in Albania, that such a woman would be an ideal target for a trafficker, particularly if she had been such a target in the past, and that the problem was pervasive throughout Albania and not limited to Cece's home village of Korçë. Dr. Fischer testified that although gang members primarily target women between the ages of sixteen and twenty-six, many women outside of the target age range are also forced into prostitution. Finally, he noted that the Albanian judicial system does not adequately enforce laws against traffickers. Reports issued by the U.S. State Department in 2004 corroborated his representations of a large-scale problem with human trafficking in Albania.

The immigration judge granted Cece asylum in 2006, concluding that she belonged to the group of "young women who are targeted for prostitution by traffickers in Albania," and that the Albanian government was unwilling or unable to protect such women. He noted in particular that Albania stands out in Europe as a major country of origin of traffickers in prostitution; the government's judicial system is not effective against the problem; Albania suffers from a major and ongoing trafficking of young women by gangs; and there is no prospect in the foreseeable future of the government being able or willing to address the problem. The immigration judge also found Cece's testimony credible and her fear reasonable.

The Board of Immigration Appeals vacated the decision of the immigration judge, however, finding that Cece failed to establish past persecution and had successfully relocated within Albania. Specifically, the Board held that the immigration judge erred in determining that Cece was a member of a social group of young women who have been targeted for prostitution by traffickers, noting its precedent that a social group must have social visibility and share a narrowing characteristic other than the risk of being persecuted.

On remand, the immigration judge expressed concern with the Board's conclusion that Cece did not belong to a protectable social group and that she could safely relocate within the country. The immigration judge, however, recognized that he was bound by the Board's determinations and denied the application for asylum. The Board dismissed Cece's second appeal, emphasizing that Cece's proposed group was defined in large part by the harm inflicted on its members and did not exist independently of the traffickers. The Board also concluded that there was insufficient evidence in the record that internal relocation was not reasonable.

Cece appealed to this Court and over one dissent, the panel denied Cece's petition for review, agreeing with the Board that Cece had not named a cognizable social group and that the Board had sufficient evidence to conclude that Cece could relocate safely within Albania. We granted Cece's petition for rehearing en banc and vacated the panel's opinion and judgment.

II.

To be eligible for asylum, an applicant must show that she is "unable or unwilling to return" to the country of his nationality "because of persecution or a well-founded fear of persecution on account of race, religion, nationality, membership in a particular social group, or political opinion." 8 U.S.C. § 1101(a)(42)(A). An applicant who successfully proves that she was subject to past persecution is presumed to have a well-founded fear of future persecution, which the Attorney General can rebut by demonstrating a change in conditions in the applicant's home country. 8 C.F.R. § 1208.13(b)(1); *Mustafa v. Holder*, 707 F.3d

743, 750-51 (7th Cir. 2013). The applicant must show that she fits within one of those categories and that there is "a nexus between her fear of future persecution and one of those five protected grounds."...

The primary question in this case is whether Cece has proffered a particular social group that is cognizable under 8 U.S.C. § 1101(a)(42)(A). Whether a group constitutes a particular social group under the Immigration and Nationality Act is a question of law that we review de novo, while giving Chevron deference to the Board's reasonable interpretation set forth in precedential opinions interpreting the statute. *Chevron, U.S.A., Inc. v. Natural Resources Def. Council, Inc.*, 467 U.S. 837, 842–43...

... Congress did not directly address what it meant by a protected "social group" in the Immigration and Nationality Act, so we look to see how the agency has interpreted the statute.

The Board took on the task of defining "social group" in *Matter of Acosta*, 19 I. & N. Dec. 211, 233-34 (1985), *overruled, in part, on other grounds* by *Matter of Mogharrabi*, 19 I. & N. Dec. 439, 439 (BIA 1987) limiting it to groups whose membership is defined by a characteristic that is either immutable or is so fundamental to individual identity or conscience that a person ought not be required to change. *Id.* This Circuit has deferred to the Board's Acosta formulation of social group. *See Lwin v. INS*, 144 F.3d 505, 512 (7th Cir. 1998)...

Members of a social group need not be swimming against the stream of an embedded cultural norm. Sometimes the characteristic is immutable because a shared past experience or status has imparted some knowledge or labeling that cannot be undone. *Acosta*, 19 I. & N. Dec. at 233...

In order to compare Cece's social group with the likes of those above, we must first determine the contours of her social group. Both the parties and the immigration courts were inconsistent, and the description of her social group varied from one iteration to the next. The inconsistencies, however, do not upset the claim. See *In re* Kasinga, 21 I. & N. Dec. 357 (BIA 1996) (the Board, recognizing that both the Immigration and Naturalization Service and the applicant "advanced several formulations of the 'particular social group' at issue"). And in one form or another, both Cece and the immigration judge articulated the parameters of the relevant social group.

On her application for asylum, Cece explains that she is a "perfect target" of forced prostitution because she is a "young Orthodox woman living alone in Albania." The immigration judge, in initially granting Cece asylum, collapsed this definition and described her social group as first, "a social group consisting of young women who are targeted for prostitution by traffickers in Albania," and then a "social group consisting of women in danger of being trafficked as prostitutes." Thus the immigration judge omitted the important characteristic that Cece lived alone. There is no doubt that it should have been included in the immigration judge's description of social group, as so much of the testimony before him centered on Cece's status as a woman living alone. Cece testified at length that women do not live alone in Albania, that she did not know anyone who lived alone; that she was afraid to live alone, and most importantly that she was targeted because she was living alone. Similarly, the Albanian expert's testimony was focused on the risk of women who lived alone in Albania. Cece's brief before this Court noted several times that the Board failed to consider this formulation of the group....

The Board's order rejects Cece's social group as being not cognizable under the Act because it "is defined in large part by the harm inflicted on the group, and does not exist independently of the traffickers." This is not a reasoned conclusion. As we have just described, the characteristics of the group consist of the immutable or fundamental traits of being young, female, and living alone in Albania. Even if the group were defined in part by the fact of persecution (and we do not believe it to be), that factor would not defeat recognition of the social group under the Act. Although it is true that "where a proposed group is defined only by the characteristic that it is persecuted, it does not qualify as a 'social group,'" the Board of Immigration Appeals has never required complete independence of any relationship to the persecutor. *Escobar*, 657 F.3d at 545 (emphasis ours). And just because all members of a group suffer persecution, does not mean that this characteristic is the only one that links them. *Id.* at 545–46. A social group "cannot be defined merely by the fact of persecution" or "solely by the shared characteristic of facing dangers in retaliation for actions they took against alleged persecutors." *Jonaitiene v. Holder*, 660 F.3d 267, 271–72 (7th Cir.2011) (emphasis ours). That shared trait, however, does not disqualify an otherwise valid social group. *Escobar*, 657 F.3d at 547 (instructing that we cannot tease out one component of the group's characteristics to defeat the definition of social group). It certainly did not invalidate the social group in *Agbor* which consisted of "women who fear being circumcised should they return to their home countries," despite the fact that the group was defined in large part by the persecution inflicted on the group. *Agbor*, 487 F.3d at 502. Nor did it disqualify "women in Jordan who have (allegedly) flouted repressive moral norms, and thus who face a high risk of honor killing." *Sarhan*, 658 F.3d at 654, 655. These women still had the immutable characteristics of gender, nationality, and the inability to alter their past labels of non-conformist.

"Women who fear female genital circumcision" sound a lot like "women who fear prostitution," thus demonstrating that it is not fair to conclude that the group is defined by the harm or potential harm inflicted merely by the language used rather than determining what underlying characteristics account for the fear and vulnerability. The Board's cases instruct that we must look to see whether the group shares "common characteristics that members of the group either cannot change, or should not be required to change, because such characteristics are fundamental to their individual identities." *Escobar*, 657 F.3d at 545 (citing *Gatimi*, 578 F.3d at 614, *In re* Kasinga, 21 I. & N. Dec. 357, 365–66 (BIA 1996)). In this case, although it is true that these women are linked by the persecution they suffer — being targeted for prostitution — they are also united by the common and immutable characteristic of being (1) young, (2) Albanian, (3) women, (4) living alone. For this reason we disagree with the Sixth Circuit's conclusion in *Rreshpja v. Gonzales*, that the social group of "young (or those who appear to be young), attractive Albanian women who are forced into prostitution" does not constitute a social group because it is circularly defined by the fact that it suffers persecution. *Id.* 420 F.3d 551, 555–56 (6th Cir.2005).

Our conclusion is consistent with a parallel line of reasoning found in mixed motive cases. The Board of Immigration Appeals and this Court have long recognized that persecution can exist in a mixed motive case in which the persecutor targets an individual for more than one reason and one of the reasons does not warrant protection under the Act. Under the mixed-motives doctrine, an applicant may qualify for asylum so long as the applicant demonstrates by either direct or circumstantial evidence that his persecutors were motivated, at least in part, by one of the enumerated grounds...

Demonstrating that an asylum applicant belongs to a cognizable social group is only the first step in determining asylum. Recall that an applicant must show not only that she fits within a cognizable social group but also that there is a nexus between the persecution and the membership in the social group. *Escobar*, 657 F.3d at 542; *Ishitiaq*, 578 F.3d at 715. Justice Alito, while on the Third Circuit, described the steps as follows:

The alien must (1) identify a group that constitutes a 'particular social group' within the interpretation just discussed, (2) establish that he or she is a member of that group, and (3) show that he or she would be persecuted or has a well-founded fear of persecution based on that membership.

Fatin v. INS, 12 F.3d 1233, 1240 (3d Cir. 1993). He then went on to note that, "to the extent that the petitioner in this case suggests that she would be persecuted or has a well-founded fear that she would be persecuted in Iran simply because she is a woman, she has satisfied the first of the three elements that we have noted." *Id.* As we are about to see, it is the nexus requirement where the rubber meets the road.

Those who fear that the slope leading to asylum has been made too slick by broad categories need not worry. The importance of the "on account of" language must not be overlooked... In order to be entitled to asylum, Cece must be able to demonstrate a particular link between her mistreatment and her membership in the stated social group. *Escobar*, 657 F.3d at 544; *Bueso-Avila*, 663 F.3d at 936. This requirement is not unique to inquiries about persecution based on "social group," but rather one that is applicable to cases of claimed persecution based on race, religion, nationality or political opinion. In other words, an ethnic Rom (gypsy) who has been mistreated by the town mayor because of a long-standing business dispute would not be eligible for asylum even if the mayor has undoubtedly and unfairly mistreated him, and even if he belongs to an ethnic group that was frequently the target of persecution in his country. The persecution must still be "on account of" the protected category.

[16] In any event, the breadth of category has never been a per se bar to protected status... Many of the groups recognized by the Board and courts are indeed quite broad. These include: women in tribes that practice female genital mutilation; *Matter of Kasinga*, 21 I. & N. Dec. at 365, *Agbor*, 487 F.3d at 502; persons who are opposed to involuntary sterilization, 8 U.S.C. § 1101(a)(42)(B); *Chen v. Holder*, 604 F.3d 324, 332 (7th Cir. 2010); members of the Darood clan and Marehan subclan in Somalia, *In re* H-, 21 I. & N. Dec. at 340, 343 (1% of the population of Somalia are members of the Marehan subclan); homosexuals in Cuba, *In re* Toboso-Alfonso, 20 I. & N. Dec. 819, 822–23 (BIA 1990); Filipinos of Chinese ancestry living in the Philippines, *Matter of V-T-S-*, 21 I. & N. Dec. 792, 798 (BIA 1997) (approximately 1.5% of the Philippines population has an identifiable Chinese background); *Singh v. INS*, 94 F.3d 1353, 1359 (9th Cir. 1996) (rejecting the notion that an applicant is ineligible for asylum merely because all members of a persecuted group might be eligible for asylum). The ethnic Tutsis of Rawanda numbered close to 700,000 before the genocide of 1994, and yet a Tutsi singled out for murder who managed to escape to the United States could surely qualify for asylum in this country. And undoubtedly any of the six million Jews ulti-

mately killed in concentration camps in Nazi-controlled Europe could have made valid claims for asylum, if only they had had that opportunity. Many of our asylum laws originated out of a need to address just such refugees from World War II. It would be antithetical to asylum law to deny refuge to a group of persecuted individuals who have valid claims merely because too many have valid claims. See *Iao*, 400 F.3d at 533; *Singh*, 94 F.3d at 1359. For this reason we also reject the Sixth Circuit's reasoning that the group of young-looking, attractive Albanian women who are forced into prostitution is not a cognizable social group because it is too broad and sweeping of a classification. *Rreshpja*, 420 F.3d at 555...

Because Cece's group cannot be distinguished from others with immutable and fundamental traits, the Board's decision is inconsistent with its own precedent... The issue of whether a particular social group is cognizable is a question of law on which the Board erred. The Board's decision cannot stand and must be reconsidered on remand: Cece has established that she belongs to a cognizable social group...

III.

The Board also found that there was insufficient evidence in the record that internal relocation was not a feasible means of avoiding the persecution of which Cece complains. The Board, however, ignored the fact, emphasized throughout the hearing and appeals, that Cece had lived safely in Tirana only while living with her sister in her sister's university dormitory. Once her sister left Tirana and Cece had to move from the dormitory, she was again at risk. The Albanian expert testified at length that Albania was a small country and that it would be difficult to hide anywhere. Even in the big city of Tirana, people tended to live in family or clan groupings, and a young single woman living alone would stick out as an anomaly. *Id.* The expert also surmised that Cece faced an increased risk of being targeted simply because of her previous status as a target, i.e. she was already known to traffickers... The only evidence in the record is that Cece felt safe in Tirana only so long as she was not living alone — a status quo that ended as soon as her last family member left the country. An asylum applicant is entitled to a reasoned analysis of her case supported by relevant, probative evidence. *Mustafa*, 707 F.3d at 754. A failure to provide such a reasoned analysis requires remand. *Kadia v. Holder*, 557 F.3d 464, 467 (7th Cir. 2009).

We therefore grant the petition for review and remand to the agency for further proceedings consistent with this opinion.

EASTERBROOK, Chief Judge, dissenting.

Cece defines, as the "social group" at risk of persecution, "young Albanian women in danger of being trafficked as prostitutes." At earlier stages of these proceedings she made different proposals, but this is the definition in her appellate briefs. My colleagues hold that the Board of Immigration Appeals erred by not treating "young Albanian women who live alone" as her social group. Put to one side the fact that Cece does not ask us to define a social group that way. Whether the group is "young Albanian women in danger of being trafficked as prostitutes" or "young Albanian women who live alone," Cece isn't in it. Her own expert defined "young" as 16 to 26 or 27. Cece is 34. The basis for her claim of asylum is future risk; she does not argue that she suffered persecution before leaving Albania, so the fact that she is not a member of her own proposed group should be dispositive. (Perhaps Cece looks younger than her age and would be targeted by mistake, but she does not argue this.)

Then there is the question "how much risk is too much?" Cece's expert did not attempt to quantify the risk that young Albanian women living alone face, nor does the majority. That many of Western Europe's prostitutes are Albanians does not tell us how many are in the sex trade involuntarily. The State Department tries to estimate risk. Its Human Trafficking Report 2012 finds that 84 complaints about trafficking were made to Albanian public agencies during 2011. Report at 64. Nongovernmental groups (NGOs) reported more: they counted 132 Albanian trafficking victims in 2011. *Ibid.* The number of young women living alone in Albania is substantially higher. The State Department ranks nations into four tiers (1, 2, 2 Watch List, and 3), with Tier 1 representing the best performance. *Id.* at 51. Albania is in Tier 2, as are Greece, Hong Kong, Japan, Switzerland, and more than 60 other nations. *Id.* at 52. Fifty-one nations are in tiers 2WL or 3, below Albania. Ibid. Deplorable as human trafficking is, any given woman's danger in Albania may be modest.

Whatever risk Cece faces comes from criminals, not from the government, yet "persecution" means mistreatment at public hands. See *Hor v. Gonzales*, 421 F.3d 497 (7th Cir. 2005); *Bitsin v. Holder*, 719 F.3d 619, 628–31 (7th Cir. 2013). Crime may be rampant in Albania, but it is common in the United States too. People are forced into prostitution in Chicago. *See, e.g., United States v. Cephus*, 684 F.3d 703 (7th Cir. 2012). Must Canada grant asylum to young women who fear prostitution in the United States, or who dread the risk of violence in or near public-housing projects? If there were reason to think the Albanian government in cahoots with the traffickers, Cece would have a better case; but when the record shows no more than ineffective law enforcement, there's no basis to infer persecution. *Meghani v. INS*, 236 F.3d 843, 847 (7th Cir. 2001).

...

The majority expresses sympathy for Cece and other applicants for asylum. Yet the choice whether to be strict or lenient belongs to the agency, not to the court. See, e.g., *INS v. Phinpathya*, 464 U.S. 183, 104 S. Ct. 584, 78 L. Ed. 2d 401 (1984); *INS v. Jong Ha Wang*, 450 U.S. 139, 101 S. Ct. 1027, 67 L. Ed. 2d 123 (1981). The Board has chosen to make "social group" do real work. This court effectively reads it out of the statute and directs the agency to ask only whether an alien faces a significant risk for any reason. This intrudes on the sort of choice Congress has committed to the Executive Branch. The Attorney General could direct the Board to ditch Acosta and C-A-, but as long as the political branches of government stand by them, Chevron requires the judiciary to implement their choices.

One final observation. Cece entered the United States by fraud, pretending to be from a nation whose citizens do not need visas to visit. See *Bayo v. Napolitano*, 593 F.3d 495 (7th Cir. 2010) (en banc). She started that journey from Rome and has never contended that she feared sex trafficking in Italy. Her fraud thus is not mitigated by a need to escape from danger. The Board has concluded that entering the United States by fraud, when danger is not imminent, is a strongly adverse factor in the discretionary decision whether to grant asylum. See *Alsagladi v. Gonzales*, 450 F.3d 700 (7th Cir. 2006); *Matter of Pula*, 19 I. & N. Dec. 467 (1987). Although the court decides today that Cece is eligible for asylum, it does not hold that she is entitled to it; that question, at least, remains open to decision on remand.

MANION, Circuit Judge, with whom EASTERBROOK, Chief Judge, joins, dissenting.

I.

. . .

In holding that "Cece has established that she belongs to a cognizable social group," Opinion at 677, the en Banc court discusses at length the complexity of defining a "social group." See Opinion at 668–77. As discussed below, I have several concerns with the court's analysis. However, even if the en Banc court is correct that "young Albanian women who live alone," is a "social group" within the meaning of the INA, her petition for review should nonetheless be denied because substantial evidence supports the Board's finding that Cece did not present sufficient evidence that internal relocation is not reasonable. That finding alone dooms Cece's asylum petition and accordingly we should deny Cece's petition for review. I DISSENT.

II.

A. Social Group

As the en Banc court explains, "Congress did not directly address what it meant to be a protected 'social group' in the Immigration and Nationality Act, so we look to see how the agency has interpreted the statute." Opinion at 668–69. The court then notes that the Board defined "social group" in *Matter of Acosta*, 19 I. & N. Dec. 211, 233–34 (1985), to be limited "to groups whose membership is defined by a characteristic that is either immutable or is so fundamental to individual identity or conscience that a person ought not be required to change." Opinion at 669. We have deferred to that definition. Opinion at 669 (citing *Lwin v. INS*, 144 F.3d 505, 512 (7th Cir. 1998)).

My first concern with the en Banc court's holding is that the court's formulation of Cece's social group as "young Albanian women who live alone" does not satisfy the Board's definition of "immutable" or "fundamental" characteristics. There is nothing immutable about "living alone." Nor is "living alone," unlike an individual's choice to be single or married, "so fundamental to individual identity or conscience that a person ought not be required to change." And there are many variations in location and type of dwelling where a woman can choose to live alone.

I also have concerns with the en Banc court defining a social group with the subjective adjective of "young." A shared characteristic of a "social group," "must provide a clear demarcation, 'permit[ting] an accurate separation of members' from non-members,' … Consequently, loose descriptive phrases that are open-ended and that invite subjective interpretation are not sufficiently particular to describe a protected social group." *Mayorga-Vidal v. Holder*, 675 F.3d 9, 15 (1st Cir. 2012) (quoting *Ahmed v. Holder*, 611 F.3d 90, 94 (1st Cir. 2010)).

…

However, in the final analysis, we need not reach these difficult questions because, as discussed below, even if Cece identified a social group within the meaning of the INA, and presented a case of persecution—as opposed to generalized lawlessness—Cece still cannot prevail on her request for asylum because the Board found that "there is [in]sufficient evidence in the record … that internal relocation is not reasonable."

B. Internal Relocation

Because Cece's application for asylum is based on a well-founded fear of future persecution, in addition to proving that she is unable or unwilling to return to Albania because of her membership in a particular social group, she also bears the added burden of proving she cannot reasonably relocate to another part of her home country to avoid persecution. *Oryakhil v. Mukasey*, 528 F.3d 993, 998 (7th Cir. 2008). "The immigration regulations contemplate two separate inquiries to determine whether an applicant could reasonably relocate within his home country: (1) whether safe relocation is possible, and if so, (2) whether it would be reasonable to expect the applicant to safely relocate." *Id.*

...

The Board then concluded: "In sum, we cannot find that there is sufficient evidence in the record ... that internal relocation is not reasonable."

The Board's conclusion that Cece failed to show that safe relocation was not reasonable was supported by substantial evidence. Following her encounter with Reqi, Cece successfully relocated to Tirane and while there obtained a job teaching English. It is true that Cece was not living alone in Tirane — she was living in a dormitory room she shared with three other single women. But Cece was not homebound. She had to go to and from work, and about her daily affairs. Not once during the year Cece lived in Tirane was she approached by Reqi or anyone else. While Cece claimed Reqi could find her anywhere, the Board could reasonably conclude, as it did, that because no one had approached Cece in Tirane, neither Reqi nor any other trafficker was motivated to pursue Cece outside of Korce. And given Cece's testimony that she had no problems in Tirane, the Board could reasonably conclude that "[t]here is insufficient indication in the record that she has a well-founded fear of persecution in Tirane or in another city within Albania, outside of Korce." True, if she were living alone in Tirane she would fit one (of the many) profiles of those targeted by criminals. But when the profile of those targeted by criminals is so broad, as it is here, something more is necessary — some evidence that the individual has a well-founded fear that she will be targeted. In her case, Cece offered no evidence that she would actually be targeted in Korce and thus that she had a well-founded fear of persecution there. Without such evidence, the Board could reasonably conclude that Cece did not meet her burden of showing that internal relocation was not reasonable. Accordingly, the Board did not err in denying Cece's application for asylum and the petition for review should be denied.

I DISSENT.

c. Non-Immigrant Visas

1) Non-Immigrants Generally

In addition to citizenship and permanent resident alien status, a third group of people coming to this country are allowed to remain. These people hold a temporary authority known as "non-immigrant" status (recall that permanent resident aliens are referred to as "immigrants"). Non-immigrant categories include, among others: students (F-visas), visitors for business or pleasure (B-visas), treaty traders and investors (E-visas), temporary workers (H-visas), and fiancées and fiancés (K-visas). The letters refer to a subsection of the Immigration and Nationality Act with its corresponding lettered subsections. These and all other non-immigrant categories are set out at 8 U.S.C.A. § 1101.

2) T-Visas

In 2000, Congress created another non-immigrant category, the T-visa. This temporary permission to live in the United States was enacted as part of the Victims of Trafficking and Violence Protection Act of 2000.[18] The Act provided that victims of trafficking who qualify, are allowed to remain and work in the United States. In order to obtain the T-visa, the victim has to demonstrate that he or she has been subjected to a "severe form of trafficking in persons," and meet the other criteria established in the statute and in 8 C.F.R. 214. Following, with a few deletions pertaining to the process for the family members of T-visa applicants, are the requirements set out in 8 C.F.R. 214. These requirements are technical and lengthy. However, anyone who is interested in assisting victims of international trafficking must be willing to read through them in a painstaking manner.

---

18. 18 U.S.C. 1581-96.

(a) Definitions. The Service shall apply the following definitions as provided in sections 103 and 107(e) of the Trafficking Victims Protection Act (TVPA) with due regard for the definitions and application of these terms in 28 CFR part 1100 and the provisions of chapter 77 of title 18, United States Code:

Bona fide application means an application for T-1 nonimmigrant status as to which, after initial review, the Service has determined that there appears to be no instance of fraud in the application, the application is complete, properly filed, contains an LEA endorsement or credible secondary evidence, includes completed fingerprint and background checks, and presents prima facie evidence to show eligibility for T nonimmigrant status, including admissibility.

Child means a person described as such in section 101(b)(1) of the Act.

Coercion means threats of serious harm to or physical restraint against any person; any scheme, plan, or pattern intended to cause a person to believe that failure to perform an act would result in serious harm to or physical restraint against any person; or the abuse or threatened abuse of the legal process.

Commercial sex act means any sex act on account of which anything of value is given to or received by any person.

Debt bondage means the status or condition of a debtor arising from a pledge by the debtor of his or her personal services or of those of a person under his or her control as a security for debt, if the value of those services as reasonably assessed is not applied toward the liquidation of the debt or the length and nature of those services are not respectively limited and defined.

Immediate family member means the spouse or a child of a victim of a severe form of trafficking in persons, and, in the case of a victim of a severe form of trafficking in persons who is under twenty-one years of age, a parent of the victim.

Involuntary servitude means a condition of servitude induced by means of any scheme, plan, or pattern intended to cause a person to believe that, if the person did not enter into or continue in such condition, that person or another person would suffer serious harm or physical restraint; or the abuse or threatened abuse of legal process. Accordingly, involuntary servitude includes "a condition of servitude in which the victim is forced to work for the defendant by the use or threat of physical restraint or physical injury, or by the use or threat of coercion through law or the legal process. This definition encompasses those cases in which the defendant holds the victim in servitude by placing the victim in fear of such physical restraint or injury or legal coercion." (*United States v. Kozminski*, 487 U.S. 931, 952 (1988)).

Law Enforcement Agency (LEA) means any Federal law enforcement agency that has the responsibility and authority for the detection, investigation, or prosecution of severe forms of trafficking in persons. LEAs include the following components of the Department of Justice: the United States Attorneys' Offices, the Civil Rights and Criminal Divisions, the Federal Bureau of Investigation (FBI), the Immigration and Naturalization Service (Service), and the United States Marshals Service. The Diplomatic Security Service, Department of State, also is an LEA.

Law Enforcement Agency (LEA) endorsement means Supplement B, Declaration of Law Enforcement Officer for Victim of Trafficking in Persons of Form I-914, Application for T Nonimmigrant Status.

Peonage means a status or condition of involuntary servitude based upon real or alleged indebtedness.

Reasonable request for assistance means a reasonable request made by a law enforcement officer or prosecutor to a victim of a severe form of trafficking in persons to assist law enforcement authorities in the investigation or prosecution of the acts of trafficking in persons. The "reasonableness" of the request depends on the totality of the circumstances taking into account general law enforcement and prosecutorial practices, the nature of the victimization, and the specific circumstances of the victim, including fear, severe traumatization (both mental and physical), and the age and maturity of young victims.

Severe forms of trafficking in persons means sex trafficking in which a commercial sex act is induced by force, fraud, or coercion, or in which the person induced to perform such act has not attained eighteen years of age; or the recruitment, harboring, transportation, provision, or obtaining of a person for labor or services, through the use of force, fraud, or coercion for the purpose of subjection to involuntary servitude, peonage, debt bondage, or slavery.

Sex trafficking means the recruitment, harboring, transportation, provision, or obtaining of a person for the purpose of a commercial sex act.

TVPA means the Trafficking Victims Protection Act of 2000, Division A of the VTVPA, *Pub. L. 106-386.*

United States means the continental United States, Alaska, Hawaii, Puerto Rico, Guam, the United States Virgin Islands, and the Commonwealth of the Northern Mariana Islands.

Victim of a severe form of trafficking in persons means an alien who is or has been subject to a severe form of trafficking in persons, as defined in section 103 of the VTVPA and in this section.

VTVPA means the Victims of Trafficking and Violence Protection Act of 2000, *Pub. L. 106-386.*

(b) Eligibility. Under section 101(a)(15)(T)(i) of the Act, and subject to section 214(n) of the Act, the Service may classify an alien, if otherwise admissible, as a T-1 nonimmigrant if the alien demonstrates that he or she:
  (1) Is or has been a victim of a severe form of trafficking in persons;
  (2) Is physically present in the United States, American Samoa, or at a port-of-entry thereto, on account of such trafficking in persons;
  (3) Either:
    (i) Has complied with any reasonable request for assistance in the investigation or prosecution of acts of such trafficking in persons, or
    (ii) Is less than 15 years of age; and
  (4) Would suffer extreme hardship involving unusual and severe harm upon removal, as described in paragraph (i) of this section.

(c) Aliens ineligible for T nonimmigrant status. No alien, otherwise admissible, shall be eligible to receive a T nonimmigrant status under section 101(a)(15)(T) of the Act if there is substantial reason to believe that the alien has committed an act of a severe form of trafficking in persons.

(d) Application procedures for T status—

(1) Filing an application. An applicant seeking T nonimmigrant status shall submit, by mail, a complete application package containing Form I-914, Application for T Nonimmigrant Status, along with all necessary supporting documentation, to the Service.

(2) Contents of the application package. In addition to Form I-914, an application package must include the following:

(i) The proper fee for Form I-914 as provided in *§ 103.7(b)(1)* of this chapter, or an application for a fee waiver as provided in *§ 103.7(c)* of this chapter;

(ii) Three current photographs;

(iii) The fingerprint fee as provided in *§ 103.7(b)(1)* of this chapter;

(iv) Evidence demonstrating that the applicant is a victim of a severe form of trafficking in persons as set forth in paragraph (f) of this section;

(v) Evidence that the alien is physically present in the United States on account of a severe form of trafficking in persons as set forth in paragraph (g) of this section;

(vi) Evidence that the applicant has complied with any reasonable request for assistance in the investigation or prosecution of acts of severe forms of trafficking in persons, as set forth in paragraph (h) of this section, or has not attained 15 years of age; and

(vii) Evidence that the applicant would suffer extreme hardship involving unusual and severe harm if he or she were removed from the United States, as set forth in paragraph (i) of this section.

(3) Evidentiary standards. The applicant may submit any credible evidence relevant to the essential elements of

the T nonimmigrant status. Original documents or copies may be submitted as set forth in *§ 103.2(b)(4)* and *(b)(5)* of this chapter. Any document containing text in a foreign language shall be submitted in accordance with *§ 103.2(b)(3)* of this chapter.

(4) Filing deadline in cases in which victimization occurred prior to October 28, 2000. Victims of a severe form of trafficking in persons whose victimization occurred prior to October 28, 2000 must file a completed application within one (1) year of January 31, 2002 in order to be eligible to receive T-1 nonimmigrant status. If the victimization occurred prior to October 28, 2000, an alien who was a child at the time he or she was a victim of a severe form of trafficking in persons must file a T status application within one (1) year of his or her 21st birthday, or one (1) year of January 31, 2002, whichever is later. For purposes of determining the filing deadline, an act of severe form of trafficking in persons will be deemed to have occurred on the last day in which an act constituting an element of a severe form of trafficking in persons, as defined in paragraph (a) of this section, occurred. If the applicant misses the deadline, he or she must show that exceptional circumstances prevented him or her from filing in a timely manner. Exceptional circumstances may include severe trauma, either psychological or physical, that prevented the victim from applying within the allotted time.

(5) Fingerprint procedure. All applicants for T nonimmigrant status must be fingerprinted for the purpose of conducting a criminal background check in accordance with the process and procedures described in *§ 103.2(e)* of this chapter. After submitting an application with fee to the Service, the applicant will be notified of the proper time and location to appear for fingerprinting.

(6) Personal interview. After the filing of an application for T nonimmigrant status, the Service may require an applicant to participate in a personal interview. The neces-

sity of an interview is to be determined solely by the Service. All interviews will be conducted in person at a Service-designated location. Every effort will be made to schedule the interview in a location convenient to the applicant.

(7) Failure to appear for an interview or failure to follow fingerprinting requirements.

(i) Failure to appear for a scheduled interview without prior authorization or to comply with fingerprint processing requirements may result in the denial of the application.

(ii) Failure to appear shall be excused if the notice of the interview or fingerprint appointment was not mailed to the applicant's current address and such address had been provided to the Service unless the Service determines that the applicant received reasonable notice of the appointment. The applicant must notify the Service of any change of address in accordance with *§265.1* of this chapter prior to the date on which the notice of the interview or fingerprint appointment was mailed to the applicant.

(iii) Failure to appear at the interview or fingerprint appointment may be excused, at the discretion of the Service, if the applicant promptly contacts the Service and demonstrates that such failure to appear was the result of exceptional circumstances.

(8) Aliens in pending immigration proceedings. Individuals who believe they are victims of severe forms of trafficking in persons and who are in pending immigration proceedings must inform the Service if they intend to apply for T nonimmigrant status under this section. With the concurrence of Service counsel, a victim of a severe form of trafficking in persons in proceedings before an immigration judge or the Board of Immigration Appeals (Board) may request that the proceedings be administratively closed (or that a motion to reopen or motion to reconsider be indefinitely continued) in order to allow

the alien to pursue an application for T nonimmigrant status with the Service. If the alien appears eligible for T nonimmigrant status, the immigration judge or the Board, whichever has jurisdiction, may grant such a request to administratively close the proceeding or continue a motion to reopen or motion to reconsider indefinitely. In the event the Service finds an alien ineligible for T-1 nonimmigrant status, the Service may recommence proceedings that have been administratively closed by filing a motion to re-calendar with the immigration court or a motion to reinstate with the Board. If the alien is in Service custody pending the completion of immigration proceedings, the Service may continue to detain the alien until a decision has been rendered on the application. An alien who is in custody and requests bond or a bond redetermination will be governed by the provisions of part 236 of this chapter.

(9) T applicants with final orders of exclusion, deportation or removal. An alien who is the subject of a final order is not precluded from filing an application for T-1 nonimmigrant status directly with the Service. The filing of an application for T nonimmigrant status has no effect on the Service's execution of a final order, although the alien may file a request for stay of removal pursuant to *§ 241.6(a)* of this chapter. However, if the Service subsequently determines, under the procedures of this section, that the application is bona fide, the Service will automatically stay execution of the final order of deportation, exclusion, or removal, and the stay will remain in effect until a final decision is made on the T-1 application. The time during which such a stay is in effect shall not be counted in determining the reasonableness of the duration of the alien's continued detention under the standards of § 241.4 of this chapter. If the T-1 application is denied, the stay of the final order is deemed lifted as of the date of such denial, without regard to whether the alien appeals the decision. If the Service grants an appli-

cation for T nonimmigrant status, the final order shall be deemed canceled by operation of law as of the date of the approval.

(e) Dissemination of information. In appropriate cases, and in accordance with Department of Justice policies, the Service shall make information from applications for T-1 nonimmigrant status available to other Law Enforcement Agencies (LEAs) with the authority to detect, investigate, or prosecute severe forms of trafficking in persons. The Service shall coordinate with the appropriate Department of Justice component responsible for prosecution in all cases where there is a current or impending prosecution of any defendants who may be charged with severe forms of trafficking in persons crimes in connection with the victimization of the applicant to ensure that the Department of Justice component responsible for prosecution has access to all witness statements provided by the applicant in connection with the application for T-1 nonimmigrant status, and any other documents needed to facilitate investigation or prosecution of such severe forms of trafficking in persons offenses.

(f) Evidence demonstrating that the applicant is a victim of a severe form of trafficking in persons. The applicant must submit evidence that fully establishes eligibility for each element of the T nonimmigrant status to the satisfaction of the Attorney General. First, an alien must demonstrate that he or she is a victim of a severe form of trafficking in persons. The applicant may satisfy this requirement either by submitting an LEA endorsement, by demonstrating that the Service previously has arranged for the alien's continued presence under *28 CFR 1100.35*, or by submitting sufficient credible secondary evidence, describing the nature and scope of any force, fraud, or coercion used against the victim (this showing is not necessary if the person induced to perform a commercial sex act is under the age of 18). An application must contain a statement by the applicant describing the facts of his or her victimization. In determining whether an applicant is a victim of a severe form of trafficking in persons, the Service will consider all credible and relevant evidence.

(1) Law Enforcement Agency endorsement. An LEA endorsement is not required. However, if provided, it must be submitted by an appropriate law enforcement official on Supplement B, Declaration of Law Enforcement Officer for Victim of Trafficking in Persons, of Form I-914. The LEA endorsement must be filled out completely in accordance with the instructions contained on the form and must attach the results of any name or database inquiry performed. In order to provide persuasive evidence, the LEA endorsement must contain a description of the victimization upon which the application is based (including the dates the severe forms of trafficking in persons and victimization occurred), and be signed by a supervising official responsible for the investigation or prosecution of severe forms of trafficking in persons. The LEA endorsement must address whether the victim had been recruited, harbored, transported, provided, or obtained specifically for either labor or services, or for the purposes of a commercial sex act. The traffickers must have used force, fraud, or coercion to make the victim engage in the intended labor or services, or (for those 18 or older) the intended commercial sex act. The situations involving labor or services must rise to the level of involuntary servitude, peonage, debt bondage, or slavery. The decision of whether or not to complete an LEA endorsement for an applicant shall be at the discretion of the LEA.

(2) Primary evidence of victim status. The Service will consider an LEA endorsement as primary evidence that the applicant has been the victim of a severe form of trafficking in persons provided that the details contained in the endorsement meet the definition of a severe form of trafficking in persons under this section. In the alternative, documentation from the Service granting the applicant continued presence in accordance with *28 CFR 1100.35* will be considered as primary evidence that the applicant

has been the victim of a severe form of trafficking in persons, unless the Service has revoked the continued presence based on a determination that the applicant is not a victim of a severe form of trafficking in persons.

(3) Secondary evidence of victim status; Affidavits. Credible secondary evidence and affidavits may be submitted to explain the nonexistence or unavailability of the primary evidence and to otherwise establish the requirement that the applicant be a victim of a severe form of trafficking in persons. The secondary evidence must include an original statement by the applicant indicating that he or she is a victim of a severe form of trafficking in persons; credible evidence of victimization and cooperation, describing what the alien has done to report the crime to an LEA; and a statement indicating whether similar records for the time and place of the crime are available. The statement or evidence should demonstrate that good faith attempts were made to obtain the LEA endorsement, including what efforts the applicant undertook to accomplish these attempts. Applicants are encouraged to provide and document all credible evidence, because there is no guarantee that a particular piece of evidence will result in a finding that the applicant was a victim of a severe form of trafficking in persons. If the applicant does not submit an LEA endorsement, the Service will proceed with the adjudication based on the secondary evidence and affidavits submitted. A non-exhaustive list of secondary evidence includes trial transcripts, court documents, police reports, news articles, and copies of reimbursement forms for travel to and from court. In addition, applicants may also submit their own affidavit and the affidavits of other witnesses. The determination of what evidence is credible and the weight to be given that evidence shall be within the sole discretion of the Service.

(4) Obtaining an LEA endorsement. A victim of a severe form of trafficking in persons who does not have an LEA endorsement should contact the LEA to which the alien

has provided assistance to request an endorsement. If the applicant has not had contact with an LEA regarding the acts of severe forms of trafficking in persons, the applicant should promptly contact the nearest Service or Federal Bureau of Investigation (FBI) field office or U.S. Attorneys' Office to file a complaint, assist in the investigation or prosecution of acts of severe forms of trafficking in persons, and request an LEA endorsement. If the applicant was recently liberated from the trafficking in persons situation, the applicant should ask the LEA for an endorsement. Alternatively, the applicant may contact the Department of Justice, Civil Rights Division, Trafficking in Persons and Worker Exploitation Task Force complaint hotline at 1-888-428-7581 to file a complaint and be referred to an LEA.

(g) Physical presence on account of trafficking in persons. The applicant must establish that he or she is physically present in the United States, American Samoa, or at a port-of-entry thereto on account of such trafficking, and that he or she is a victim of a severe form of trafficking in persons that forms the basis for the application. Specifically, the physical presence requirement reaches an alien who: is present because he or she is being subjected to a severe form of trafficking in persons; was recently liberated from a severe form of trafficking in persons; or was subject to severe forms of trafficking in persons at some point in the past and whose continuing presence in the United States is directly related to the original trafficking in persons.

(1) In general. The evidence and statements included with the application must state the date and place (if known) and the manner and purpose (if known) for which the applicant entered the United States, American Samoa, or a port-of-entry thereto, and demonstrate that the applicant is present now on account of the applicant's victimization as described in paragraph (f) of this section and section 101(a)(15)(T)(i)(I) of the Act.

(2) Opportunity to depart. If the alien has escaped the traffickers before law enforcement became involved in the

matter, he or she must show that he or she did not have a clear chance to leave the United States in the interim. The Service will consider whether an applicant had a clear chance to leave in light of the individual applicant's circumstances. Information relevant to this determination may include, but is not limited to, circumstances attributable to the trafficking in persons situation, such as trauma, injury, lack of resources, or travel documents that have been seized by the traffickers. This determination may reach both those who entered the United States lawfully and those who entered without being admitted or paroled. The Service will consider all evidence presented to determine the physical presence requirement, including asking the alien to answer questions on Form I-914, about when he or she escaped from the trafficker, what activities he or she has undertaken since that time, including the steps he or she may have taken to deal with the consequences of having been trafficked, and the applicant's ability to leave the United States.

(3) Departure from the United States. An alien who has voluntarily left (or has been removed from) the United States at any time after the act of a severe form of trafficking in persons shall be deemed not to be present in the United States as a result of such trafficking in persons unless the alien's reentry into the United States was the result of the continued victimization of the alien or a new incident of a severe form of trafficking in persons described in section 101(a)(15)(T)(i)(I) of the Act.

(h) Compliance with reasonable requests from a law enforcement agency for assistance in the investigation or prosecution. Except as provided in paragraph (h)(3) of this section, the applicant must submit evidence that fully establishes that he or she has complied with any reasonable request for assistance in the investigation or prosecution of acts of severe forms of trafficking in persons. As provided in paragraph (h)(3) of this section, if the victim of a severe form of trafficking in persons is under age 15, he or she is not required to comply with any reasonable request for assistance in order to be eligible for T nonimmigrant status, but may cooperate at his or her discretion.

(1) Primary evidence of compliance with law enforcement requests. An LEA endorsement describing the assistance provided by the applicant is not required evidence. However, if an LEA endorsement is provided as set forth in paragraph (f)(1) of this section, it will be considered primary evidence that the applicant has complied with any reasonable request in the investigation or prosecution of the severe form of trafficking in persons of which the applicant was a victim. If the Service has reason to believe that the applicant has not complied with any reasonable request for assistance by the endorsing LEA or other LEAs, the Service will contact the LEA and both the Service and the LEA will take all practical steps to reach a resolution acceptable to both agencies. The Service may, at its discretion, interview the alien regarding the evidence for and against the compliance, and allow the alien to submit additional evidence of such compliance. If the Service determines that the alien has not complied with any reasonable request for assistance, then the application will be denied, and any approved application based on the LEA endorsement will be revoked pursuant to this section.

(2) Secondary evidence of compliance with law enforcement requests; Affidavits. Credible secondary evidence and affidavits may be submitted to show the nonexistence or unavailability of the primary evidence and to otherwise establish the requirement that the applicant comply with any reasonable request for assistance in the investigation or prosecution of that severe form of trafficking in persons. The secondary evidence must include an original statement by the applicant that indicates the reason the LEA endorsement does not exist or is unavailable, and whether similar records documenting any assistance provided by the applicant are available. The statement or evidence must show that an LEA that has responsibility

and authority for the detection, investigation, or prosecution of severe forms of trafficking in persons has information about such trafficking in persons, that the victim has complied with any reasonable request for assistance in the investigation or prosecution of such acts of trafficking, and, if the victim did not report the crime at the time, why the crime was not previously reported. The statement or evidence should demonstrate that good faith attempts were made to obtain the LEA endorsement, including what efforts the applicant undertook to accomplish these attempts. In addition, applicants may also submit their own affidavit and the affidavits of other witnesses. The determination of what evidence is credible and the weight to be given that evidence shall be within the sole discretion of the Service. Applicants are encouraged to describe and document all applicable factors, since there is no guarantee that a particular reason will result in a finding that the applicant has complied with reasonable requests. An applicant who never has had contact with an LEA regarding the acts of severe forms of trafficking in persons will not be eligible for T-1 nonimmigrant status.

(3) Exception for applicants under the age of 15. Applicants under the age of 15 are not required to demonstrate compliance with the requirement of any reasonable request for assistance in the investigation and prosecution of acts of severe forms of trafficking in persons. Applicants under the age of 15 must provide evidence of their age. Primary evidence that a victim of a severe form of trafficking in persons has not yet reached the age of 15 would be an official copy of the alien's birth certificate, a passport, or a certified medical opinion. Secondary evidence regarding the age of the applicant also may be submitted in accordance with *§ 103.2(b)(2)(i)* of this chapter. An applicant under the age of 15 still must provide evidence demonstrating that he or she satisfies the other necessary requirements, including that he or she is the

victim of a severe form of trafficking in persons and faces extreme hardship involving unusual and severe harm if removed from the United States.

(i) Evidence of extreme hardship involving unusual and severe harm upon removal. To be eligible for T-1 nonimmigrant status under section 101(a)(15)(T)(i) of the Act, an applicant must demonstrate that removal from the United States would subject the applicant to extreme hardship involving unusual and severe harm.

(1) Standard. Extreme hardship involving unusual and severe harm is a higher standard than that of extreme hardship as described in § 240.58 of this chapter. A finding of extreme hardship involving unusual and severe harm may not be based upon current or future economic detriment, or the lack of, or disruption to, social or economic opportunities. Factors that may be considered in evaluating whether removal would result in extreme hardship involving unusual and severe harm should take into account both traditional extreme hardship factors and those factors associated with having been a victim of a severe form of trafficking in persons. These factors include, but are not limited to, the following:

(i) The age and personal circumstances of the applicant;

(ii) Serious physical or mental illness of the applicant that necessitates medical or psychological attention not reasonably available in the foreign country;

(iii) The nature and extent of the physical and psychological consequences of severe forms of trafficking in persons;

(iv) The impact of the loss of access to the United States courts and the criminal justice system for purposes relating to the incident of severe forms of trafficking in persons or other crimes perpetrated against the applicant, including criminal and civil redress for acts of trafficking in persons, criminal prosecution, restitution, and protection;

(v) The reasonable expectation that the existence of laws, social practices, or customs in the foreign country to which the applicant would be returned would penalize the applicant severely for having been the victim of a severe form of trafficking in persons;

(vi) The likelihood of re-victimization and the need, ability, or willingness of foreign authorities to protect the applicant;

(vii) The likelihood that the trafficker in persons or others acting on behalf of the trafficker in the foreign country would severely harm the applicant; and

(viii) The likelihood that the applicant's individual safety would be seriously threatened by the existence of civil unrest or armed conflict as demonstrated by the designation of Temporary Protected Status, under section 244 of the Act, or the granting of other relevant protections.

(2) Evidence. An applicant is encouraged to describe and document all factors that may be relevant to his or her case, since there is no guarantee that a particular reason or reasons will result in a finding that removal would cause extreme hardship involving unusual and severe harm to the applicant. Hardship to persons other than the alien victim of a severe form of trafficking in persons cannot be considered in determining whether an applicant would suffer extreme hardship involving unusual and severe harm.

(3) Evaluation. The Service will evaluate on a case-by-case basis, after a review of the evidence, whether the applicant has demonstrated extreme hardship involving unusual or severe harm. The Service will consider all credible evidence submitted regarding the nature and scope of the hardship should the applicant be removed from the United States, including evidence of hardship arising from circumstances surrounding the victimization as described in section 101(a)(15)(T)(i)(I) of the Act and

any other circumstances. In appropriate cases, the Service may consider evidence from relevant country condition reports and any other public or private sources of information. The determination that extreme hardship involving unusual or severe harm to the alien exists is to be made solely by the Service.

(j) Waiver of grounds of inadmissibility. An application for a waiver of inadmissibility under section 212(d)(13) or section 212(d)(3) of the Act must be filed in accordance with *§ 212.16* of this chapter, and submitted to the Service with the completed application package.

(k) Bona fide application for T-1 nonimmigrant status—

(1) Criteria. Once an application is submitted to the Service, the Service will conduct an initial review to determine if the application is a bona fide application for T nonimmigrant status. An application shall be determined to be bona fide if, after initial review, it is properly filed, there appears to be no instance of fraud in the application, the application is complete (including the LEA endorsement or other secondary evidence), the application presents prima facie evidence of each element to show eligibility for T-1 nonimmigrant status, and the Service has completed the necessary fingerprinting and criminal background checks. If an alien is inadmissible under section 212(a) of the Act, the application will not be deemed to be bona fide unless the only grounds of inadmissibility are those under the circumstances described in section 212(d)(13) of the Act, or unless the Service has granted a waiver of inadmissibility on any other grounds. All waivers are discretionary and require a request for a waiver. Under section 212(d)(13), an application can be bona fide before the waiver is granted. This is not the case under other grounds of inadmissibility.

(2) Determination by USCIS. An application for T-1 status under this section will not be treated as a bona fide application until USCIS has provided the notice described in paragraph (k)(3) of this section. In the event that an application is incomplete or if the application is complete but does not present sufficient evidence to establish

prima facie eligibility for each required element of T nonimmigrant status, USCIS will follow the procedures provided in *8 CFR 103.2(b)* for requesting additional evidence, issuing a notice of intent to deny, or adjudicating the case on the merits.

(3) Notice to alien. Once an application is determined to be a bona fide application for a T-1 nonimmigrant status, the Service will provide written confirmation to the applicant.

(4) Stay of final order of exclusion, deportation, or removal. A determination by the Service that an application for T-1 nonimmigrant status is bona fide automatically stays the execution of any final order of exclusion, deportation, or removal. This stay shall remain in effect until there is a final decision on the T application. The filing of an application for T nonimmigrant status does not stay the execution of a final order unless the Service has determined that the application is bona fide. Neither an immigration judge nor the Board of Immigration Appeals (Board) has jurisdiction to adjudicate an application for a stay of execution, deportation, or removal order, on the basis of the filing of an application for T nonimmigrant status.

(l) Review and decision on applications—

(1) De novo review. The Service shall conduct a de novo review of all evidence submitted and is not bound by its previous factual determinations as to any essential elements of the T nonimmigrant status application. Evidence previously submitted for this and other immigration benefits or relief may be used by the Service in evaluating the eligibility of an applicant for T nonimmigrant status. However, the Service will not be bound by its previous factual determinations as to any essential elements of the T classification. The Service will determine, in its sole discretion, the evidentiary value of previously or concurrently submitted evidence.

(2) Burden of proof. At all stages of the processing of an application for any benefits under T nonimmigrant sta-

tus, the burden shall be on the applicant to present to the Service evidence that fully establishes eligibility for the desired benefit.

(3) Decision. After completing its review of the application, the Service shall issue a written decision granting or denying the application. If the Service determines that the applicant has met the requirements for T-1 nonimmigrant status, the Service shall grant the application, subject to the annual limitation as provided in paragraph (m) of this section. Along with the approval, the Service will include a list of nongovernmental organizations to which the applicant can refer regarding the alien's options while in the United States and resources available to the alien.

(4) Work authorization. When the Service grants an application for T-1 nonimmigrant status, the Service will provide the alien with an Employment Authorization Document incident to that status, which shall extend concurrently with the duration of the alien's T-1 nonimmigrant status.

(m) Annual cap. In accordance with section 214(n)(2) of the Act, the total number of principal aliens issued T-1 nonimmigrant status may not exceed 5,000 in any fiscal year.

(1) Issuance of T-1 nonimmigrant status. Once the cap is reached in any fiscal year, the Service will continue to review and consider applications in the order they are received. The Service will determine if the applicants are eligible for T-1 nonimmigrant status, but will not issue T-1 nonimmigrant status at that time. The revocation of an alien's T-1 status will have no effect on the annual cap.

(2) Waiting list. All eligible applicants who, due solely to the cap, are not granted T-1 nonimmigrant status shall be placed on a waiting list and will receive notice of such placement. While on the waiting list, the applicant shall maintain his or her current means to prevent removal (deferred action, parole, or stay of removal) and any employment authorization, subject to any limits imposed

on that authorization. Priority on the waiting list is determined by the date the application was properly filed, with the oldest applications receiving the highest priority. As new classifications become available in subsequent years, the Service will issue them to applicants on the waiting list, in the order in which the applications were properly filed, providing the applicant remains admissible. The Service may require new fingerprint and criminal history checks before issuing an approval. After T-1 nonimmigrant status has been issued to qualifying applicants on the waiting list, any remaining T-1 nonimmigrant numbers will be issued to new qualifying applicants in the order that the applications were properly filed.

(n) [Reserved]

(o) Admission of the T-1 applicant's immediate family members—

(1) Eligibility. Subject to section 214(n) of the Act, an alien who has applied for or been granted T-1 nonimmigrant status may apply for admission of an immediate family member, who is otherwise admissible to the United States, in a T-2 (spouse) or T-3 (child) derivative status (and, in the case of a T-1 principal applicant who is a child, a T-4 (parent) derivative status), if accompanying or following to join the principal alien. The applicant must submit evidence sufficient to demonstrate that:

(i) The alien for whom T-2, T-3, or T-4 status is being sought is an immediate family member of a T-1 nonimmigrant, as defined in paragraph (a) of this section, and is otherwise eligible for that status; and

(ii) The immediate family member or the T-1 principal would suffer extreme hardship, as described in paragraph (o)(5) of this section, if the immediate family member was not allowed to accompany or follow to join the principal T-1 nonimmigrant.

...

(5) Evidence demonstrating extreme hardship for immediate family members. The application must demonstrate

that each alien for whom T-2, T-3, or T-4 status is being sought, or the principal T-1 applicant, would suffer extreme hardship if the immediate family member was not admitted to the United States or was removed from the United States (if already present). When the immediate family members are following to join the principal, the extreme hardship must be substantially different than the hardship generally experienced by other residents of their country of origin who are not victims of a severe form of trafficking in persons. The Service will consider all credible evidence of extreme hardship to the T-1 recipient or the individual immediate family members. The determination of the extreme hardship claim will be evaluated on a case-by-case basis, in accordance with the factors outlined in § 240.58 of this chapter. Applicants are encouraged to raise and document all applicable factors, since there is no guarantee that a particular reason or reasons will result in a finding of extreme hardship if the applicant is not allowed to enter or remain in the United States. In addition to these factors, other factors that may be considered in evaluating extreme hardship include, but are not limited to, the following:

(i) The need to provide financial support to the principal alien;

(ii) The need for family support for a principal alien; or

(iii) The risk of serious harm, particularly bodily harm, to an immediate family member from the perpetrators of the severe forms of trafficking in persons.

. . .

(p) Duration of T nonimmigrant status.

(1) In general. An approved T nonimmigrant status shall expire after 4 years from the date of approval. The status may be extended if a Federal, State, or local law enforcement official, prosecutor, judge, or other authority investigating or prosecuting activity relating to human trafficking certifies that the presence of the alien in the United States is necessary to assist in the investigation or

prosecution of such activity. At the time an alien is approved for T nonimmigrant status or receives an extension, USCIS shall notify the alien when his or her nonimmigrant status will expire. The applicant shall immediately notify USCIS of any changes in the applicant's circumstances that may affect eligibility under section 101(a)(15)(T)(i) of the Act and this section.

(2) Information pertaining to adjustment of status. USCIS will notify an alien granted T nonimmigrant status of the requirement to timely apply for adjustment of status, and that the failure to apply for adjustment of status in accordance with *8 CFR 245.23* will result in termination of the alien's T nonimmigrant status at the end of the 4-year period unless that status is extended in accordance with paragraph (p)(1) of this section. Aliens who properly apply for adjustment of status to that of a person admitted to permanent residence in accordance with *8 CFR 245.23* shall remain eligible for adjustment of status.

(q) De novo review. The Service shall conduct a de novo review of all evidence submitted at all stages in the adjudication of an application for T nonimmigrant status. Evidence previously submitted for this and other immigration benefits or relief may be used by the Service in evaluating the eligibility of an applicant for T nonimmigrant status. However, the Service will not be bound by its previous factual determinations as to any essential elements of the T classification. The Service will determine, in its sole discretion, the evidentiary value of previously or concurrently submitted evidence.

(r) Denial of application. Upon denial of any T application, the Service shall notify the applicant, any LEA providing an LEA endorsement, and the Department of Health and Human Service's Office of Refugee Resettlement in writing of the decision and the reasons for the denial in accordance with *§ 103.3* of this chapter. Upon denial of an application for T nonimmigrant status, any benefits derived as a result of having filed a bona fide application will automatically be revoked when the denial becomes final. If an applicant chooses to appeal the denial pursuant to the provisions of *§ 103.3* of this chapter, the denial will not become final until the appeal is adjudicated.

(s) Revocation of approved T nonimmigrant status. The alien shall immediately notify the Service of any changes in the terms and conditions of an alien's circumstances that may affect eligibility under section 101(a)(15)(T) of the Act and this section.

(1) Grounds for notice of intent to revoke. The Service shall send to the T nonimmigrant a notice of intent to revoke the status in relevant part if it is determined that:

(i) The T nonimmigrant violated the requirements of section 101(a)(15)(T) of the Act or this section;

(ii) The approval of the application violated this section or involved error in preparation procedure or adjudication that affects the outcome;

(iii) In the case of a T-2 spouse, the alien's divorce from the T-1 principal alien has become final;

(iv) In the case of a T-1 principal alien, an LEA with jurisdiction to detect or investigate the acts of severe forms of trafficking in persons by which the alien was victimized notifies the Service that the alien has unreasonably refused to cooperate with the investigation or prosecution of the trafficking in persons and provides the Service with a detailed explanation of its assertions in writing; or

(v) The LEA providing the LEA endorsement withdraws its endorsement or disavows the statements made therein and notifies the Service with a detailed explanation of its assertions in writing.

(2) Notice of intent to revoke and consideration of evidence. A district director may revoke the approval of a T nonimmigrant status at any time, even after the validity of the status has expired. The notice of intent to revoke shall be in writing and shall contain a detailed statement of the grounds for the revocation and the time period allowed for the T nonimmigrant's rebuttal. The alien may submit evidence in rebuttal within 30 days of the date of the notice. The director shall consider all relevant evidence pre-

sented in deciding whether to revoke approval of the T nonimmigrant status. The determination of what is relevant evidence and the weight to be given to that evidence shall be within the sole discretion of the director.

(3) Revocation of T nonimmigrant status. If, upon reconsideration, the approval previously granted is revoked, the director shall provide the alien with a written notification of the decision that explains the specific reasons for the revocation. The director also shall notify the LEA that supplied an endorsement to the alien, any consular officer having jurisdiction over the applicant, and HHS's Office of Refugee Resettlement.

(4) Appeal of a revocation of approval. The alien may appeal the decision to revoke the approval within 15 days after the service of notice of the revocation. All appeals of a revocation of approval will be processed and adjudicated in accordance with *§ 103.3* of this chapter.

(5) Effect of revocation of T-1 status. In the event that a principal alien's T-1 nonimmigrant status is revoked, all T nonimmigrant status holders deriving status from the revoked status automatically shall have that status revoked. In the case where a T-2, T-3, or T-4 application is still awaiting adjudication, it shall be denied. The revocation of an alien's T-1 status will have no effect on the annual cap as described in paragraph (m) of this section.

(t) Removal proceedings without revocation. Nothing in this section shall prohibit the Service from instituting removal proceedings under section 240 of the Act for conduct committed after admission, or for conduct or a condition that was not disclosed to the Service prior to the granting of nonimmigrant status under section 101(a)(15)(T) of the Act, including the misrepresentation of material facts in the applicant's application for T nonimmigrant status.

(u) [Reserved]

(v) Service officer referral. Any Service officer who receives a request from an alien seeking protection as a victim of a severe form of trafficking in persons or seeking information regarding

> T nonimmigrant status shall follow the procedures for protecting and providing services to victims of severe forms of trafficking outlined in *28 CFR 1100.31*. Aliens believed to be victims of a severe form of trafficking in persons shall be referred to the local Service office with responsibility for investigations relating to victims of severe forms of trafficking in persons for a consultation within 7 days. The local Service office may, in turn, refer the victim to another LEA with responsibility for investigating or prosecuting severe forms of trafficking in persons. If the alien has a credible claim to victimization, he or she will be given the opportunity to submit an application for T status pursuant to section 101(a)(15)(T) of the Act and any other benefit or protection for which he or she may be eligible. An alien determined not to have a credible claim to being a victim of a severe form of trafficking in persons and who is subject to removal will be removed in accordance with Service policy.

3) U-Visas

Another non-immigrant category which might be available to victims of trafficking is the U- (victims of crime) visa, pursuant to 8 C.F.R. 214 and 8 U.S.C.A. 1101. However, aliens can only apply for one status at a time. A U application could theoretically be a fallback option to a T-visa.

Congress created U-visas in the year 2000 as part of the VTVPA, intending to assist not only alien victims of crime, but also to assist law enforcement in prosecuting those crimes. There are 10,000 visas set aside under this category each year, and it protects people who are victims of crime other than trafficking as well as those who are victims of trafficking. 8 C.F.R section 214.14 (b) sets for the grounds for eligibility of a U-visa:

> (b) Eligibility. An alien is eligible for U-1 nonimmigrant status if he or she demonstrates all of the following in accordance with paragraph (c) of this section:
>
> (1) The alien has suffered substantial physical or mental abuse as a result of having been a victim of qualifying criminal activity. Whether abuse is substantial is based on a number of factors, including but not limited to: The nature of the injury inflicted or suffered; the severity of

the perpetrator's conduct; the severity of the harm suffered; the duration of the infliction of the harm; and the extent to which there is permanent or serious harm to the appearance, health, or physical or mental soundness of the victim, including aggravation of pre-existing conditions. No single factor is a prerequisite to establish that the abuse suffered was substantial. Also, the existence of one or more of the factors automatically does not create a presumption that the abuse suffered was substantial. A series of acts taken together may be considered to constitute substantial physical or mental abuse even where no single act alone rises to that level;

(2) The alien possesses credible and reliable information establishing that he or she has knowledge of the details concerning the qualifying criminal activity upon which his or her petition is based. The alien must possess specific facts regarding the criminal activity leading a certifying official to determine that the petitioner has, is, or is likely to provide assistance to the investigation or prosecution of the qualifying criminal activity. In the event that the alien has not yet reached 16 years of age on the date on which an act constituting an element of the qualifying criminal activity first occurred, a parent, guardian or next friend of the alien may possess the information regarding a qualifying crime. In addition, if the alien is incapacitated or incompetent, a parent, guardian, or next friend may possess the information regarding the qualifying crime;

(3) The alien has been helpful, is being helpful, or is likely to be helpful to a certifying agency in the investigation or prosecution of the qualifying criminal activity upon which his or her petition is based, and since the initiation of cooperation, has not refused or failed to provide information and assistance reasonably requested. In the event that the alien has not yet reached 16 years of age on the date on which an act constituting an element of the qualifying criminal activity first occurred, a parent, guardian or next friend of the alien may provide the re-

quired assistance. In addition, if the petitioner is incapacitated or incompetent and, therefore, unable to be helpful in the investigation or prosecution of the qualifying criminal activity, a parent, guardian, or next friend may provide the required assistance; and

(4) The qualifying criminal activity occurred in the United States (including Indian country and U.S. military installations) or in the territories or possessions of the United States, or violated a U.S. federal law that provides for extraterritorial jurisdiction to prosecute the offense in a U.S. federal court.

What is "qualifying criminal activity" that would qualify an alien for a U-visa? 8 C.F.R section 214.14(a)(9) provides the definition:

> (9) Qualifying crime or qualifying criminal activity includes one or more of the following or any similar activities in violation of Federal, State or local criminal law of the United States: Rape; torture; trafficking; incest; domestic violence; sexual assault; abusive sexual contact; prostitution; sexual exploitation; female genital mutilation; being held hostage; peonage; involuntary servitude; slave trade; kidnapping; abduction; unlawful criminal restraint; false imprisonment; blackmail; extortion; manslaughter; murder; felonious assault; witness tampering; obstruction of justice; perjury; or attempt, conspiracy, or solicitation to commit any of the above mentioned crimes. The term "any similar activity" refers to criminal offenses in which the nature and elements of the offenses are substantially similar to the statutorily enumerated list of criminal activities.

As noted, because applications cannot be filed for more than one status at a time, trafficking victims will need to elect which to pursue. U-visa holders will likely spend more time in contact with law enforcement agencies. There are provisions for admitting family members of U-visa holders, and waivers of grounds of inadmissibility.

4) Inadmissibility

Just because an alien qualifies for admission under the T-visa (or any other non-immigrant visa), that does not mean that the alien is automatically qualified to remain in this country and be awarded the non-immigrant status. 8 U.S.C. 1182 precludes people who otherwise would be eligible if they fall into "ineligibility" grounds. Among these grounds are health related grounds, those convicted of certain crimes, controlled substance traffickers, and those involved in prostitution and commercialized vice. A new ground of inadmissibility, "significant traffickers in persons" was added in the year 2000 as 8 U.S.C. 1182 (H) Significant traffickers in persons.

> (i) In general
> Any alien who commits or conspires to commit human trafficking offenses in the United States or outside the United States, or who the consular officer, the Secretary of Homeland Security, the Secretary of State, or the Attorney General knows or has reason to believe is or has been a knowing aider, abettor, assister, conspirator, or colluder with such a trafficker in severe forms of trafficking in persons, as defined in the *section 7102 of Title 22,* is inadmissible.
>
> (ii) Beneficiaries of trafficking
> Except as provided in clause (iii), any alien who the consular officer or the Attorney General knows or has reason to believe is the spouse, son, or daughter of an alien inadmissible under clause (i), has, within the previous 5 years, obtained any financial or other benefit from the illicit activity of that alien, and knew or reasonably should have known that the financial or other benefit was the product of such illicit activity, is inadmissible.
>
> (iii) Exception for certain sons and daughters
> Clause (ii) shall not apply to a son or daughter who was a child at the time he or she received the benefit described in such clause.

5) Waivers

However, even if a ground of ineligibility applies, the T-visa applicant might also be able to obtain a waiver. Waivers can be granted if they are in the national interest (8 U.S.C. 1182(d)(13)) or as an exercise of discretion for other reasons (8 U.S.C. 1182(d)(3)(B)).

This is undoubtedly very confusing to law students, and to lawyers who are unfamiliar with the complexities (and sometimes the absurdities) of United States immigration law. Imagine how impenetrable this would all seem to a trafficking victim from another country. In order to create an approach that might assist your understanding of the process, consider asking these questions.

1. Is there an immigration category for which the trafficking victim qualifies? If so, you must still explore the next question.
2. Are there any grounds that would make the victim (who otherwise qualifies for permanent resident status or T-visa or other visa status) inadmissible? If the answer is no, the victim is eligible for the immigration status. However, even if the answer to this second question is "yes," ask the next question.
3. Are there any grounds or bases for seeking a waiver of the grounds of inadmissibility? If so, the trafficking victim will be able to obtain the immigration status he/she seeks in this country.

If the T-visa is granted, it remains in effect for four years. (8 C.F.R. 214.11(p)). Not only is the alien allowed to remain, but her parents may also be granted a T-visa if the victim is under twenty-one. The victim's children who are under twenty-one, her spouse, and her siblings are also eligible for the T-visa. However, those family members must show that they, or the T-visa applicant would suffer extreme hardship if the family members were not allowed to join the trafficking victim in the United States (8 C.F.R. 214.11(o)(3)). It is important to note that even if someone qualifies for a T-visa, is able to show that she is not ineligible, or that if she is ineligible but a waiver applies, that still does not guarantee the issuance of a visa. The reason is that Congress has set a limit of 5,000 visas in the T-category each year. If more than 5,000 T-visas are granted in one year, those whose petitions have been approved "wait in line" until another 5,000 visas become available in the following year.

3. Immigration Options Ultimately Available to Victims of Trafficking

Recall that citizenship can be acquired by birth or through the naturalization process. It is possible that some victims of trafficking who are brought into the United States are actually citizens of the United States.

It might be that the victim was born in this country but is unaware of that fact. It is also possible that even if the victim is born abroad, one or both of her parents might be U.S. citizens. If that is the case, she acquired U.S. citizenship at her birth. These options should always be explored with any trafficking victim (or indeed, with any other alien) seeking to remain in the United States.

Some aliens who are victims of trafficking will be eligible for permanent resident alien status if a successful application for asylum or refugee status can be pursued. Someone who receives a non-immigrant T-visa is also eligible to apply for permanent resident alien status under a process known as "Adjustment of Status" (8 U.S.C. 1255(1)). The victim must be of good moral character. She must have either assisted in prosecution of her trafficker or demonstrate extreme hardship if she were removed from the United States. (8 C.F.R. 245.23) Note also that the application for adjustment of status can only occur after the victim has been in this country for three years under her status.

If a trafficking victim becomes a permanent resident either through the route of asylum, or the route of adjustment of status from her T-Visa, she may ultimately apply to become a citizen of the United States. Generally, the trafficking victim must have served as a permanent resident alien for five years, or for only three years if she is married to a U.S. citizen. See the requirements for naturalization set out at 8 U.S.C. 1427, 1429. Finally, when counseling a trafficking victim, the attorney should not overlook the possibility that the alien might qualify for either permanent residency or a temporary non-immigrant visa, under one of the many other categories. In other words, the trafficking victim should not be looked upon solely as a victim. The attorney attempting to assist her should explore all immigration and other lawful benefits available to those who have not suffered the misfortune of trafficking.

C. For Further Thought

1. Compare the definition of "Trafficking in Persons" set out in Article 3(a) of the United Nations Protocol, with the "Severe Forms of Trafficking," "Debt Bondage," "Involuntary Servitude," and "Peonage," as defined in 8 C.F.R. 214. How are the definitions by the United Nations

and the United States consistent? How do they differ? What do you think explains the differences?

2. Do the opportunities available for trafficking victims under United States law meet or exceed the aspirations of Article 7 of the United Nations Protocol?
3. A wealthy resident of a foreign country seeks to enter another country as a treaty investor. In the past, that resident has assisted in trafficking. What provisions would apply under both the United Nations Protocol and United States immigration law?
4. For each of the hypothetical fact patterns presented at the beginning of this chapter, assume that you are representing the alien. What additional information would you seek in order to determine how best to proceed to assist the alien? Outline your approach to attempting to obtain permission for the alien to live and work in the United States. What opportunities exist, if any, for family members of the alien?
5. In 2015, Congress, at the urging of U.S. Senator Cornyn, R-TX, passed legislation to create a fund to assist trafficking victims. Money from fines assessed against traffickers, together with Congressional appropriations, will be used for that purpose. What other measures could be implemented by federal, state, and local governments in this regard? Should states adopt a Uniform Act? (*See* Andrew Hall, *The Uniform Act on Prevention of and Remedies for Human Trafficking*, 56 Ariz. L. Rev. 853 (2014).)
6. What role could private charitable organizations continue to play in assisting trafficking victims? How might individuals assist in these efforts?

Selected Bibliography

Books

Bill Piatt, Catholic Legal Perspectives (Carolina Academic Press 3d ed. 2018).

Bill Piatt, Immigration Law: Cases and Materials (The Michie Company 1994).

Articles

Janet Beck, Human Trafficking and the T Visa Process, 75 Tex. B.J. 770 (2012).

Jennifer Chacón, Tensions and Trade-offs: Protecting Trafficking Victims in the Era of Immigration Enforcement, 158 U. Pa. L. Rev. 1609 (2010).

Aretha Chakraborti, Alien Human-Trafficking Victims in the United States: Examining the Constitutionality of the TVPA and INA's Assistance Requirements, 17 U. Pa. J. L. & Soc. Change 55 (2014).

Emily Davis, Cece v. Holder: An Unprecedented Look at the Asylum Claim for Victims of Attempted Sex Trafficking, 29 Emory Int'l L. Rev. 379 (2014).

Sally Green, Protection for Victims of Child Sex Trafficking in the United States: Forging the Gap Between U.S. Immigration Laws and Human Trafficking Laws, 12 U.C. Davis J. Juv. L. & Pol'y 309 (2008).

Andrew Hall, The Uniform Act on Prevention of and Remedies for Human Trafficking, 56 Ariz. L. Rev. 853 (2014).

Britta Loftus, Coordinating U.S. Law on Immigration and Human Trafficking: Lifting the Lamp to Victims, 43 Colum. Hum. Rts. L. Rev. 143 (2011).

Diana Squillante, Single, Young Female-Seeking Asylum: The Struggles Victims of Sex Trafficking Face Under Current States Refugee Law, 88 St. John's L. Rev. 223 (2014).

Chapter 5

Should Prostitution Be Legalized?

Most people would agree that the current system of laws criminalizing prostitution in this country and abroad do not prevent prostitution and trafficking, and have not eliminated the harms associated with them. Are there other models that might be effective?

A. Experiments in Legalization

Efforts to eliminate sex trafficking inevitably turn to a discussion of whether legalization of prostitution would be the best method of addressing these problems. An analogy might be drawn to recent efforts to decriminalize the use of marijuana. Advocates have urged that marijuana will continue to be bought and sold, even in the face of laws making such activity criminal. They argue that criminal statutes have not eliminated the use of the drug. Removing the criminality of transactions regulated and even taxed by the state would theoretically drive the criminal element out of drug transactions, allowing law enforcement to focus efforts on crimes that are not "victimless." The public welfare and safety would be enhanced, because theoretically the state would insure that the drugs being sold met minimal safety standards. Revenues earned in the form of taxes would fund the state's regulatory scheme. In addition to the safety issues, advocates have adopted a libertarian position that the individual should be free to decide whether to use marijuana. Some states have recently de-criminalized the use of small amounts of marijuana. Studies on whether there has been any health and safety benefits or whether the increased use of marijuana has led to unforeseen harms are not yet conclusive.

Similar rationales have been advanced for the legalization of prostitution. Advocates refer to prostitution, at least where it involves consenting adults, as a victimless crime. They would argue that prostitution has remained a human phenomenon throughout history notwithstanding the existence of laws which make it a crime. They urge that allowing the state to license and regulate sex workers removes the criminal element from prostitution guaranteeing that public safety concerns are addressed. One civil rights attorney, Ameer Benno, argues, "Sexual commerce should be treated like other kinds of work, and sex workers like workers in other occupations.... [T]hat means that they should be afforded the full panoply of rights, protections and responsibilities that come along with that, without stigma. Look, abuse, exploitation, and violence are unquestionably bad things that we all should aspire to eradicate, but they are by no means inherent in prostitution."[1]

These views have actually been implemented. In the year 2000, prostitution in the Netherlands was legalized. At that point, revenues in prostitution were already exceeding $1 billion a year. The expectation was that legalizing sex trade would make it safer for the women involved.[2] Germany followed in the year 2002 by legalizing prostitution. The purpose of the law included providing access for sex workers to employment benefits and health insurance and protect other employment rights.[3] By 2013, more than one million men were lawfully paying for sex each day in Germany.[4]

---

1. Diana Falzone, *Amnesty International's Legalized Prostitution Push Turning Off Celeb Supporters*, Fox News (July 30, 2015), http://www.foxnews.com/entertainment/2015/07/30/amnesty-international-legalized-prostitution-push-turning-off-celeb-supporters.

2. Brief for Petitioner at 19, Agency for Int'l Development v. Alliance for Open Society Int'l, 133 S. Ct. 2321 (2013) (No. 12-10), 2013 WL 860449; *see also* Peter Cluskey, *Abuse, Misery and Criminality Behind the Legal Sex Trade,* Irish Times (Mar. 17, 2012), http://www.irishtimes.com/newspaper/world/2012/0317/1224313471972.html.

3. Louise Osborne, *Why Germany is Now Europe's Biggest Brothel,* The Guardian (June 12, 2013), http://www.theguardian.com/world/shortcuts/2013/jun/12/germany-now-europes-biggest-brothel.

4. *Id.*

These European efforts were preceded in the Western world by legislation in Victoria, Australia, which legalized prostitution in licensed brothels.[5] The purpose of the legislation was to enable "harm minimization."[6] The hope was that limiting prostitution to licensed brothels would reduce street prostitution. It was also hoped that these efforts would reduce the risk of sexually transmitted diseases. The idea was to provide a safer environment for both prostitutes and their clients. New Zealand followed suit by decriminalizing prostitution in 2003.[7]

While the regulatory schemes are complex, and some countries provide criminal penalties for the procurement, as opposed to the purchase of sexual services. Acts of prostitution are not criminal in these countries:

> Andorra, Angola, Antigua/Barbuda, Argentina, Aruba, Azerbaijan, Bangladesh, Barbados, Belgium, Belize, Benin, Bermuda, Bhutan, Bolivia, Bosnia and Herzegovina, Brazil, Burkina Faso, Burma, Canada, Cape Verde, Cayman Islands, Central African Republic, Chad, Chile, Colombia, Democratic Republic of Congo, Republic of Congo, Costa Rica, Cote D'Ivoire, Croatia, Cuba, Cyprus, Czech Republic, Denmark, Djibouti, Dominica, Dominican Republic, Ecuador, El Salvador, Equatorial New Guinea, Estonia, Ethiopia, Europa Island, Falkland Islands, Faroe Islands, Fiji, Finland, France, French Guiana, French Polynesia, French So and Antarctica Lands, French and South Antigua, Gaza Strip, Georgia, Germany, Guatemala, Guinea-Bissau, Guyana, Haiti, Hong Kong, India, Indonesia, Ireland, Italy, Japan, Kazakhstan, Kenya, Kiribati, Latvia, Lesotho, Liberia, Luxembourg, Macedonia, Madagascar, Malawi, Marshall Islands, Martinique, Mauritius, Mayotte, Mexico, Moldova, Monaco, Montenegro, Montserrat, Namibia, Nauru,

---

5. Mary Sullivan & Sheila Jeffreys, *Legalizing Prostitution is Not the Answer: the Example of Victoria, Australia*, COALITION AGAINST TRAFFICKING IN WOMEN (AUSTRALIA), Dec. 1, 2001.

6. *Id.* at 2.

7. Melissa Farley, *The Real Harms of Prostitution*, CATHOLIC EDUCATION RESEARCH CENTER (Oct. 2010), www.catholiceducation.org/en/controversy/persecution/the-real-harms-of-prostitution.html.

> Nepal, Netherlands, Netherlands Antilles, New Caledonia, New Zealand, Nicaragua, Niger, Niue, Norfolk Islands, North Korea, Norway, Palau, Panama, Papua New Guinea, Paracel Islands, Paraguay, Peru, Pitcaim Island, Poland, Portugal, Reunion, St. Kitts and Nevis, St. Lucia, Samoa, San Marino, Sao Tome and Principe, Senegal, Serbia, Seychelles, Sierra Leone, Slovak Republic, So. Georgia and So. Sandwich Islands, South Korea, Spain, Suriname, Svalbard, Swaziland, Switzerland, Taiwan, Tajikistan, Tanzania, Togo Tokelau, Tonga, Trinidad and Tobago, Turkey, Turkmenistan, Turks/Caicous Island, Tuvalu, Uganda, United Kingdom, Uruguay, Uzbekistan, Venezuela, Vietnam, Virgin Islands (UK), Virgin Islands (U.S.), Wallis and Futuna, Yugoslavia, Zambia, and Zimbabwe.[8]

Refer back to the citation to detailed discussion of the state of human trafficking in individual countries prepared by the U.S. State Department, presented in Chapter 3.

And of course, as noted in Chapter 1, some areas of the state of Nevada in the United States provide that legalized prostitution can occur in state-licensed brothels.

Efforts at legalization of prostitution continue. Amnesty International took under consideration a new policy which would urge decriminalization of sex trafficking worldwide. Amnesty's deputy executive director Cammie Crofts stated, "Sex workers are one of the most marginalized groups in the world so it is important that we understand how, as Amnesty International, we can work to support their human rights. The violations that sex workers can be exposed to include physical and sexual violence, arbitrary arrest and detention, extortion and harassment, human trafficking, forced HIV testing and medical interventions.... They can also be excluded from health care and housing services and other social and legal protection."[9] While indicating that the issue was still

8. Mohamed Y. Mattar, *Trafficking in Persons, Especially Women and Children, in Countries of the Middle East: The Scope of the Problem and the Appropriate Legislative Responses*, 26 FORDHAM INT'L L.J. 721 (2002–2003).

9. Falzone, *supra* note 1.

under study, Crofts made it clear that the legalization approach was one method under consideration for protecting the rights of sex workers.[10]

However, critics and scholars have identified some serious inadequacies in this approach. For example, as Melissa Farley notes in "Examining the Legalization Scheme in the Netherlands," sexual violence and physical assault are the norm for women in legal prostitution. In one Dutch study, 60% of women in legal prostitution were physically assaulted, 70% were threatened with physical assault, 40% experienced sexual violence and 40% had been coerced into legal prostitution. Another study of the Netherlands approach indicates that 80% are foreigners, which indicates the Dutch women do not want to work as prostitutes. The majority of prostitutes, working in the Netherlands remain unlicensed.[11] Difficulties have led to the mayor of Amsterdam stating, "We realize this hasn't worked, that trafficking in women continues."[12] In Germany, two-thirds of the 400,000 sex workers are foreigners. The volume of the sex traffic in Germany has led some to consider it a national brothel.[13] Legalization in Victoria, Australia did not initially deal with trafficking or child prostitution. Not only that, while legalization led to a growth in legal prostitution, a tripling of unlicensed sex businesses sprung up.[14]

B. Can the U.S. Government Require That Organizations Receiving Federal Funding Oppose Prostitution?

The United States has not, and almost certainly will not, legalize prostitution. Similarly, states in the United States are unlikely to endorse the legalization of prostitution for reasons of morality, and for the practical reason that legalization has not been proven to eliminate trafficking. Assume, then, that the United States will resist such legalization efforts.

---

10. *Id.*

11. Brief for Petitioner, *supra* note 2, at 19.

12. Brief for Petitioner, *supra* note 2, at 20; *see also* Marlise Simons, *Amsterdam Tries Upscale Fix for Red-Light District Crime*, NEW YORK TIMES (Feb. 24, 2008), http://www.nytimes.com/2008/02/24/world/europe/24amsterdam.html?pagewanted=print&_r=0.

13. *Id.*

14. Sullivan & Jeffreys, *supra* note 5.

Does this mean that federal funds can be denied to organizations which do not adopt policies expressly opposing prostitution?

133 S. Ct. 2321
Supreme Court of the United States

AGENCY FOR INTERNATIONAL DEVELOPMENT, et al., Petitioners
v.
ALLIANCE FOR OPEN SOCIETY INTERNATIONAL, INC., et al.

No. 12-10. Argued April 22, 2013. Decided June 20, 2013.

Opinion

Chief Justice ROBERTS delivered the opinion of the Court.

The United States Leadership Against HIV/AIDS, Tuberculosis, and Malaria Act of 2003 (Leadership Act), 117 Stat. 711, as amended, 22 U.S.C. § 7601 et seq., outlined a comprehensive strategy to combat the spread of HIV/AIDS around the world. As part of that strategy, Congress authorized the appropriation of billions of dollars to fund efforts by nongovernmental organizations to assist in the fight. The Act imposes two related conditions on that funding: First, no funds made available by the Act "may be used to promote or advocate the legalization or practice of prostitution or sex trafficking." § 7631(e). And second, no funds may be used by an organization "that does not have a policy explicitly opposing prostitution and sex trafficking." § 7631(f). This case concerns the second of these conditions, referred to as the Policy Requirement. The question is whether that funding condition violates a recipient's First Amendment rights.

Congress passed the Leadership Act in 2003 after finding that HIV/AIDS had "assumed pandemic proportions, spreading from the most severely affected regions, sub-Saharan Africa and the Caribbean, to all corners of the world, and leaving an unprecedented path of death and devastation." 22 U.S.C. § 7601(1). According to congressional findings, more than 65 million people had been infected by HIV and more than 25 million had lost their lives, making HIV/AIDS the fourth highest cause of death worldwide. In sub-Saharan Africa alone, AIDS had claimed the lives of more than 19 million individuals and was projected to kill a full quarter of the population of that area over the next decade. The disease not only directly endangered those infected, but also increased the potential for social and political instability and economic devastation, posing a security issue for the entire international community. § 7601(2)–(10).

In the Leadership Act, Congress directed the President to establish a "comprehensive, integrated" strategy to combat HIV/AIDS around the world. § 7611(a). The Act sets out 29 different objectives the President's strategy should seek to fulfill, reflecting a multitude of approaches to the problem. The strategy must include, among other things, plans to increase the availability of treatment for infected individuals, prevent new infections, support the care of those affected by the disease, promote training for physicians and other health care workers, and accelerate research on HIV/AIDS prevention methods, all while providing a framework for cooperation with international organizations and partner countries to further the goals of the program. §§ 7611(a)(1)–(29).

The Act "make[s] the reduction of HIV/AIDS behavioral risks a priority of all prevention efforts." § 7611(a)(12); *see also* § 7601(15) ("Successful strategies to stem the spread of the HIV/AIDS pandemic will require... measures to address the social and behavioral causes of the problem"). The Act's approach to reducing behavioral risks is multifaceted. The President's strategy for addressing such risks must, for example, promote abstinence, encourage monogamy, increase the availability of condoms, promote voluntary counseling and treatment for drug users, and, as relevant here, "educat[e] men and boys about the risks of procuring sex commercially" as well as "promote alternative livelihoods, safety, and social reintegration strategies for commercial sex workers." § 7611(a)(12). Congress found that the "sex industry, the trafficking of individuals into such industry, and sexual violence" were factors in the spread of the HIV/AIDS epidemic, and determined that "it should be the policy of the United States to eradicate" prostitution and "other sexual victimization." § 7601(23).

The United States has enlisted the assistance of nongovernmental organizations to help achieve the many goals of the program. Such organizations "with experience in health care and HIV/AIDS counseling," Congress found, "have proven effective in combating the HIV/AIDS pandemic and can be a resource in... provid[ing] treatment and care for individuals infected with HIV/AIDS." § 7601(18). Since 2003, Congress has authorized the appropriation of billions of dollars for funding these organizations' fight against HIV/AIDS around the world. § 2151b-2(c); § 7671.

Those funds, however, come with two conditions: First, no funds made available to carry out the Leadership Act "may be used to promote or advocate the legalization or practice of prostitution or sex trafficking." § 7631(e). Second, no funds made available may "provide assistance to any group or organization that does not have a policy explicitly opposing prostitution and sex trafficking, except... to the Global Fund to Fight AIDS, Tuberculosis and Malaria, the World Health Organization, the International AIDS Vaccine Initiative or to any United Nations agency." § 7631(f). It is this second condition — the Policy Requirement — that is at issue here.

The Department of Health and Human Services (HHS) and the United States Agency for International Development (USAID) are the federal agencies primarily responsible for overseeing implementation of the Leadership Act. To enforce the Policy Requirement, the agencies have directed that the recipient of any funding under the Act agree in the award document that it is opposed to "prostitution and sex trafficking because of the psychological and physical risks they pose for women, men, and children." 45 CFR § 89.1(b) (2012); USAID, Acquisition & Assistance Policy Directive 12-04, p. 6 (AAPD 12-04).

Respondents are a group of domestic organizations engaged in combating HIV/AIDS overseas. In addition to substantial private funding, they receive billions annually in financial assistance from the United States, including under the Leadership Act. Their work includes programs aimed at limiting injection drug use in Uzbekistan, Tajikistan, and Kyrgyzstan, preventing mother-to-child HIV transmission in Kenya, and promoting safer sex practices in India. Respondents fear that adopting a policy explicitly opposing prostitution may alienate certain host governments, and may diminish the effectiveness of some of their programs by making it more difficult to work with prostitutes in the fight against HIV/AIDS. They are also concerned that the Policy Requirement may require them to censor their privately funded discussions in publications, at conferences, and in other forums about how best to prevent the spread of HIV/AIDS among prostitutes.

In 2005, respondents Alliance for Open Society International and Pathfinder International commenced this litigation, seeking a declaratory judgment that the Government's implementation of the Policy Requirement violated their First Amendment rights. Respondents sought a preliminary injunction barring the Government from cutting off their funding under the Act for the duration of the litigation, from unilaterally terminating their cooperative agreements with the United States, or from otherwise taking action solely on the basis of respondents' own privately funded speech. The District Court granted such a preliminary injunction, and the Government appealed....

The Court of Appeals affirmed, concluding that respondents had demonstrated a likelihood of success on the merits of their First Amendment challenge under this Court's "unconstitutional conditions" doctrine. 651 F.3d 218 (C.A.2 2011). Under this doctrine, the court reasoned, "the government may not place a condition on the receipt of a benefit or subsidy that infringes upon the recipient's constitutionally protected rights, even if the government has no obligation to offer the benefit in the first instance." *Id.*, at 231 (citing *Perry v. Sindermann*, 408 U.S. 593, 597, 92 S. Ct. 2694, 33 L. Ed. 2d 570 (1972)). And a condition that compels recipients "to espouse the government's position" on a subject of international debate could not be squared with the First Amendment. 651 F.3d, at 234. The court concluded that "the Policy Requirement, as implemented by the Agencies, falls well beyond what the Supreme Court... ha[s] upheld as permissible funding conditions." *Ibid.*

Judge Straub dissented, expressing his view that the Policy Requirement was an "entirely rational exercise of Congress's powers pursuant to the Spending Clause." *Id.*, at 240.

We granted certiorari....

III

The Policy Requirement mandates that recipients of Leadership Act funds explicitly agree with the Government's policy to oppose prostitution and sex trafficking. It is, however, a basic First Amendment principle that "freedom of speech prohibits the government from telling people what they must say." (cites omitted in this paragraph—ed). "At the heart of the First Amendment lies the principle that each person should decide for himself or herself the ideas and beliefs deserving of expression, consideration, and adherence."... ("The government may not... compel the endorsement of ideas that it approves.") Were it enacted as a direct regulation of speech, the Policy Requirement would plainly violate the First Amendment. The question is whether the Government may nonetheless impose that requirement as a condition on the receipt of federal funds.

A

The Spending Clause of the Federal Constitution grants Congress the power "[t]o lay and collect Taxes, Duties, Imposts and Excises, to pay the Debts and provide for the common Defence and general Welfare of the United States." Art. I, § 8, cl. 1. The Clause provides Congress broad discretion to tax and spend for the "general Welfare," including by funding particular state or private programs or activities. That power includes the authority to impose limits on the use of such funds to ensure they are used in the manner Congress intends....

As a general matter, if a party objects to a condition on the receipt of federal funding, its recourse is to decline the funds.

This remains true when the objection is that a condition may affect the recipient's exercise of its First Amendment rights. *See, e.g., United States v. American Library Assn., Inc.*, 539 U.S. 194, 212, 123 S. Ct. 2297, 156 L. Ed. 2d 221 (2003) (plurality opinion) (rejecting a claim by public libraries that conditioning funds for Internet access on the libraries' installing filtering software violated their First Amendment rights, explaining that "[t]o the extent that libraries wish to offer unfiltered access, they are free to do so without federal assistance"); *Regan v. Taxation With Representation of Wash.*, 461 U.S. 540, 546, 103 S. Ct. 1997, 76 L. Ed. 2d 129 (1983) (dismissing "the notion that First Amendment rights are somehow not fully realized unless they are subsidized by the State" (internal quotation marks omitted)).

At the same time, however, we have held that the Government "'may not deny a benefit to a person on a basis that infringes his constitutionally protected ... freedom of speech even if he has no entitlement to that benefit.'" *Forum for Academic and Institutional Rights, supra*, at 59, 126 S. Ct. 1297 (quoting American Library Assn., *supra*, at 210, 123 S. Ct. 2297). In some cases, a funding condition can result in an unconstitutional burden on First Amendment rights. See Forum for Academic and Institutional Rights, *supra*, at 59, 126 S. Ct. 1297 (the First Amendment supplies "a limit on Congress' ability to place conditions on the receipt of funds")....

B

As noted, the distinction drawn in these cases—between conditions that define the federal program and those that reach outside it—is not always self-evident. As Justice Cardozo put it in a related context, "Definition more precise must abide the wisdom of the future." *Steward Machine Co. v. Davis*, 301 U.S. 548, 591, 57 S. Ct. 883, 81 L. Ed. 1279 (1937). Here, however, we are confident that the Policy Requirement falls on the unconstitutional side of the line.

To begin, it is important to recall that the Leadership Act has two conditions relevant here. The first—unchallenged in this litigation—prohibits Leadership Act funds from being used "to promote or advocate the legalization or practice of prostitution or sex trafficking." 22 U.S.C. § 7631(e). The Government concedes that § 7631(e) by itself ensures that federal funds will not be used for the prohibited purposes. Brief for Petitioners 26–27.

The Policy Requirement therefore must be doing something more — and it is. The dissent views the Requirement as simply a selection criterion by which the Government identifies organizations "who believe in its ideas to carry them to fruition." Post, at 2332. As an initial matter, whatever purpose the Policy Requirement serves in selecting funding recipients, its effects go beyond selection. The Policy Requirement is an ongoing condition on recipients' speech and activities, a ground for terminating a grant after selection is complete. *See* AAPD 12-04, at 12. In any event, as the Government acknowledges, it is not simply seeking organizations that oppose prostitution. Reply Brief 5. Rather, it explains, "Congress has expressed its purpose 'to eradicate' prostitution and sex trafficking, 22 U.S.C. § 7601(23), and it wants recipients to adopt a similar stance." Brief for Petitioners 32 (emphasis added). This case is not about the Government's ability to enlist the assistance of those with whom it already agrees. It is about compelling a grant recipient to adopt a particular belief as a condition of funding.

By demanding that funding recipients adopt — as their own — the Government's view on an issue of public concern, the condition by its very nature affects "protected conduct outside the scope of the federally funded program." *Rust*, 500 U.S., at 197, 111 S. Ct. 1759. A recipient cannot avow the belief dictated by the Policy Requirement when spending Leadership Act funds, and then turn around and assert a contrary belief, or claim neutrality, when participating in activities on its own time and dime. By requiring recipients to profess a specific belief, the Policy Requirement goes beyond defining the limits of the federally funded program to defining the recipient. *See ibid.* ("our 'unconstitutional conditions' cases involve situations in which the Government has placed a condition on the recipient of the subsidy rather than on a particular program or service, thus effectively prohibiting the recipient from engaging in the protected conduct outside the scope of the federally funded program")....

Pressing its argument further, the Government contends that "if organizations awarded federal funds to implement Leadership Act programs could at the same time promote or affirmatively condone prostitution or sex trafficking, whether using public or private funds, it would undermine the government's program and confuse its message opposing prostitution and sex trafficking." Brief for Petitioners 37 (emphasis added). But the Policy Requirement goes beyond preventing recipients from using private funds in a way that would undermine the federal program. It requires them to pledge allegiance to the Government's policy of eradicating prostitution. As to that, we cannot improve upon what Justice Jackson wrote for the Court 70 years ago: "If there is any fixed star in our constitutional constellation, it is that no official, high or petty, can prescribe what shall be orthodox in politics, nationalism, religion, or other matters of opinion or force citizens to confess by word or act their faith therein." *Barnette*, 319 U.S., at 642, 63 S. Ct. 1178.

* * *

The Policy Requirement compels as a condition of federal funding the affirmation of a belief that by its nature cannot be confined within the scope of the Government program. In so doing, it violates the First Amendment and cannot be sustained. The judgment of the Court of Appeals is affirmed.

It is so ordered.

KAGAN, J., took no part in the consideration or decision of this case.

Justice SCALIA, with whom Justice THOMAS joins, dissenting.[15]

---

15. Agency for Int'l Development v. Alliance for Open Society Int'l, 133 S. Ct. 2321 (2013).

Numerous scholars and studies have concluded that legalizing prostitution does not decrease sex trafficking human beings. Legalization likely has resulted in an increase in the prostitution of children.[16] She also suggests that the phenomenon of legalization increases the demand on the part of sex buyers for "unrestricted" sex acts. Legalization does not seem to reduce violence directed at prostitutes.[17]

C. The Nordic Approach

While most countries outlaw prostitution, and while some are experimenting with legalizing it, there is a middle ground. In 1999, Sweden enacted a plan which decriminalizes prostitution on the part of the sex worker. However, it imposes criminal penalties on their customers. Following this lead, the countries of Norway, Iceland, and South Korea have enacted variations of this Nordic approach. It is under study in other nations as well. Follow up studies on the effects of the law indicate that there has been a 50% decrease of street prostitution in the country of Sweden. However, a resulting increase in neighboring countries has occurred, leading to the possibility that Sweden is exporting its difficulties with street prostitution. More than 70% of those surveyed in Sweden approve of the legislation. One important feature is that women who choose to leave the practice of prostitution are afforded exit services by the state. Farley notes that "[t]hose who have extricated themselves from prostitution take a positive view of criminalization, while those who are still exploited in prostitution are critical of the ban."[18]

A French variation on the Nordic approach was enacted in 2014. Those favoring the legislation argue that the Nordic model best serves societal interests. Not all agree. Opponents believe that this approach will push prostitutes even further to the margin endangering them. Another concern is the fact that 90% of prostitutes in France were foreign-born.[19]

---

16. Sullivan, Making Sex Work: A Failed Experiment With Legalized Prostitution (2007) (cited in Farley).

17. *Id.*

18. *Id.*

19. *Id.*

Even in the Netherlands, where prostitution remains legal, there is a recognition that some changes need to occur. Recently the mayor of Amsterdam noted, "Prostitution is a vulnerable profession. It often involves an unequal power relationship between owners and prostitutes. We need to change that power relationship."[20] However, rather than moving to the Nordic model, Amsterdam instead has introduced language skills tests and brothels and is considering raising the lawful age of prostitution from eighteen to twenty-one.[21]

The logic of attacking the purchasers of prostitution is illustrated in the following excerpt from the 2012 article of co-author Professor Cheryl Taylor Page (formerly Cheryl George) which appears at 13 *Fla. Coastal L. Rev.* 293, *Jailing the Johns: The Issue of Demand in Human Sex Trafficking*:[22]

> II. The "Johns"
>
> For sex trafficking to be successful, there has to be a demand.[15] Without demand, the multibillion-dollar industry would not prosper or even exist.[16] In this industry, victims emanate from countries where the victims are easily brought in as sex slaves.[17] Traffickers then send these victims to the destination country where men use these women and children as instruments for their own sexual pleasure.[18]
>
> While much research and discussion has focused on the supply side of sex trafficking, the demand side of sex trafficking rarely receives attention.[19] Focusing on the demand side of sex trafficking is a key component in eradicating this problem.[20] We need to investigate why there is a demand for women and children for use as sexual instruments for sexual deviants.
>
> As we explore the demand side of sex trafficking, we need to investigate what initiates this industry.[21] It is clear that the de-

---

20. Taina Bien-Aime, *France Takes First Steps Towards Abolition of Prostitution*, CATW INTERNATIONAL, (Feb. 13, 2014) http://www.huffingtonpost.com/taina-bienaime/france-prostitution-laws_b_4775608.html (last visited Sept. 2, 2015).

21. *Id.*

22. Cheryl George, *Jailing the Johns: The Issue of Demand in Human Sex Trafficking*, 13 FLA. COASTAL L. REV. 293 (2012). Reprinted with permission from the Florida Coastal Law Review.

mand for victims begins with them being used as either prostitutes or for free sexual favors.[22] When there is a demand for sexual slaves, there are pimps that will find these victims and supply them to the "Johns."[23] Demand is the first link in the chain of sex trafficking.[24]

Four components comprise the demand for human sex trafficking: (1) the men purchasing commercial sex acts; (2) "the exploiters who make up the sex industry;" (3) the states that serve as destination countries; and (4) the cultures and environments that tolerate and promote sexual exploitation.[25]

The concept that the demand originates from lonely men in unsatisfying relationships is merely a myth.[26] The truth is these men actually have a greater number of sexual partners than those men who are not purchasing sex.[27] The men who purchase sex are not unsatisfied; they simply seek something more and find excitement in the idea of finding a woman that "they can buy for a short time."[28] Many of these young women are purchased for as short as fifteen minutes at a time.[29] The arousal stems from the thought of a sexual relationship without any attached responsibility.[30] Further, the men seek entertainment, sexual gratification, and acts of violence as they crave control and refuse to respect women.[31] Finally, the demand group "is comprised of men of all colors, races, and cultural, educational and socio-economic backgrounds."[32] More often than not, these men develop the idea that they have a specific "right to sexual services in a way that results in ignorance regarding the development of relationships based on equality, truth, intimacy and commitment."[33]

There is a school of thought that espouses the theory that the sexual exploitation of women who are trafficked, as well as prostituted, is behavior that the male representatively created and designed to reinforce control and power over the female, one gender dominating another.[34] Another indication of gender domination is the brutal treatment and torture of women, where men consistently use rape as a weapon of war.[35] This tool has been used "to terrorize, degrade, and destroy its female victims."[36]

The "Johns" are average citizens from every walk of life.[37] They are doctors, lawyers, judges, celebrities, chief executive officers, construction workers, and plumbers.[38] "Rich and poor, young and old, the men who buy the women and girls in prostitution are from every race/ethnicity in the world."[39] Many tend to think that these "Johns" are sadistic, psychotic men, as society naturally tends to vilify and demonize them.[40] However, these "Johns" are our fathers, brothers, husbands, and sons.[41] Until we realize that fact, we will not see where the demand side of this industry stems from and the problem will continue to run rampant.[42]

Many experts have attempted to categorize and estimate the number of men participating in the sex industry.[43] The problem is that "Johns" do not advertise who they are.[44] They are secretive and not easy to research or interview.[45] "It is almost impossible to estimate how many men in the world have bought women for sex."[46] Even in countries where prostitution is legal, many aspects of the "Johns'" behavior are unknown and undiscoverable.[47] Melissa Farley, in her essay for the 2003 Captive Daughters Conference, notes that:

Estimates of the numbers of men who have ever purchased women in prostitution range from 16%–80%. A conservative guess at the percentage of US johns is probably around 50% of all men. This includes purchase of trafficked women. Johns don't ask for a "trafficked woman" in a massage parlor. We do know, however, that they often demand "something different," which keeps up the demand for so-called "exotic" women.[48]

Another expert, Elina Penttinen, has espoused one theory of the root cause of this demand for victims used for sexual gratification.[49] In her book, Globalization, Prostitution and Sex-Trafficking: Corporeal Politics, she explains that the sex bars "rely on hedonistic individualism, consumer culture and male rights to consume commercial sex."[50] She elaborates that some men believe they have an "individualistic freedom and right to buy commercial sexual services."[51]

One of the factors that contributes to the proliferation of the sex trafficking industry is the male demand for the prostitute for sexual gratification.[52] The kind of men that frequent brothels, sex bars, strip clubs that offer sex for their customers, escort dating services, massage parlors, and similar types of establishments "want unlimited access to a supply of women and girls from different countries, cultures and backgrounds."[53] This steady desire for variety and the exotic is what causes the human trafficking industry, fueled by the sex trafficking component, to proliferate and be the second largest organized criminal activity in the world,[54] and while sex slaves comprise only four percent of all slaves in existence today, they generate approximately forty percent of the money earned by the slave owners and exploiters.[55] Were it not for men that have this sense of sexual entitlement (that they have the implicit right to purchase and sexually exploit women and children), the trade of sex trafficking would collapse and be nonexistent.[56] Scholars in the field of researching sex trafficking and its many causes recognize "the male demand for the sex of prostitution as the most immediate and proximate cause of the expansion of the sex industry, without which it would be unprofitable for pimps, recruiters and traffickers to seek out a supply of women."[57] As basic as the notion might sound, a sex market devoid of the male consumers would go bankrupt.[58]

The males that desire and demand these victims of sexual abuse find that their sexual desires, fetishes, and needs are not or cannot be satisfied within the ordinary confines of legitimate sexual relationships such as the traditional marital relationship, and as such, prostitutes and sex slaves fill that void.[59] This leads men to use women in prostitution "as sexualized, commodified bodies to be appropriated, dissected, fragmented, used and abused in the interests of male biology and its need for variety, sexual fantasy and hegemony."[60]

Basically, "Johns" are paying to dehumanize a human being (the prostitute); the embodiment of the deal is for her to be "an object, not a subject."[61] Society as a whole has turned a blind eye to the plight of victims of the slave trade.[62] We tend to not want to identify these "Johns" as the monsters that they are,[63] but we must acknowledge that in this heinous crime "men use women's and girls' bodies, vaginas, anuses, mouths for their sexual pleasures and as vessels of ejaculation, over and over and over again."[64] Scholar Gunilla S. Ekberg has referred to prostitution as humiliation, torture, sexual exploitation, and rape.[65] When we view this crime in the right scope, we realize that the men that create the demand for the victims "are sexual predators and rapists."[66]

Many of the "Johns" explain away their involvement in the seedy business of sex trafficking by believing they are the object of desire for the victims and that somehow the victims "desire and want" them as their sexual partners.[67] Many reason that their sexual drive, and their human nature as men, causes them to have this insatiable urge to abuse women and children in this way.[68] Some articulate that it is an expression of masculinity, a consensual act between adults, or part of a cultural ritual and is an experience that the victims welcome and appreciate.[69]

15. Donna M. Hughes, Professor & Carlson Endowed Chair in Women's Studies at Univ. of R.I., *The Demand: Where Sex Trafficking Begins at the Pontifical Gregorian University "A Call to Action: Joining the Fight Against Trafficking in Persons,"* Conference 1 (June 17, 2004), *available at* http://www.uri.edu/artsci/wms/hughes/demand_rome_june04.pdf.

16. *See id.*

17. *Id.*

18. *See id.* at 2–3.

19. *Id.* at 1.

20. *See infra* note 24 and accompanying text.

21. *See infra* notes 22–69 and accompanying text.

22. *See* Hughes, *supra* note 15, at 1.

23. *Id.*

24. *See id.*

25. DONNA M. HUGHES, THE DEMAND FOR VICTIMS OF SEX TRAFFICKING 7 (2005), *available at* http://www.uri.edu/artsci/wms/hughes/demand_for_victims.pdf.

26. *Id.*

27. *Id.*

28. *Id.*

29. Peter Landesman, *The Girls Next Door*, N.Y. TIMES, Jan. 25, 2004, at 630 (illustrating that fifteen minutes of intercourse costs a mere four dollars and fifty cents).

30. *See* Hughes, *supra* note 15, at 2.

31. *Id.*

32. Norma Hotaling & Leslie Levitas-Martin, *Increased Demand Resulting in the Flourishing Recruitment and Trafficking of Women and Girls: Related Child Sexual Abuse and Violence Against Women*, 13 Hastings Women's L.J. 117, 121 (2002).

33. *Id.*

34. *See, e.g.*, Jonathan Todres, *The Importance of Realizing "Other Rights" to Prevent Sex Trafficking*, 12 Cardozo J.L. & Gender 885, 889–90 (2006) (discussing how gender-based discrimination and violence leads to human trafficking); *see also* Lisa Avery, *The Women and Children in Conflict Protection Act: An Urgent Call for Leadership and the Prevention of Intentional Victimization of Women and Children in War*, 51 Loy. L. Rev. 103, 107–10 (2005) (explaining the effects of armed conflict on women and children). *See generally* Andrea Dworkin, *Against the Male Flood: Censorship, Pornography, and Equality*, 8 Harv. Women's L.J. 1 (1985) (discussing the negative effect of the pornography industry on women).

35. Elisabeth Rehn & Ellen Johnson Sirleaf, Women War Peace: The Independent Experts' Assessment on the Impact of Armed Conflict on Women and Women's Role in Peace-Building 11–12 (2002).

36. Avery, *supra* note 34, at 108.

37. Melissa Farley, 2003 Conference: *Demand Dynamics: The Forces of Demand in International Sex Trafficking: The Demand for Prostitution, Captive Daughters*, http://www.captivedaughters.org/2003conf.html (last visited Mar. 29, 2012).

38. *Id.*

39. *Id.*

40. *See id.*

41. Hotaling & Levitas-Martin, *supra* note 32, at 121.

42. *See* Farley, *supra* note 37.

43. *See id.*

44. *Id.*

45. *Id.*

46. *Id.*

47. *Id.*

48. *Id.*

49. Elina Penttinen, Globalization, Prostitution and Sex-Trafficking: Corporeal Politics 115 (2008).

50. *Id.*

51. *Id.*

52. *See* Monica O'Connor & Grainne Healy, The Links Between Prostitution and Sex Trafficking: A Briefing Handbook 6 (2006), *available at* http://ewl.horus.be/SiteResources/data/MediaArchive/Violence Centre/News/handbook.pdf.

53. *Id.* at 10.

54. *Child Sex-Trafficking: The Facts*, Oprah (Nov. 15, 2005), http://www.oprah.com/oprahshow/Child-Sex-Trafficking-The-Facts.

55. *Sex Trafficking: Inside the Business of Modern Slavery, Stop Trafficking: Anti-Human Trafficking*, Newsl., June 2009, at 2, *available at* http://homepage.mac.com/srjeanschafersds/stoptraffic/archives/stoptraff706.pdf ("Hence sex trafficking is more

profitable for criminals than drug trafficking. It carries many of the same overhead costs, such as bribing local policemen and border guards, but far lower risks of getting caught.").

56. O'Connor & Healy, *supra* note 52, at 10.

57. *Id.*

58. *Id.*

59. *See id.*

60. *Id.*

61. *Id.*

62. *See, e.g.*, Kathleen A. McKee, *Modern-Day Slavery: Framing Effective Solutions for an Age-Old Problem*, 55 Cath. U. L. Rev. 141, 144–45 (2005) (discussing the general public's disinclination to believe human trafficking is a form of slavery existing in this day and age); Moira Heiges, Note, *From the Inside Out: Reforming State and Local Prostitution Enforcement to Combat Sex Trafficking in the United States and Abroad*, 94 Minn. L. Rev. 428, 445 (2009) ("[W]ithin the United States… many people still view prostitution as a voluntary 'victimless' crime…").

63. *See* Heiges, *supra* note 62, at 437 ("Unfortunately, rather than focusing on reducing the market for sex trafficking, police, prosecutors, and courts have typically viewed pimps and purchasers as trivial or derivative offenders, while targeting prostituting persons for arrest and prosecution.") (citations omitted).

64. O'Connor & Healy, *supra* note 52, at 11.

65. *Id.* (citing Gunilla S. Ekberg, The International Debate About Prostitution and Trafficking in Women: Refuting the Arguments (2002) (unpublished paper presented at the Seminar on the Effects of Legalization of Prostitution Activities, Stockholm, Sweden).

66. *Id.*

67. *Id.*

68. *Id.*

69. *Id.*[23]

D. Particular Problems Involving Children

One particularly difficult problem associated with legalization of prostitution, as noted, is the reality that it seems to result in an increase in the sexual exploitation of children. The sex tourism industry in particular raises the danger to children. The following excerpt from Pro-

23. *Id.*

fessor Page's 2014 article, *Where Has Their Innocence Gone? Addressing Child Sex Tourism,* examines this problem.[24]

> INTRODUCTION
>
> Safety and security don't just happen, they are the result of collective consensus and public investment. We owe our children, the most vulnerable citizens in our society, a life free of violence and fear.
>
> —Nelson Mandela (as cited in U.S. Government International Assistance for Children in Adversity, 2014)
>
> On October 12, 2012, Malala Yousafzai was shot by a known terrorist organization (Husain, 2013). Her crime or offense? She was attending school. This brave and courageous young lady has become a world-renowned figure for advocating for the rights of children (Sagan, 2013). She has spoken before the United Nations and other places about injustices toward children, especially girls, and she has advocated tirelessly for people to take note to the injustices that are being done to children. One such injustice is child sex trafficking.
>
> If someone thinks that slavery is a thing of the past, they are simply unaware of what is going on around them. It is amazingly easy to "buy" a child. Given the incredible advances in technology and the pervasiveness of the Internet, one could obtain practically any product with a simple click of a mouse. While these technological advances have made life easier in many respects, it has also made it easier for sex predators to have access to buy and sell children. These children are exploited sexually just as easily as ordering a pizza ("Child Sex Trafficking," 2013).
>
> Children around the world are used as objects to satisfy the perverted sexual desires of deviants. The bulk of these children reside in poor and vastly uneducated countries around the

24. Cheryl George, *Where Has Their Innocence Gone?, Addressing Child Sex Tourism*, Law Enforcement Executive Forum 14.3 (2014): 98–111. Reprinted with permission from the Illinois Law Enforcement Training and Standards Board. Citations to the sources cited in the excerpt may be found in the original publication.

globe (Fisher, 2013) and their innocence is stolen and shattered on a daily basis (Hume, Cohen, & Sorvino, 2013).

This article addresses the already rampant problem of sex tourism with special attention on child sex tourism. The focus will be to inform the who, what, and where of sex tourism, its history, the economics of it, the laws — both domestic and international — concerning sex tourism, court cases involving sex tourism, the problems associated with combating sex tourism, and also possible solutions in eliminating sex tourism.

THE THREE Ws OF SEX TOURISM: WHAT, WHERE, AND WHO

Traveling for the purpose of purchasing a sex acts is known as sex tourism (Hughes, 2004). Quite logically, child sex tourism would imply traveling for the purpose of purchasing sex acts with a child or as the ECPAT (2013) (an international organization aimed at ending child prostitution, pornography, and trafficking for sexual purposes) defines it, "the commercial sexual exploitation of children by men or women who travel from one place to another... and there engage in sexual acts with children." Congress integrates sex tourism as part of the definition of "trafficking" (Cotter, 2009, p. 497).

Where does sex tourism take place? The answer to that is found in the definition: wherever someone can travel and engage in sex acts (Cotter, 2009, p. 497). Traditionally, when people think of sex tourism, they associate it with exotic destinations such as the Caribbean, Southeast Asia, or Amsterdam's "red light district," but sex tourism is not limited to only those destinations. How far one must travel varies from region to region or town to town, but it can be a much shorter distance. These destination countries are often less developed, have a poorer economy and a favorable exchange rate for the traveler, and also offer anonymity due to being in an entirely foreign location. Many of these tourists have traveled from a wealthier country, region, or town to these less-developed destinations (ECPAT, 2013).

Who are involved in sex tourism? There are numerous players involved in this trade—specifically, there are the victims who are primarily women and children from rural communities and poor families that lack educational and economic opportunities (Mathews, 2005, pp. 658–59). Those victims who are children are mostly between the ages of 13 and 18, but those victims that fall in the category of under 13 are growing (Fredette, 2009, p. 5).

There are the facilitators of this "flesh trade"—the sex tour operators, brothel owners, traffickers, and so forth. Traffickers obtain their supply of these sex workers through recruitment via employment opportunities in remote locations or by abduction (Fredette, 2009, pp. 5–6). When the traffickers have control over the victims, they are removed from their communities and sold to vendors or marketed directly to sex tourists. The victims are then held against their will and made to perform sexual acts (p. 6). Traffickers are able to get the victims to fall in line through coercive methods, including fabricating debt (from travel expenses, lodging, and/or feeding them), seizing identity documents (birth certificates, passports, and/or driver's licenses), forcing the victims to take drugs and thus become dependent on them, and threatening or actually committing violence (p. 6).

Brothels used to be the main place to procure children for sex, but because brothels are stationary, they are obvious targets for law enforcement (Atwell, 2008–2009, p. 173). Because of the law enforcement presence around brothels, sex tourists have been forced to find victims on their own and commit their crimes in private homes or hotel rooms (Fredette, 2009, p. 6). Traffickers sometimes work in conjunction with sex tour operators. These tour operators have created and set up trafficking "travel agencies" that arrange tour packages for tourists who desire sexual encounters with adults, children, or both. In addition, the operators arrange local guides to facilitate sexual encounters at brothels (p. 6).

There are also customers who are referred to as "Johns and James" (according to the ECPAT [2013], women comprise only 5% of the sexual offenders). These customers like the anonymity of these above-mentioned locations. Some may rationalize sexually exploiting children by thinking such behavior is culturally acceptable in the place they are visiting. Twenty-five percent of international child sex tourists come from the U.S. (Patterson, 2007, p. 17). According to the Federal Bureau of Investigation (FBI), half of those from the U.S. who engaged in sex tourism were between the ages of 40 and 60 with nearly one-fourth over 60 years old (p. 19). The FBI also has data showing that most offenders were either divorced or separated from their spouses.

HISTORY

The beginnings of the sex tourism industry can be traced back to the Vietnam War. Brothels, bars, and massage parlors popped up around U.S. bases in Thailand, the Philippines, and Taiwan in the late 1960s. Many of these places used underage prostitutes. After the war, demand decreased, and the U.S. withdrew or downsized its forces. The governments in these countries did not attack prostitution but, instead, encouraged it, planning and promoting international tourism with sex tourism as part of the getaway (Beyer, 2000–2001, pp. 302, 304–05). As sex tourism received more international attention, some of the sex tourism packages moved into the shadows. For example, arranged fishing expeditions to the Amazon were organized for the purpose of child sex tourism for European and American exploiters (Shepherd, 2010).

Demand for women and children prostitutes continued to rise until Asia could not support it, resulting in the sex tourism industry spreading to other areas of the world. Several countries have become preferred destinations for sex tourists. Some of these destinations include Brazil, Costa Rica, the Dominican Republic, Kenya, Morocco, the Netherlands, the Philippines, Colombia, and Thailand (Beyer, 2000–2001).

In an article on sex tourism, Nancy Beyer (2000–2001) identifies five reasons behind the existence of sex tourism: (1) poverty, (2) materialism, (3) inaction of the government, (4) gender discrimination, and (5) beliefs of sex tourists. The impoverished environment of developing countries is one of the main causes of child prostitution (pp. 306–08). Families are struggling to provide their children the necessities of life. Sex procurement agents seek out these struggling families telling them there are jobs for these children and offering cash advances. The children repay these advances with their labor. Some parents are aware of the fate awaiting their children. Economic benefits are not limited to these families. It goes all the way up the chain from the recruiter, to the pimps, to the brothel owner, and finally to the local police who turn a blind eye. The profitability of this trade keeps some governments from taking action to relieve the problem (p. 306).

In regards to parents of these abused children, they look to the sex trade for materialistic reasons. They use money gained from these cash advancements to attain modern indulgences. Children enter the industry believing the economic rewards for prostitutes to be great (Beyer, 2000–2001, p. 307). An income as a sex worker can be up to 25 times greater than legitimate rural wages, which also has the effect of tempting families to force their children into the flesh trade (Fredette, 2009, p. 11).

Government inaction increases the trade. As already mentioned, the trade provides the local economy with a source of revenue, but there are also corrupt officials taking bribes from sex tourists who are caught (Beyer, 2000–2001, p. 307).

Gender discrimination is also a big factor. Females continue to be viewed as sexual objects. In many developing nations, girls have fewer educational opportunities than boys, leaving them with little job opportunity available to them. Traditional gender roles have an effect, too, because men are seen as providers and women are seen as house-keepers who bear children for their husbands (Beyer, 2000–2001, p. 308).

There are two beliefs common among sex tourists promoting sexual exploitation of minors: (1) having sex with minors will allow them to remain sexually active farther into their later years, and (2) sexual intercourse with children poses a decreased risk of contracting the HIV virus. These children are often marketed as virgins both for the decreased risk and more money. However, these sex tourists face greater risks of contracting these diseases with young prostitutes both because of failure to use condoms and the child's body is not ready for sexual activity, so the anus or vagina are extremely susceptible to rupturing (Beyer, 2000–2001).

ECONOMICS

Worldwide, there are nearly two million children in the commercial sex industry. Not surprisingly, sex tourism generates in excess of $32 billion dollars (Compassion International, 2014). In the countries of Indonesia, Malaysia, Thailand, and the Philippines, sex industries account for 2 to 14% of these countries' gross domestic product (Cotter, 2009, p. 506). INTERPOL (which is the official representative to the International Criminal Organization) numbers suggest that a woman being sexually exploited can bring in from $75,000 to $250,000 per year (Beyer, 2000–2001, pp. 304–05). It is estimated that 600,000 to 800,000 people (including children) are trafficked internationally. Children, who are highly valued for their virginity and decreased risk of sexually transmitted diseases, can bring in even more money (Compassion International, 2014).

Kevin Bales (2004), in his book Disposable People, provides charts that illustrate the costs of brothels in Thailand. He shows that it costs $2.00 to $3.20 to feed a prostitute per day (p. 54). Also, the brothel owners avoid trouble with the law through bribes, and these bribes cost around $8.00 to $16.00 a day. Even with these costs, these girls are very profitable. Bales studies show that each girl has between 10 and 18 clients a day at $50.00 to $90.00. Thus, the brothel owner has profits between $1,000 and $1,800 on just sex alone (p. 55). Selling sex is not the only way the brothel owner makes money. The owner also makes money through bar sales, condom sales, and rent the girls have to pay. General expenses of running a brothel in Thailand, on average, are approximately $10,280 a month (p. 55). Minus expenses, these brothels can profit on average $81,280 a month. This is just one of many brothels all over the world, but, specifically, Thailand has an estimated two million prostitutes, with 800,000 of these being children or adolescents (British National Policy, 2013).

With profits like these, it is easy to see why sex tourism is flourishing. The brothel owners are getting paid very well, and police are getting paid well to look away where illegalities exist. This is a billion dollar industry for the countries involved — a billion dollar industry in which the sex worker is risking the most, putting up with the most inhumane treatment, and receiving only a fraction if any of the profits (Fredette, 2009, p. 9).[25]

E. For Further Thought

1. Recall from Chapter 1 that the international and domestic prohibitions on trafficking involve the element of coercion. Should adult human beings have the right to decide for themselves if they wish to accept money for engaging in non-coerced sexual activity? Why or why not? How would it be possible to determine if such conduct has any impact on anyone other than the immediate participants? Would the feelings of the immediate friends or relatives of the participants be relevant in your answer?
2. Is it possible that some prostitutes were sexually abused as children, and have turned to commercial sexual activity because they feel a loss of self-worth? If some of those individuals learned that acting in a sexual manner resulted in some type of reward, are they truly making a free choice to engage in prostitution as adults? In other words, are the victims of childhood abuse who participate in prostitution as adults truly making a non-coerced choice?
3. Do many choices regarding non-sexual labor involve an element of coercion? For example, is the worker whose family is starving, and who can only find employment in a job involving very difficult working

25. *Id.*

conditions truly making a free choice in accepting the employment? On a less dramatic note, what about the worker who suffers under an obnoxious boss? At what point, if any, should any such coercion be addressed, and by whom or by what entity? How does this coercion differ, if at all, from coercion regarding sexual labor?

4. Many police entities have used "sting" operations to arrest sex buyers. These arrests are often highly-publicized, with the object of deterring other potential buyers from participating in the prostitution business. Note that those arrested have not actually engaged in sexual activity for money. Rather, they have engaged in conversations about that activity, usually with undercover police agents. Should states criminalize these conversations? If not, how else could police make arrests for purchasing or attempting to purchase sex? How effective do you think this public shaming will be in reducing prostitution?

Chapter 6

The Lingering Effects of African Slavery in the United States

A. The Double Whammy of Being Female and African American

A complete discussion of the horrible lingering effects of slavery imposed upon Africans who were forcibly removed from their native countries and transported to this country would take volumes. Yet it is obvious that the effects continue. The African American descendants of their enslaved Africans ancestors continue to bear the burdens of the racist trafficking and social structure which existed with the force of law in this country. Professor Page has written and lectured regarding these concerns. One of her recent articles focuses on "The Double Whammy of Being Female and African American: How Black Women are More Vulnerable to Trafficking and Other Forms of Discrimination." We include the entire article, including footnotes, which appears at 22 GONZAGA JOURNAL OF INTERNATIONAL LAW 114 (2019).

The Double Whammy of Being Female and African-American: How Black Women Are More Vulnerable to Trafficking and Other Forms of Discrimination

Professor Cheryl Page*

I. INTRODUCTION

> "Black women and girls represent 30 percent of all women incarcerated but make up just 13 percent of the population. In addition, Black girls continue to be treated as criminals in the justice system in instances where they should be treated as victims."
>
> The Congressional Caucus on Black Women & Girls[1]

Commercial sexual exploitation discriminates even among those that fall prey to this heinous criminal enterprise. It is impossible to comprehensively discuss this topic without addressing the fact that the majority of victims are female, females of color, traditionally are from a lower economic status, tend to not have as many educational opportunities, have experienced some form of abuse and trauma, have been a part of the foster

---

* Professor Page has worked in the area of human trafficking (international and domestic) since 2005. She has spoken and taught internationally and domestically in Austria, China, Czech Republic, Greece and Turkey, to name a few. She has been a law professor since 2004 and currently works at Florida A&M University College of Law where she teaches, amongst other courses, Human Trafficking. Hoping to shed light on the subject and the scourge that is human trafficking, Professor Page co-authored a textbook entitled *Human Trafficking*, with Professor Bill Piatt. Prof. Page sees herself as a modern-day abolitionist and works tirelessly to see the eradication of modern day slavery.

1. *Black Women and Girls in the Criminal Justice System*, The Congressional Caucus on Black Women and Girls, https://watsoncoleman.house.gov/cbwgcaucus/criminal justice system.htm.

care system, and have other vulnerabilities that make them even more susceptible to being trafficked.

This discussion would be incomplete without also addressing how trafficking is connected to race and racial discrimination, poverty, the foster care system, gender, migration and inadequate access to real educational opportunities.[2] Each of these factors contributes to the flourishing and lucrative business of trafficking.[3] As a result, those subject to these conditions are more vulnerable and more likely to be trafficked.

The vast majority of victims of human trafficking victims are African-American females.[4] Many states prosecute victims of sex trafficking as "prostitutes" and do not distinguish between adults and children.[5] This article addresses how our criminal justice system failed Cyntoia Brown and is also failing countless other women of color in the same or similar situations. This article may refer to "African American youth," not distinguishing between males and females; this is because so few studies break down statistics between the sexes. This only solidifies the point regarding intersectionality and oppression referred to in the article.

---

2. Jamaal Bell, *Race and Human Trafficking in the U.S.: Unclear but Undeniable*, HUFFPOST (May 10, 2010), https://www.huffingtonpost.com/Jamaal-bell/race-and-human-trafficking_b_569795.html (last updated Dec. 6, 2017).

3. *ILO Action Against Trafficking in Human Beings*, INTERNATIONAL LABOUR OFFICE (2008), http://www.ilo.org/www.ilo.org/wcmsp5/groups/public/@ed_norm/@declaraion/documents/publication/wcms_090356.pdf (estimating annual profits as high as $32 billion dollars generated from trafficking in human beings).

4. Karla Jacbos, *Who's Disproportionately a Victim of Human Trafficking? Young Black Women*, WASHINGTON EXAMINER (Jan. 30, 2019), https://www.washingtonexaminer.com/opinion/oo-eds/whos-disproportionately-a-victim-of-human-trafficking-young-black-women (stating 94% of trafficking victims served in Georgia were female; 59% of those females were African Americans).

5. Cynthia Soohoo, *Criminalization of Trafficking Victims*, UNITED NATIONS UNIVERSAL PERIODIC REV. U.S. AM. 2 (May 2015), http://www.law.cuny.edu/academics/clinics/iwhr/publications/Criminalization-of-TraffickingVictims.pdf.

II. CYNTOIA BROWN: ONE CASE ILLUSTRATES HISTORICAL STEREOTYPES AND DISCRIMINATION AGAINST YOUNG WOMEN OF COLOR

Unfortunately, the facts of Cyntoia Brown's case are not unusual. She was born to a mother who drank heavily throughout her pregnancy and began using drugs just before Cyntoia was born.[6] She was born with fetal alcohol syndrome, which can cause impulse control problems.[7] Between the ages of six months and three years, Cyntoia bounced between seven or eight different homes and was kidnapped by a member of her family.[8] At sixteen, she ran away from home and found herself under the control of a pimp who went by the name of "Cut Throat."[9] This man, eight years her senior, was physically, emotionally, sexually, and verbally abusive to Cyntoia.[10] He told her she needed to "learn to be a good whore," because no one else would want her but him, and that she was born to be a whore.[11]

Traffickers are master manipulators and have a way of grooming a victim into believing that they alone are their savior. This predator was able to do just that with Cyntoia. Traffick-

6. Tom Jacobs, *Life in Prison Begins at 16*, review of PBS documentary *Me Facing Life: Cyntoia's Story*, Pacific Standard (June 14, 2017), https://psmag.com/social-justice/life-in-prison-begins-at-16-27624.

7. Basics about FASDs, Centers for Disease Control and Prevention, https://www.cdc.gov/ncbddd/fasd/facts.html (last visited May 21, 2019).

8. Jamie Catacosinos, Evaluating the Role of Trauma: Case of Cyntoia Brown, DANIELLE ROUSSEAU (December 16, 2017), http://sites.bu.edu/daniellerousseau/2017/12/16/evaluating-the-role-of-trauma-case-of-cyntoia-brown/ (last visited May 21, 2019).

9. Benjamin Goggin, *Cyntoia Brown, a Trafficking Victim Jailed for Killing a Man Using her for Sex, was Granted Clemency Following a Social Media Campaign. Here's Everything You Need to Know.* Insider (Jan. 8, 2019, 2:55 AM), https://www.insider.com/cyntoia-brown-timeline-clemency-story-kim-kardashian-2019-1#brown-ran-away-from-her-adoptive-home-in-2004-when-she-was-16-she-was-forced-into-prostitution-by-a-24-year-old-man-named-garion-mcglothen-who-went-by-cut-throat-2 (last visited May 21, 2019).

10. *Id.*

11. Demetria D. Frank, *Cyntoia Brown Case Reveals Entrenched Problems with Tennessee Juvenile Justice*, The Appeal (Dec. 1, 2017), https://theappeal.org/cyntoia-brown-case-reveals-entrenched-problems-with-tennessee-juvenile-justice-b4dd46e416e0/.

ers are able to spot vulnerable young women and capitalize on their weaknesses. Cyntoia came from an insecure and unstable background, a risk factor for sex trafficking. In 2013 the FBI reported that 60% of child sex trafficking victims had been in the foster care system, while the DOJ reported that the figure was 85% for female victims.[12] On average, children in foster care are moved between seven different homes.[13] This instability causes the smooth words of a pimp promising a better life to become more appealing, so traffickers target foster children.[14] Their words are steeped in lies and deception and filled with promises of the life every child and young person dreams of.[15] Many traffickers will offer food, alcohol (despite knowledge that the child is a minor), clothing, rides in fancy cars, life in a nice residence, drugs, love and affection.[16] Victims quickly realize the promises are complete lies, designed to mislead and defraud, but by the time the victims come to this realization, it is often too late to leave the trafficker. By then, many pimps have threatened victims and their families, caused violent physical harm, forced them to watch others being dehumanized and harmed, or forced victims to take drugs, which creates an addiction and a dependence on the trafficker.[17] This grooming process is a deliberate, methodical act that completely paralyzes the victim and makes her believe that she has no one else to run to for help.[18]

---

12. Aliya Kuykendall, *New Report Shows Why Foster Care Often Leads to Sex Trafficking*, The Stream (2018), https://stream.org/new-report-shows-why-foster-care-often-leads-to-sex-trafficking/ (last visited May 21, 2019).

13. Kenneth A. Camp, *How Many Times on Average Does a Child in Foster Care Move?*, Kenneth A Camp (Jan. 14, 2015) http://kennethacamp.com/how-many-times-on-average-does-a-child-in-foster-care-move/ (stating many families lack the resources to properly care for the child).

14. Kuykendall, *supra* note 11.

15. Kajal Patel, *Child Prostitutes or Sexually Exploited Minors: The Deciding Debate in Determining How Best to Respond to Those Who Commit Crimes as a Result of Their Victimhood*, 2017 U. Ill. L. Rev. 1545, 1555 (2017).

16. *Id.*

17. *Id.*

18. *Id.* at 1565.

The laws as enforced do not provide adequate protection. Traffickers benefit from these laws, as they are able to more easily manipulate their victims by capitalizing on their fear of law enforcement.[19] While there are statutes that criminalize child sex trafficking, over 700 children in the United States are arrested each year for prostitution.[20] As Yasmin Vafa has noted:

> In any other instance what happens to these youth would be considered statutory rape or sexual assault of a minor, landing their abusers behind bars. But because their abuse is paid for, it is the child who ends up in handcuffs and detention instead of their exploiters, making this the only form of child abuse where our response is to criminalize the abused child.[21]

Our criminal justice system treats prostitution as a "victimless crime." Nothing could be further from the truth.

Studies on the American education system often focus on gender and/or race. This perspective excludes the intersectionality females of color face, as members of both groups, and compounds the problems and ignores the possible solutions. It also makes a female of color feel as if she does not fit in anywhere, as if her specific issues are not valid or worthy of being discussed and validated. This is made worse by disparities between races: drop out/graduation rates, separate but unequal educations, a lack of credentialed educators (inexperienced and uncertified), inequitable facilities, technology, books, and computers, as well as differences in discipline based on race.[22]

---

19. Matthew Myatt, *The "Victim Perpetrator" Dilemma: The Role of State Safe Harbor Laws in Creating a Presumption of Coercion for Human Trafficking Victims*, 25 William & Mary Journal of Race, Gender, and Social Justice 555, 564 (2019).

20. Yasmin Vafa, There is No Such Thing as a "Child Prostitute," NATIONAL COUNCIL OF JUVENILE AND FAMILY COURT JUDGES, http://www.ncjfcj.org/there-no-such-thing-child-prostitute (last visited May 21, 2019).

21. *Id.*

22. *See generally* Adaku Onyeka-Crawford, Kayla Patrick & Neena Chaudhry, *Let Her Learn: Stopping School Push Out for Girls of Color*, National Women's Law Center (2017), https://nwlc-ciw49tixgw5lbab.stackpathdns.com/wp-content/uploads/2017/04/

African-American females are five and a half times more likely to be suspended than white females.[23] African-American females attend schools that are under-funded and ill equipped to educate them and prepare them for a productive life after high school.[24] This lack of meaningful education negatively affects their financial future and further educational opportunities.[25]

A disproportionate number of African-American females attend schools that are overpopulated by inexperienced educators and lack adequate staffing for counselors.[26] In schools where there are 90% African-American students, the student to counselor ratio is 309:1.[27] The likelihood that a student will receive adequate professional counseling under these circumstances is highly unlikely. Counseling is an invaluable resource for students coming from communities and neighborhoods that can create toxic stress.[28] The lack of counseling, and the higher rates of sexual assault experienced by African American women[29] who lack the resources to properly process the stress, creates a cauldron of additional problems.

Schools with higher percentages of students of color are more likely to have law enforcement officials present, which helps explain the disproportionately high school-based student arrests and referrals to law enforcement among students of color.[30] The increased arrests and encounters with the juvenile justice system lead to increased numbers of African American females dropping out and becoming entangled in the adult

---

final_nwlc_Gates_GirlsofColor.pdf_ (discussing barriers to success in education for teenage girls of color).

23. *Id.* at 13.

24. *Id.* at 1.

25. *Id.*

26. *Id.* at 9.

27. *Id.* at 11.

28. Onyeka-Crawford, Patrick & Chaudhry, *supra* note 22, at 11.

29. *African-American Women and Sexual Assault Fact Sheet*, MARYLAND COALITION AGAINST SEXUAL ASSAULT, https://mcasa.org/assets/files/African-American-Women-and-Sexual-Assaultl.pdf (2019).

30. Onyeka-Crawford, Patrick & Chaudhry, *supra* note 22, at 11–12.

criminal justice system.[31] This is what is referred to as the "school to prison pipeline."[32]

Further, society still stereotypes young African-American women. A stereotype is defined as "conforming to a fixed or general pattern, especially: a standardized mental picture that is held in common by members of a group and that represents an oversimplified opinion, prejudiced attitude, or uncritical judgement."[33] Many of the stereotypes that society has regarding African-American women revolves around their sexuality.[34] There are stereotypes that portray African-American women as "Jezebels," "loose/unscrupulous" women, sex addicts, promiscuous and having an insatiable sexual appetite.[35] These misconceived and fallacious notions help to perpetuate the idea that African American women are somehow to blame for their victimization or that they "deserve" it.[36]

When a jury evaluates a case like Cyntoia's — a sixteen-year-old African American female who was being sexually violated by a white man, feared for her life, shot, and killed him — one must wonder whether they allow those stereotypes to play in their minds. This concern is particularly pressing when that child is ultimately sentenced to what amounts to life in prison and brings to mind a troubling question: would the ruling and sentence would have been the same for a sixteen-year-old white girl?[37] It would even be more of a question if the rapist were African American. Race, particularly the race of the victim and perpetrator, plays a role in every phase of the criminal process,

---

31. *Id.*

32. *School to Prison Pipeline*, ACLU, https://www.aclu.org/issues/juvenile-justice/school-prison-pipeline (accessed May 22, 2019).

33. *Stereotype*, MERRIAM-WEBSTER, https://www.merriam-webster.com/dictionary/stereotype.

34. MARYLAND COALITION AGAINST SEXUAL ASSAULT, *supra* note 29.

35. *Id.*

36. *Id.*

37. MARYLAND COALITION AGAINST SEXUAL ASSAULT, *supra* note 29. A study of college students showed that participants were more likely to believe a white assault victim over a black assault victim. *Id.*

from charging decisions to sentencing.[38] These factors cause some victims of violence to not even report their case because they know that they may not be believed or will be blamed for their own assaults.[39]

Since the birth of this nation, our criminal justice system has historically meted out racially biased, unfair, and harsher laws, judgements, and sentences to African Americans. United States Supreme Court rulings included blatant racism in cases such as *Dred Scott* (1856),[40] *Plessy v. Ferguson* (1896),[41] and *Cumming v. Richmond* (1899).[42] These cases are just the beginning of the unfair and unjust ways in which African Americans have been treated.

A more recent egregious case of unfair sentencing and bias is the case of an African American female, with no prior criminal record, Sharanda Purlette Jones.[43] Jones lived in Terrell, Texas and was sentenced to life in prison for a drug offense.[44] The evidence was circumstantial, as there was no direct evi-

---

38. ACLU, *Written Submission on Racial Disparities in Sentencing*, INTER AM. COMM'N H.R. (2014).

39. *See id.* at 1. Our criminal justice system has a history of treating white victims better than people of color. *Id.*; *see also* Feminista Jones, *Why Black Women Struggle More with Domestic Violence*, TIME, Sept. 10, 2014.

40. Dred Scott v. Sandford, 60 U.S. (19 How.) 393 (1857), *superseded by constitutional amendment*, U.S. CONST. amend. XIV. Dred Scott was seeking his freedom; the Court ruled against him saying slaves could not be citizens and therefore lacked the ability to sue in federal court, hence the Court lacked jurisdiction. One Justice said that slaves were property under the Fifth Amendment and any law that deprived owners of their property was unconstitutional. *See id.*

41. Plessy v. Ferguson, 163 U.S. 537 (1896), *overruled by* Brown v. Bd. of Ed. of Topeka, Shawnee Cty., Kan., 347 U.S. 483 (1954). This case sanctioned segregation and said that separate was equal. *See id.*

42. Cumming v. Bd. of Ed. of Richmond Cty., 175 U.S. 528 (1899). When the school in their area was shut down, African American families asked the Court to allow their children to finish their schooling at the local white school. The Court ruled against them and said if there was no suitable school in the African American community, that their children would not be educated. *See id.*

43. *See* ACLU *supra* note 38, at 9.

44. *Id.*

dence tying Jones to the alleged crime.[45] She was convicted based on the testimony of a drug user and drug dealer, who were both offered a reduced sentence for their testimony.[46] Jones' sister and paraplegic mother were also convicted.[47] Jones' mother died while in prison after spending her entire sentence in a prison ward for the disabled and handicapped.[48] All of their convictions were part of a task force in a town of roughly 13,500 that netted 105 arrests of solely African Americans.[49]

Our criminal justice system has a proven track record of being unfair and discriminatory towards African Americans. Another factor that plays a role in the unfair treatment of African American women is the fact that they are charged as "adults" when similarly situated white females are not charged as adults. The people that decide whether or not to try a juvenile as an adult are the prosecutors (the State requests it) and the judges (have to approve it).[50] A very small percentage of prosecutors are women of color (which could include African Americans, Asians, Latinas, Pacific Islanders, West Indians, or Native Americans).[51]

Who gets tried as an adult depends upon the race of the defendant (and perhaps to a lesser extent, the race of the prosecutor and judge).[52]

---

45. *Id.*

46. *Id.*

47. ACLU, *A Living Death: Life without Parole for Nonviolent Offenses* 43, ACLU Foundation (2013).

48. *Id.*

49. *See* ACLU *supra* note 38, at 9.

50. Sarah Gonzalez, *Kids in Prison: Getting Tried as an Adult Depends on Skin Color*, WNYC News, (Oct. 10, 2016) https://www.wnyc.org/story/black-kids-more-likely-be-tried-adults-cant-be-explained/.

51. Amita Kelly, *Does It Matter That 95 Percent of Elected Prosecutors Are White?*, NPR (July 8, 2015, 4:59 PM), https://www.npr.org/sections/itsallpolitics/2015/07/08/420913118/does-it-matter-that-95-of-elected-prosecutors-are-white.

52. *Id.* In the United States 95% of elected prosecutors are white; 83% men; 1% are women of color. *Id.*

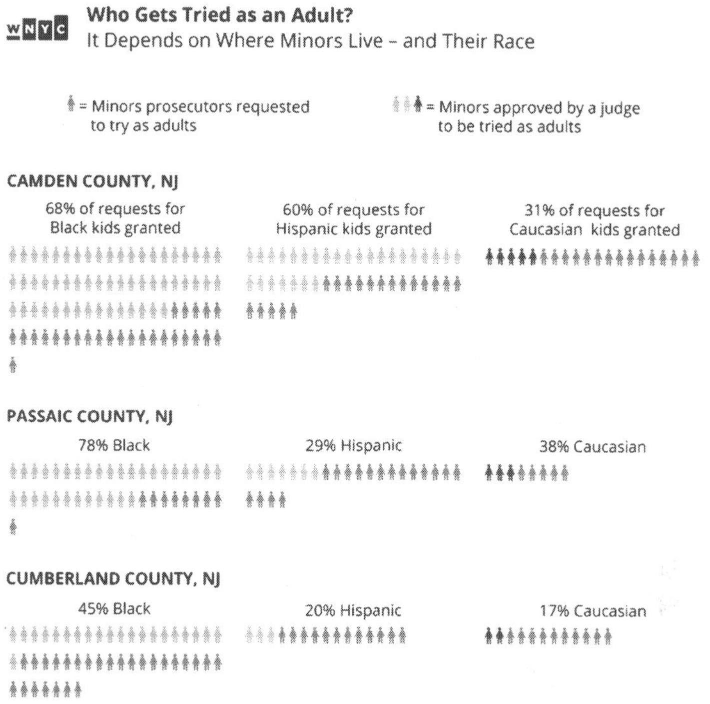

Source: Administrative Office of the Courts, NJ from July 1, 2011 through May 19, 2016. (Clarisa Diaz, WNYC Data News Team)

The chart above illustrates how juveniles are charged as adults in specific counties in New Jersey.[53] Prosecutors have a considerable amount of power:

> [I]n the U.S. legal system prosecutors may wield even more power than cops. Prosecutors decide whether to bring a case or drop charges against a defendant; charge a misdemeanor or felony; demand a prison sentence or accept probation. Most cases are resolved through plea bargains, where prosecutors, not judges, negotiate whether and for how long a defendant goes to prison. And prose-

53. *See* Gonzalez, *supra* note 50.

cutors make these judgments almost entirely outside public scrutiny.[54]

White youth commit the same types of crimes as African American youth, but prosecutors do not seek to try them as adults at the same rate as they do young African Americans.[55] When all factors considered by prosecutors when making charging decisions (educational and familial background, economic status, type and severity of the crime, any past criminal history, likelihood to re-offend) are similar, "there are still disparities, significant disparities, that cannot be explained by anything other than race."[56]

The systematic oppression of African American women is seen in every aspect of the criminal process. One can harken back to the horrid story of Sandra Bland.[57] How does a simple traffic stop end in the death of an unarmed African American woman?

A study commissioned by Georgetown Law Center on Poverty found that African American females as young as 5 and up to 14 are seen as "less innocent and more adult-like" than their white counterparts.[58] The results are disheartening and disconcerting. It showed a perception that African American girls need less nurturing, protection, support, and comfort; are more independent; and know more about adult topics and sex.[59] These results give some insight into how African American fe-

---

54. Jeffrey Toobin, *The Milwaukee Experiment: What can one prosecutor do about the mass incarceration of African-Americans*, The New Yorker, May 4, 2015.

55. *See* Gonzalez, *supra* note 50.

56. *Id.* This statement was provided by Laura Cohen, Director of the Criminal and Youth Justice Clinic at Rutgers Law School. *Id.*

57. *See* Danny Cevallos, *Was the Sandra Bland Traffic Stop Legal—and Fair?*, CNN (July 23, 2015), https://www.cnn.com/2015/07/23/opinions/cevallos-sandra-bland-traffic-stop/index.html.

58. Rebecca Epstein, Jamilia Blake & Thalia Gonzalez, *Girlhood Interrupted: The Erasure of Black Girls' Childhood*, Georgetown Law Ctr. on Poverty and Inequality (June 27, 2017), https://www.law.georgetown.edu/poverty-inequality-center/wp-content/uploads/sites/14/2017/08/girlhood-interrupted.pdf.

59. *Id.*

males receive disproportionately severe penalties in school compared to their white classmates for similar conduct. It also suggests why African American females are treated in a racist and discriminatory fashion in the criminal justice system.

Abusing and mistreating another human being requires the abuser to dehumanize and degrade the person being victimized.[60] It makes the mistreatment more palatable and acceptable when they are abusing someone perceived as "less" characteristics to a child. The abuser is placing the victim in another category, thereby justifying the disparities in their minds. By attributing these character traits to victims, abusers and even third parties justify the plight of the victim. That is how a white prosecutor, jury, and judge could charge a sixteen-year-old for murder, convict her, and sentence her to prison essentially for life. This, without taking into consideration any mitigating factors—which may include mental disabilities, childhood trauma, poverty, and a lack of a stable home environment; to name a few.

Cyntoia Brown's case was not easily overturned.[61] She was convicted in 2006 of the 2004 fatal shooting of a white male child rapist (Johnny Allen, 43).[62] The child predator picked up sixteen-year-old Cyntoia Brown, and then he raped her.[63] He took her to his home and threatened her with physical violence by brandishing a gun.[64] Brown said that she feared for her life when Allen appeared to be reaching for his gun. It was at this

---

60. *See* Deborah Doherty & Dorothy Berglund, *Psychological Abuse: A Discussion Paper*, GOV'T OF CAN. (July 26, 2012), https://www.canada.ca/en/public-health/services/health-promotion/stop-family-violence/prevention-resource-centre/family-violence/psychological-abuse-discussion-paper.html.

61. Leah Carroll, *How The Justice System Failed Cyntoia Brown*, REFINERY 29 (Jan. 7, 2019, 9:39 AM), https://www.refinery29.com/en-us/2018/12/219015/cyntoia-brown-case-facts-real-story.

62. *Id.*

63. *Id.*

64. *Id.*

point that she shot him in the back of the head and killed him.[65] After killing him, she stole some of his guns and his wallet.[66]

Prosecutors elected to charge her as an adult, and the presiding judge approved it.[67] She was found guilty and sentenced to two concurrent sentences.[68] There is no doubt that Brown's attorneys were ineffective in their assistance as her legal advocates. She was not allowed to testify on her own behalf and her attorneys failed to offer evidence that she had a severe neurodevelopmental disorder and suffered from fetal alcohol syndrome.[69]

Brown, at the time of the shooting, was living under the control of a violent, vicious pimp, "Cut Throat."[70] He told her on the evening of the shooting to make some money.[71] Brown knew what that meant. That is how she ended up in the car of a stranger, who paid to rape her.[72] Five years after being in prison, a filmmaker produced a film about Brown's case, *Me Facing Life: Cyntoia's Story*, which brought national attention to the facts of the case and to the child prostitution laws at that time.[73] This movie helped to change that law. It also highlighted the fact that there were not many social programs designed to help children like Brown, who are statistically more likely to be sex trafficked.

New attorneys took on Brown's case and represented her 2012 appeal of the 2006 conviction.[74] Her new defense team put forth new evidence concerning her traumatic and violent past, the fetal alcohol syndrome, her diminished mental capacity,

---

65. *Id.*
66. *Id.*
67. Carroll, *supra* note 61.
68. *Id.*
69. *Id.*
70. *Id.*
71. *Id.*
72. *Id.*
73. *Me Facing Life: Cyntoia's Story* (PBS, Mar. 1, 2011).
74. Travis Loller, *Attorneys Seek New Trial for Teenage Killer*, SPOKESMAN REVIEW, Nov. 13, 2012, http://www.spokesman.com/stories/2012/nov/13/attorneys-seek-new-trial-for-teenage-killer/.

and her abusive relationship with Cut Throat.[75] Her attorneys also argued that her sentence was unconstitutional in light of a 2012 Supreme Court case[76] holding that mandatory life sentences for minors are unconstitutional.[77] Despite new and compelling evidence and new legal precedent, Brown's conviction and sentence were upheld.[78]

In 2017, Rihanna shared a social media post about Cyntoia Brown that read, "Imagine at the age of 16 being sex-trafficked by a pimp named 'cutthroat.' After days of being repeatedly drugged and raped by different men you were purchased by a 43-year-old child predator who took you to his home to use you for sex. You end up finding enough courage to fight back and shoot and kill him."[79] Other celebrities, including Kim Kardashian, Amy Shumer, Alyssa Milano, and Ashley Judd, began to advocate on Brown's behalf for her release from prison. Rihanna's post brought global awareness and attention to Brown's case and began the social media firestorm that would eventually lead Brown's case to the desk of the Tennessee governor, Bill Haslam.

After she had served fifteen years in prison, in January 2019, Governor Haslam granted Cyntoia Brown clemency.[80] She is set to be released in August 2019.[81] In granting Brown clemency, the governor effectively reduced her sentence and is allowing her to get out of prison sooner than expected. Her conviction, however, remains intact. The governor's act is not a pardon, which would have effectively "forgiven" her for the crime.[82]

---

75. *Id.*

76. Miller v. Alabama, 567 U.S. 460 (2012).

77. Dakin Andone, *Cyntoia Brown Must Serve 51 Years Before She's Eligible for Release, Tennessee Supreme Court Says*, CNN (Dec. 8, 2018, 8:20 AM), https://www.cnn.com/2018/12/07/us/cyntoia-brown-prison-release/index.html.

78. *Id.*

79. *See* Carroll *supra* note 61.

80. Bill Chappell, *Cyntoia Brown, In Prison For Murder, Is Granted Clemency By Tenn. Governor*, NPR (Jan. 7, 2019), https://www.npr.org/2019/01/07/682938808/cyntoia-brown-jailed-for-murder-is-granted-clemency-by-tenn-governor.

81. *Id.*

82. *Id.*

Another example of institutional discriminatory treatment of African American females is that they are suspended from school in greater numbers than their white counterparts.[83] Their suspension rate is not attributed to higher disciplinary rates, acting out in greater frequency, or for more egregious or serious behavior.[84]

A belief that African American females are less innocent would lend to the fact that they receive harsher treatment by educators, law enforcement, and school resource officers. Recently, many were outraged when a video surfaced showing a high school resource officer wrapping his arm around the neck of an African American female student and tossing her to the ground in front of the entire class, and then handcuffing her for refusing to stand and hand over her cell phone.[85] The officer's behavior was deemed not to warrant reprimand.[86] Many acts committed by African American is viewed as "criminal" or "aggressive' but are not considered in that light when committed by whites.[87]

Stereotypical views of African American females needing less support or nurturing and being more independent could also explain why they are offered fewer leadership positions in school as well as not receiving more opportunities to be mentored.[88] African American women historically receive a lesser quality of healthcare and die in greater numbers in this coun-

---

83. *See, e.g.*, Onyeka-Crawford, Patrick & Chaudhry, *supra* note 22 (showing the suspension rate is greater in every single state).

84. *Id.*

85. Associated Press, *Deputy Who Tossed a S.C. High School Student Won't Be Charged*, N.Y. TIMES (Sept. 2, 2016), https://www.nytimes.com/2016/09/03/afternoonupdate/deputy-who-tossed-a-sc-high-school-student-wont-be-charged.html.

86. *Id.*

87. Jeremy Bauer-Wolf, *Going to Class While Black*, INSIDE HIGHER ED (Nov. 14, 2018), https://www.insidehighered.com/news/2018/11/14/ut-san-antonio-investigates-whether-student-escorted-out-class-having-feet-propped. A female allegedly had her feet up on the chair in front of her; the professor called the police and the student was escorted out of class by the campus police. *Id.*

88. Epstein, Blake, & González, *supra* note 58.

try.[89] Astoundingly, African American women are three to four times more likely to die from "pregnancy or delivery complications" than white women.[90]

In the American criminal justice system, African American women receive harsher sentences than their white counterparts, for the same criminal acts.[91] Every case is different, but this statistical trend cannot be ignored. There is clearly more to these sentencing disparities than a coincidence.

Further, African American women earn less money on the dollar than white females.[92] It takes an African American women roughly nineteen months to earn what a white man earns in twelve.[93] African American women earn 61% of what non-Latino white men earn, while women in general earn 80%.[94]

These are just a few ways that African American women experience disparate treatment, and these issues go to the heart of basic societal values and norms. Financial well-being, access to good quality health care, freedom to grow and learn and live, the ability to drive or walk down the street free from harassment from law enforcement, the ability to attend school and not be treated in a discriminatory fashion: these values and systems of beliefs are bedrocks of our society. They are principles that people have lived by since the dawn of this nation but not all races and peoples have enjoyed such benefits. The entitlements

---

89. Wayne J. Riley, *Health Disparities: Gaps in Access, Quality and Affordability of Medical Care*, 123 Transactions of the Am. Clinical and Climatological Assoc. 67, 168–69 (2012).

90. Jacqueline Howard, *Childbirth is Killing Black Women in the US, and Here's Why*, CNN (Nov. 15, 2017), https://www.cnn.com/2017/11/15/health/black-women-maternal-mortality/index.html.

91. Radley Balko, *There's Overwhelming Evidence that the Criminal Justice System is Racist. Here's the Proof*, Wash. Post (Sept. 18, 2018), https://www.washingtonpost.com/news/opinions/wp/2018/09/18/theres-overwhelming-evidence-that-the-criminal-justice-system-is-racist-heres-the-proof/?noredirect=on&utm_term=dld40db567b9.

92. Raina Nelson, *Black Women and the Pay Gap*, AAUW (Aug. 1, 2018), https://www.aauw.org/article/black-women-and-the-pay-gap/.

93. *Id.*

94. *Id.*

that many whites enjoy and take for granted, many People of Color never experience or expect to see in a lifetime.

Cyntoia Brown grew up in a world that showed her repeatedly that she would not experience the privileges that white people enjoy and bask in daily. She knew early on in life that her life mattered less than other lives simply because of her race and sex. She knew that that to be a fact as she saw it manifested in her life every single day. She saw that in how she was rejected by her family and shuttled through the foster care system, how she was alienated and felt the need to run away from her adopted family, how she was treated by her pimp and by men that exploited her for their sexual purposes. She saw it in how she was represented by legal counsel in her first trial and how she was treated by the jury, the judges, and the prosecution at all levels in this criminal episode. She saw and read the message loud and clear: "your life is not valued. You do not count."

III. CONCLUSION

African American women are valued less than their white counterparts and this is borne out in the statistics. And when a group of individuals are singled out repeatedly and treated in a discriminatory fashion for conduct "condoned" when done by others of a different race, it shows the targeted individuals that they are somehow "less than" or devalued and unworthy. When this treatment is pervasive, consistent, continual and present throughout one's life and that is shown across the board in varying systems (schools, banking institutions, educational settings, the justice system, places of employment, the healthcare field, etc.), the message is one that cannot be ignored or shunned. The message is crystal clear: you are somehow "subhuman," you are not valued, and you do not matter.

We must place a value on all people and treat everyone with dignity and respect. Cyntoia Brown is a prime example of the disparate treatment African American females receive in our public institutions. But there are many other Cyntoia Browns who have gone unnoticed and unrecognized. They matter. They are valuable too. Every life matters, but currently that is not what the data shows.

Many say that justice is blind. In reality, her vision is skewed and tainted by classism, racism, sexism, and a system that maintains the dominant structure. Lady Justice sees. She sees African American females as less than, expendable and not as valuable or worthy. Cyntoia Brown is symptomatic of how our criminal justice system fails African American women and allows systematic oppression and injustice to continue unchecked."

B. For Further Thought

1. List areas (employment, etc.) where you believe that there is a disparity between African Americans and the white population in this country. Now make a second list comparing the disparity between African American males and females. What do you believe contributes to these disparities?
2. Does addressing the horrors of human trafficking include addressing the lingering effects of African slavery? How might this process begin?
3. Another overlooked facet of slavery in the United States involves the slavery of Native Americans. The legacy of this slavery lingers, notwithstanding the Thirteenth Amendment to the Constitution of the United States, and notwithstanding a specific statute aimed at eliminating the "peonage" or forced labor into which Native slavery had morphed. The "Peonage Abolition Act of 1867" was not completely successful. Litigation as late as 1967 sought to free a "peon" from his thirty-three years of forced, unpaid labor. Professor Piatt and his co-author Professor Moises Gonzales explore the history of this horror in their book *Slavery in the Southwest: Genizaro Identity, Dignity and the Law*, published in 2019 by Carolina Academic Press.
4. Piatt continues exploring the theme of the lingering effects of Native slavery in his article, *Recognizing the Identity and Dignity of All Indigenous Americans*, 6 Howard Human & Civil Rights Law Review 83 (2022). Were you aware that European slavery regarding Natives preceded the transatlantic slave trade of Africans? Were you aware that even before the arrival of the Spaniards, Natives captured other Natives and held them as slaves? Were you aware that slave markets

involving Indians were held at Taos Pueblo and at other iconic locations throughout what is now New Mexico?

5. Examine Piatt's books and articles and the sources they cite for a more complete understanding of the history, and the lingering effects of the slavery of Indigenous people in what is now the United States. You might also access a documentary by Native filmmaker Gary Medina Cook, *The Genízaro Experience: Shadows in Light*. The documentary features interviews with Piatt, Gonzales, and others. The trailer to the film can be accessed on YouTube.

Chapter 7

What Else Can Be Done?

Throughout this book we have examined the legal protections aimed at reducing or eliminating the scourge of human trafficking world-wide. These approaches have met with some successes, yet nobody could seriously argue that the problems have been resolved. What else can or should we be doing? Perhaps the first step involves understanding the limitations of what we are now doing. Then, we can consider additional avenues for addressing these problems.

A. Current Efforts Are Not Enough

Co-author Cheryl Taylor Page provides a critique of current efforts in a portion of her article, *Jailing the Johns*.[1]

> V. Application
>
> In spite of all the laws on the books that address sex trafficking, those laws have been woefully inadequate at addressing and reducing the demand for sex trafficking victims.[250] It would appear that the United States is ill equipped to effectively address the demand issue of sex trafficking, and a direct consequence of that is the lack of any substantive, concrete legal efforts aimed at reducing or ending the demand.[251] In order to change the direction of its current trajectory, the demand has to

---

1. Cheryl George, *Jailing the Johns — The Issue of Demand in Human Sex Trafficking*, 13 FLA. COASTAL L. REV. 293–347 (2012), http://works.bepress.com/cheryl_george/5, excerpt reprinted with permission from the Florida Coastal Law Review.

be addressed and stopped.[252] Moreover, legislation needs "policies aimed at decreasing the demand for commercial sex."[253] As stated previously, if a businessman selling candy has no customers, he will eventually go out of business. We must create laws that will curb the demand and cause sex traffickers to go out of business.[254]

In an effort to combat sex trafficking both at home and abroad, the United States Departments of State, Labor, Justice, Homeland Security, and Health and Human Services and the United States Agency for International Development contributed approximately $375,000,000 toward antitrafficking programs between 2001 and 2006.[255] While there were 3000 trafficking convictions globally in 2004, much more needs to be done on a worldwide scale to end this modern day system of slavery.[256]

There are specific countries that are attempting to take steps to address and end sex trafficking.[257] In contrast, with a Tier 2 government, South Africa has not yet fully complied with the minimum standards as set forth for the elimination of human trafficking.[258] South Africa's lack of action in eradicating sex trafficking must be pointed out, hopefully, in an effort to bring about much needed change.[259] Sporting events are notorious for attracting even more sex trafficking incidents than are normally present.[260] Prior to the 2010 World Cup (which was held in South Africa), this country had ample opportunity to pass and enact an antitrafficking bill.[261] What was more frustrating to the antitrafficking community was that the South African government had been promising the bill would become law since 2008.[262] South Africa also had another opportunity to positively impact those affected by sex trafficking by enforcing and/or financing the 2007 Children's Amendment Act.[263] Sadly, South Africa contributed sparse funding for law enforcement geared toward sex trafficking or protecting victims of sex trafficking.[264] Even more egregious was the fact that NGOs and foreign donors gave large amounts of money to South Africa for this very purpose.[265] The country's financial contributions towards law enforcement aimed at sex trafficking or protecting victims are minimal and practically nonexistent.[266]

Notably, when evaluating the prosecution of these kinds of offenses, the South African government barely increased its law enforcement efforts to target sex trafficking during the 2008–2009 tracking period.[267] The government has a law on the books, the South African Sexual Offenses Act (SOA), which criminalizes sex trafficking.[268] This law also has penalties that are practically equivalent to penalties prescribed for similarly serious offenses.[269] The South African government began to formalize the Prevention and Combating of Trafficking in Persons Bill in March 2010, but as of the date of this publication, the law is still not in effect.[270]

Sadly, many of the cases initiated in 2006–2009 against alleged sex traffickers were still unresolved as of the publication date of the 2010 Trafficking in Persons Report.[271] An example is the 2008 trial of "Diana," a woman charged with sexually exploiting three young girls from Mozambique.[272] Another case, the only South African human trafficking conviction (as of the 2010 Trafficking in Persons Report), was a prosecution of a husband and wife.[273] They were convicted on seventeen counts of "racketeering, money laundering, and [other] offenses under the SOA."[274] However, as of the date of this publication, there has not been a sentencing.[275]

Another country that has a poor record of sex trafficking is Singapore.[276] Singapore is a Tier 2 Watch List country and has yet to make any significant steps towards reaching Tier 1.[277] One of the many ways that women are lured from their countries of origin is by way of false promises for a job, an education, and a better future.[278] When these unsuspecting women arrive in the host country, they are met with the sad reality of life as a prostitute in a brothel, massage parlor, or strip club.[279] That is how many young women and girls arrive in Singapore, lured by deceitful and fabricated stories that entice them away from home, family, and friends, to live a life of torture and abuse.[280] These promises of a fairytale life are soon crushed by the reality of life as a sex slave.[281]

The Singaporean government has shown little evidence of a desire to positively affect this industry.[282] One example of the utter lack of care or concern is evidenced by "convicting and punishing [only] two trafficking offenders."[283] Eradicating the scourge of sex trafficking should be a top priority for the Singaporean government, but their proactive measures taken to identify and assist victims, as well as prosecute perpetrators, are lacking and proving to be inefficient and ineffective.[284]

Many NGOs rightfully question Singapore's ability and willingness to locate and identify victims, initiate serious investigations, and prosecute those running and operating criminal enterprises.[285] During the 2008–2009 reporting period, "[t]he government investigated 32 [cases] of sex trafficking."[286] A case involving five Thai women forced into prostitution netted the perpetrator one year and seven months in prison.[287] This case illustrates the seriously inadequate punishment for sex traffickers.[288]

In a separate case, an individual was sentenced to nine weeks in jail and received a $20,000 fine.[289] The perpetrator was a brothel owner who had a Thai girl as a prostitute.[290] To further illustrate the lack of effort by the government to effectively attack this industry, during searches of brothels and other related businesses, the police arrested 7614 women for "prostitution violations."[291] Of these women, the government identified only one woman as a sex trafficking victim.[292] The rest of the women were sent back to their countries of origin after their arrests, some were deported at the end of the police investigations, and some were even prosecuted for violating certain immigration laws.[293] This is the typical way Singapore has dealt with sex trafficking.[294] It is clearly neither a sensitive nor effective manner of dealing with the problem.[295] To say that Singapore's efforts to impact the sex trafficking industry are lacking and leave much to be desired is an understatement.[296] There is much candy being sold and many purchasers of that product. We have to encourage countries like Singapore to close the candy store.

Another country with a trafficking problem is Greece.[297] Greece, a Tier 2 country, has women arriving mainly from "Eastern Europe, the Balkans, and Nigeria."[298] Many traffickers reportedly use "emotional abuse and financial harm as tools of coercion, instead of physical force, in attempts to evade law enforcement prosecution."[299] Concerns involving police and government complicity, inadequate protection and identification of victims, as well as insufficient funding for antitrafficking exist among NGOs.[300] There are laws on the books in Greece that, if enforced, would make a dent in the sex trafficking industry, but, like in many countries, those laws are evident only on paper without any real enforcement.[301] In 2006, the Greek government learned of a case where three police officers allegedly raped a woman while she was in custody.[302] For at least two years after the alleged assault, the officers "remained free on bail."[303] In 2009, in another case of alleged police involvement in sex trafficking, "one active and one retired [police] officer were held without bail" while awaiting trial.[304] In an effort to curtail this activity, the Greek government, collaborating with NGOs, provided antitrafficking training to law-enforcement officials.[305] The Greek government also made this training available to judges, prosecutors, and police of neighboring countries.[306]

Although many countries still have work to do to eradicate their trafficking problems, if no "Johns" demanding sexual acts existed in the first place, the denial of women and children's basic human right to be free from slavery would end.[307] Without anyone to view or purchase online pornographic images, commercial exploitation of persons portrayed in those materials would also cease.[308] If the state did not profit financially from the trafficking of women and children, the state would reinforce the dignity and self-worth of all people through serious enforcement of the laws on the books.[309] If education and valid (legal) employment opportunities were available for victims of sex trafficking, traffickers would be unable to trick women or children into believing sexual slavery is a legitimate job.[310] If there was no candy, there would be no business.

VI. CONCLUSION

If our global community is serious about paving a path to freedom for these victims, governments must make serious efforts to draft (where applicable) and implement comprehensive antitrafficking laws.[311] Local, state, and national governments must fully fund antitrafficking laws and antitrafficking efforts of NGOs.[312] NGOs' prevention strategies that address the issue of demand in this field need to be promulgated and publicized.[313]

Governments must take steps to increase officials' ability to recognize, identify, and assist victims of sex trafficking.[314] When governmental officials are implicated or found to have taken an active role in the trafficking, governments must prosecute the officials to the fullest extent of the law.[315]

Governments should also research ways to make legal assistance affordable and accessible to victims of trafficking.[316] Victims should know that prosecuting governments will not place unreasonable demands on them.[317] Governments should design laws to work in the favor of these innocent people.[318] We can hope to decrease the demand for commercial sex acts by strictly enforcing unutilized laws that are currently on the books.[319] These unenforced laws prohibit the importation of women for commercial sexual services, such as prostitution and working in brothels, massage parlors, nightclubs, and strip clubs.[320] "Johns" might be less likely to partake in this industry if the penalties for doing so were more severe and if "Johns" understood that law enforcement would target the "Johns," instead of the victim, as the offender.[321] A step in the right direction would be ensuring that victims receive the help and assistance they need and are not treated as common criminals for acts committed in connection to being trafficked.[322] At the very least, a country must take steps to create a nationwide database to monitor, collect, and evaluate statistics involving sex trafficking, antitrafficking efforts, and effective solutions.[323] This database could include a "Most Wanted List" of convicted sex traffickers.[324] This "list" should be prominently displayed to discourage future "Johns" from soliciting the services of trafficked women or children, thus curbing the demand for such services.[325]

Governments should make frequent public service announcements to keep sex trafficking and its ever-evolving face in the minds of citizens and to make citizens aware of how fluid the industry is.[326] Governments must always have specific, highly trained groups of professionals in place to deal with the youngest victims of commercial sex trafficking.[327] These children need specialized attention, if it is not already too late, to prevent them from being scarred for life.[328]

We must take a hard look at how we ingratiate males into that "all-boys" society by teaching males that all people have value, dignity, and self-worth.[329] Commercialized and glamorized sex in the media has to be brought into perspective and recognized for its role in the industry of sex trafficking.[330] Women and children must not face dehumanization and portrayal as sex objects.[331] This process lessens the humanity, dignity, and value in people, and victims are no longer seen as people but objects.[332]

Society must evaluate education, poverty, and status to address the deep divides and chasms in our global community.[333] Poverty drives individuals to desperate, unthinkable acts of grave inhumanity.[334] By educating and creating economic opportunities, we might decrease the number of impoverished individuals that turn to committing those inhumane acts.[335]

The unending and consistent struggles of the United States and most of the world with sex trafficking are intimately tied to questions concerning the "rule of law" and "good governance."[336] Many have called this fight against modern-day slavery the "new abolitionist movement."[337] As a caring, compassionate global community, we should all be encouraged and strongly motivated to join in this fight to save countless, faceless, nameless victims.[338] The goal should be to dismantle the demand and end this system of slavery forever.[339]

In the end, global sex trafficking or "slavery is a moral [dilemma] that forces confrontation with one's commitment to human dignity."[340] As such, we must recognize that as a global community we will be able to significantly decrease the number of victimized sex slaves if governments institute stringent enforcement policies, punish "Johns," and create penalties to decrease the demand for the services of those trafficked by "Johns."[341]

Demand is the grease that spins the wheels of a well-oiled and operating sex trafficking machine.[342] This demand is creating a living hell for innocent women and children around the globe; society can no longer turn a deaf ear to their plight and the brutality to which they are subjected.[343]

We must remember that the victims are real people who deserve recognition and protection.[344] To illustrate this point, one victim's letter pleads with Pastor Chun Ki-won and implores, "I want to live like a human being for one day. I am a human being. How can I be sold like this? I need freedom."[345] Another child victim recalls how scared and alone she felt when "clients" raped and brutalized her.[346] In testimony given to a Senate Committee, Luis CdeBaca reasoned, "With all of us, and those who we will touch, young people need to know that they are not alone: that we will not turn a blind eye to their abuse."[347]

250. Michelle R. Adelman, Note, *International Sex Trafficking: Dismantling the Demand*, 13 S. Cal. Rev. L. & Women's Stud. 387, 396 (2004).

251. Angela D. Giampolo, Comment, *The Trafficking Victims Protection Reauthorization Act of 2005: The Latest Weapon in the Fight Against Human Trafficking*, 16 Temp. Pol. & Civ. Rts. L. Rev. 195, 210 (2006).

252. *Id.*

253. *Id.*

254. *Id.*

255. *Combating Human Trafficking in China: Domestic and International Efforts: Hearing Before the Cong.-Exec. Comm'n on China*, 109th Cong. 39 (2006), *available at* http://frwebgate.access.gpo.gov/cgi-bin/getdoc.cgi?dbname=109_house_hearings&docid=f:26671.pdf (statement of Hon. John R. Miller).

256. *Id.*

257. U.S. Dep't of State, *supra* note 94, at 5.

258. *Id.* at 297 (noting that South Africa has moved forward in convicting its first sex traffickers and has created laws at the provincial and national levels that are designed to protect children, enacted interministerial operating policies, trained government employees on antitrafficking laws, enhanced their victim identification process, and strengthened agency roles in fighting sex trafficking).

259. *See id.* at 297–98 (highlighting the continuing problems with passing legislation, sentencing convicted human traffickers, and funding antitrafficking organizations).

260. *See generally* Victoria Hayes, Note, *Human Trafficking for Sexual Exploitation at World Sporting Events*, 85 Chi.-Kent L. Rev. 1105 (2010) (discussing the correlation between human trafficking and world sporting events).

261. U.S. Dep't of State, *supra* note 94, at 297.

262. *Id.*
263. *Id.* at 297–98.
264. *Id.* at 298.
265. *Id.*
266. *Id.*
267. *Id.*
268. *Id.*
269. *Id.* (requiring twenty years of imprisonment for sex trafficking, which is proportional to a rape sentence in South Africa).
270. *Id.*
271. *Id.*
272. *Id.*
273. *Id.*
274. *Id.*
275. *Id.*
276. *Id.* at 292.
277. *Id.*
278. *See id.*
279. *Id.*
280. *Id.*
281. *Id.*
282. *Id.* at 292–94.
283. *Id.* at 292.
284. *Id.*
285. *Id.* at 293.
286. *Id.*
287. *Id.*
288. *See id.*
289. *Id.*
290. *Id.*
291. *Id.*
292. *Id.*
293. *Id.* at 293–94.
294. *See id.* at 294.
295. *See id.* (deporting victims does not provide incentive for victims to report trafficking).
296. *See supra* notes 278–95 and accompanying text.
297. *See infra* notes 298–306 and accompanying text.
298. U.S. Dep't of State, *supra* note 94, at 158.
299. *Id.*
300. *Id.* at 159.
301. *Id.*
302. *Id.*
303. *Id.*
304. *Id.*

305. *Id.*

306. *Id.*

307. *See, e.g., id.* at 170 (noting countries that have and have not instituted programs to "reduce demand for commercial sex acts" as a means of prevention).

308. *See* Hughes, *supra* note 25, at 64 ("Demand reduction is part of prevention of sex trafficking.").

309. *See, e.g., id.* at 8 (discussing proliferation or acceptance of sex trafficking because governments can profit from the business).

310. *See* Prevention, humantrafficking.org, http://www.humantrafficking.org/combat_trafficking/prevention (last visited Apr. 1, 2012).

311. *See, e.g.*, U.S. Dep't of State, *supra* note 94, at 331 (recommending governments implement comprehensive anti-trafficking laws to reduce sex trafficking).

312. *See id.* at 14 ("At its best, victim protection is a series of laws and policies that are broadly funded, understood, and implemented. . . .").

313. *See, e.g., id.* at 298 (recommending South Africa "continue to support prevention strategies developed by NGOs" and broadly recommending programs to educate and inform the public to reduce sex trafficking).

314. Hughes, *supra* note 25, at 64–65 (discussing various improvements to law enforcement in this area).

315. *Id.* at 64.

316. U.S. Dep't of State, *supra* note 94, at 113 (recommending China "support legal assistance programs that assist both foreign and Chinese trafficking victims").

317. *See id.* at 5 (heralding the United States' introduction of the TVPA as a "key milestone [ ] in the fight against modern slavery").

318. *See id.* (applauding the United Nations' adoption of the Palermo Protocol, which instructs governmental response to focus on "prevention, criminal prosecution, and victim protection") (emphasis removed).

319. *See* Hughes, *supra* note 25, at 22 ("As commercial sexual activity is more openly advertised and laws against illegal activity are not enforced, the standards become unclear.").

320. *See, e.g.*, 22 U.S.C. §§7101(b)(2), 7106 (Supp. IV 2010).

321. *See* Hughes, *supra* note 25, at 64 (advocating for prosecution of "purchasers of sex... to eliminate the markets for victims").

322. *See id.* ("End discrimination against victims in arrest and prosecution of trafficking and prostitution-related offenses.").

323. *See* U.S. Dep't of State, *supra* note 94, at 36 ("There is growing government support for evidence-based research that suggests effective strategies for combating the crime and highlights successes among current countertrafficking initiatives.").

324. *See id.* at 113 (highlighting China's success in arresting "19 of the country's 20 most wanted traffickers").

325. *See, e.g., id.* at 116 (recommending countries continued efforts to "raise public awareness about the dangers of human trafficking").

326. *See, e.g., id.* at 80 (discussing how public service announcements are an effective means to educate the public about human trafficking).

327. *See id.* at 72, 125 (implying one of the ways to improve countries' responses to sex trafficking is to create specialized shelters to assist victims).

328. *See id.* at 72, 124.

329. *See supra* Part II.

330. *See supra* Part IV.

331. *See supra* Part IV.

332. *See supra* note 61 and accompanying text.

333. *See* Prevention, *supra* note 310.

334. *See* Hughes, *supra* note 25, at 24 ("[C]onditions such as aggravated poverty... have created a large pool of potential victims.").

335. *See* Prevention, *supra* note 310.

336. Mark P. Lagon, *Congressional Human Rights Caucus Briefing: Trafficking in China*, U.S. *Diplomatic Mission to It* (Oct. 31, 2007), http://www.usembassy.it/viewer/article.asp?article=/file2007_11/alia/a7110108.htm.

337. Condoleezza Rice, Letter from Condoleezza Rice: Trafficking in Persons Report, U.S. Dep't of State (June 12, 2007), http://www.state.gov/g/tip/rls/tiprpt/2007/82798.htm.

338. *Id.*

339. *See supra* notes 15–16 and accompanying text.

340. Kathleen Parker, *Slavery by Any Other Name*, Jewish World Rev. (Oct. 1, 2007), http://www.jewishworldreview.com/kathleen/parker100107.php3?printer_friendly (emphasis added).

341. *See supra* Part II.

342. *See supra* Part II.

343. *See supra* note 60 and accompanying text; *supra* Part IV.

344. *See supra* notes 200–01 and accompanying text ("Our culture needs to treat women, men, girls, and boys as autonomous individuals that have value and worth outside of and apart from their sexuality. Women (and all people) deserve dignity and respect as individuals who are intelligent, worthy, hardworking human beings.").

345. Hughes, *supra* note 116.

346. Cdebaca, *supra* note 159.

347. *Id.*

Even the landmark "Trafficking Victims Protection Act" has not been able to make enough strides in the removal of eradication of human trafficking, as Co-author Cheryl Taylor Page explains in the following excerpt from her article, *The Strong Arm of the Law is Weak: How the Trafficking Victims Protection Act Fails to Assist Effectively Victims of the Sex Trade.*[*]

---

* Associate Professor at the Lincoln Memorial University Duncan School of Law. The author would like to thank Rachelle Douglas Breckenridge and Lorraine Elzia for taking the time to read and give feedback on this Article. The author would also like to thank to the entire Creighton Law Review editorial staff for all of the time and effort they put

I. INTRODUCTION

Acts that occur in the underbelly of our global community can be shocking to many, but they occur every night and day right in our own neighborhoods. Sex trafficking, a derivative of human trafficking, is occurring in epidemic proportions on a global scale while the victims are suffering in silence. Sexual exploitation has taken the media forefront in recent years.[1] Much legislation has been passed to try to curb this illegal marketing of innocent women and children. Laws in various countries have been evaluated, studied, and researched and lead to the sad conclusion that these laws alone are insufficient in adequately providing the protection and relief so desperately needed by those victimized.[2] Trafficking in persons is the recruitment, transportation, transfer, harboring or receipt of persons, by means of the threat or use of force or other forms of coercion, of abduction, of fraud, of deception, of the abuse of power or of a position of vulnerability or of the giving or receiving of payments or benefits to achieve the consent of a person having control over another person, for the purpose of exploitation.[3]

Sex trafficking "is the demand for prostitution and commercial sexual services that is a central cause of trafficking for sexual exploitation."[4] Experts agree that trafficking patterns flow with "the global supply of and demand for trafficked women."[5] Just "like any other capitalist industry," the sex industry is subject "to the natural pulls of supply and demand."[6] Scholars such as Siddharth Kara have focused on the economic aspects of sex trafficking.[7] Kara espouses the belief that the demand structure and the supply aspect of the worldwide economy make trafficking a profitable business that will be extremely difficult to eradicate.[8]

Too often, however, "the customer's role in sex trafficking [is] invisible" because the demand side of the equation is never addressed.[9] Since the mid-1970s, approximately thirty million

---

into transforming this Article into what you see today. A form of this paper was first presented at the 8th International Conference on Law Sponsored by the Athens Institute for Education and research in Athens, Greece (July 2011). The author would like to thank those individuals at the conference that helped to form and mold the thesis of this Article.

women and young girls have been subjected to the worldwide trade of sex trafficking.[10]

Trafficking victims traditionally came from Latin America and Southeast Asia; now, however, victims originate in Eastern and Central Europe.[11] Experts note that "trafficking generally originates in impoverished areas that lack viable economic opportunities for women."[12] Studies also indicate that wealthier countries are the main sources of exploitation and demand.[13] According to a study released on December 5, 2007, "California is a top destination for human traffickers who coerce people into the sex trade or hard labor through force or fraud."[14] Apparently, California is vulnerable to trafficking due to its nature as an international border of various ports and airports and a popular destination for immigrants.[15]

The United Nations estimates that "2.5 million people are in forced labor (including sexual exploitation) at any given time as a result of trafficking."[16] The Polaris Project estimates that the sex trafficking industry generates approximately $32 billion a year.[17] This industry has turned into a sexually derived industry encompassed by the exploitation of women through pornography, mail-order brides, sex tourism, and forced prostitution.[18]

In 2003, the United States government estimated that the number of people annually trafficked was between 800,000 and 900,000.[19] Even more harrowing, it is estimated that 50,000 women and children from all around the world are annually trafficked into the United States "specifically for the sex trade."[20] A 2007 study estimated the number of people trafficking within the United States every year is anywhere between 14,500 and 17,500.[21]

[S]ex trafficking [is] a "special evil," a multi-billion dollar "underground of brutality and lonely fear," ... "[T]hose who create these victims and profit from their suffering must be severely punished and ... those who patronize this industry debase themselves and deepen the misery of others. And governments that tolerate this trade are tolerating a form of slavery."[22]

In 2000, the U.S. Congress determined that sex trafficking is a form of modern slavery, affecting nearly 700,000 women and children yearly.[23] Accordingly, the profits of the trafficking industry are estimated to be around $9.5 billion, with at least $4 billion attributed to the brothel and prostitution industries.[24] In 2004, one scholar predicted that human trafficking, which ballooned after the fall of the Soviet Union in the 1990s, would become the most profitable criminal activity in the world, surpassing narcotics and weapons trafficking.[25] According to research completed in 2008 and sponsored by the U.S. government, "approximately 800,000 people are trafficked across national borders," and this staggering figure is not including those trafficked within their own countries.[26]

In 2011, the State Department released a report showing numerous countries that were not doing enough to combat trafficking in their countries.[27] Some of the countries on the list are Algeria, Cambodia, Bolivia, Curacao, and the Democratic Republic of Congo.[28] In some countries trafficking has led to governmental corruption and organized crime.[29] This corruption of politicians and law enforcement officials is crucial for mass trafficking of women and children to be successful.[30]

One might think that our global community would be outraged over the atrocious acts being committed against children, but as a whole, our global community has remained silent. And as such, children continue to be brutalized, beaten, dehumanized, raped, and trafficked across country lines. There are many reasons that this happens. Two common sources of sexual exploitation of children are exploitation by a family member or exploitation by the country itself through a corrupt government.[31] One of the main reasons that children are the chosen targets of trafficking is that there is no consensus of the definition of "child" among the countries.[32] If countries are not able to determine or verify victims' ages, it is even more difficult to protect children from trafficking because their consent becomes an issue.[33]

Another reason trafficking occurs is poverty within a country. The lack of resources within a country harbors vulnerability of persons and the people are not adequately protected.[34] Those victims who lack monetary resources to escape their situations are ultimately "stuck" and easy "prey" for the traffickers.[35] Poverty is not the only reason for being easy prey. Often times trafficking gangs take advantage of women and children who are traveling by arranging for travel documents, such as passports and visas, to be confiscated.[36] The victims are then left stranded in a foreign country without money or proper travel documentation and are forced into prostitution to work off their debt.[37] This, many times, is a debt so inflated and fabricated, that it may take years to work off. Asian countries are particularly popular in the sexual tourism category; countries such as China and Japan are at the top of the sex trafficking lists for markets for women. Around 225,000 people are trafficked out of South Asia each year.[38]

Japan provides the largest market for the trafficking of Asian women for sexual purposes.[39] Approximately 150,000 non-Japanese women work as prostitutes in Japan.[40] Accordingly, "[t]he Japanese government disseminated 500,000 copies of a brochure in many languages for trafficking victims seeking help and 25,000 that describe the link between prostitution and sex trafficking."[41]

Thailand is another country that has a high rate of women being forced into the sex industry. The difference between Thailand and other Asian countries is the amount of children forced to become prostitutes. Many men, women, and children are trafficked from Cambodia, Laos, and Burma to Thailand for both sexual and labor exploitation.[42] The Thai government enacted the Prostitution Prevention and Suppression Act 43 in 1996 in order to arrest the scourge of forced prostitution and trafficking.[44] This law criminalized those involved in the sexual exploitation of men, women, and children.[45] Penalties for trafficking in children ranged according to the victims' ages.[46] As of 2008, if a child is fifteen to eighteen years old, the penalty ranges from six to twelve years plus a fine.[47] If the victim is less than fifteen years of age, the offender runs the risk of being jailed for eight to fifteen years plus a fine.[48] Between September 2005 and February 2007, the Thai government reported eighty-eight arrests in cases against traffickers.[49] The Thai government provides shelters for trafficking victims in which the victims can receive board, food, counseling, and medical care.[50]

One of the many positives of the Trafficking in Persons Report, which is produced yearly by the United States government, is the information that it makes available regarding trafficking in various countries around the world. The 2011 Trafficking in Persons Report stated that Afghanistan "is a source, transit, and destination country for men, women, and children subjected to forced labor and sex trafficking."[51] Afghani parents sometimes knowingly sell their children.[52] In Japan, the trafficking report noted that trafficking is a big problem and Japanese organized crime groups, known as Yakuza, are at the root of the problem.[53] The Philippines also has a sex trafficking problem. In the Philippines, which "is a source country and, to a much lesser extent, a destination and transit country for men, women, and children who are subjected to sex trafficking and forced labor. A significant number of Filipino men and women who migrate abroad for work are subjected to conditions of involuntary servitude worldwide."[54] Additionally, internal trafficking also remains a serious problem.[55]

Millions of women were easily trafficked into the sex industry when the Soviet Union collapsed and an economic depression followed.[56] According to a 2001 article, "Eastern European countries, particularly Russia, Ukraine, and the Czech Republic, became the predominant source countries from which traffickers procure women."[57] Over 100,000 women from Ukraine alone have been forced into the sex trade in the last ten years.[58]

Before the statutory analysis is commenced, it must be noted that until 2000, many countries, including the United States, had failed to address this global issue. In the landmark legislation, the Trafficking Victims Protection Act of 2000,[59] the United States addressed these crimes against humanity in the form of prevention, prosecution, protection, and partnership. And while this first of its kind legislation is a step in the right direction, there is still much room for improvement and even more work to be done.

II. THE UNITED STATES CONGRESS ADDRESSES HUMAN TRAFFICKING IN LANDMARK FEDERAL LEGISLATION

A. The Trafficking Victims Protection Act of 2000

The Trafficking Victims Protection Act of 2000[60] ("TVPA") defines "sex trafficking" as "the recruitment, harboring, transportation, provision, or obtaining of a person for the purpose of a commercial sex act."[61] The TVPA is considered modern anti-slavery legislation in the United States.[62] This law recognizes the fact that trafficking in humans is concurrently a problem within the United States as well as a crisis internationally.

The TVPA has three levels: prevention, protection, and prosecution.[63] Prevention is governed by the TVPA's promise to put out an annual report assessing the efforts of governments in meeting minimum standards in preventing trafficking.[64] For those countries that did not meet minimum standards, President Bush made specific requirements regarding United States funding.[65] The TVPA also incorporates protection measures.[66] Assistance programs provide medical services and housing to victims.[67] The Department of Homeland Security, Bureau of Immigration and Customs Reform, and Department of Justice handle prosecution. These departments ultimately identify and prosecute sex traffickers.

The TVPA created three tiers in which to place countries based on their efforts to reduce sex trafficking.[68] Tier one is for those countries whose governments fully comply with the Act's minimum requirement standards for eliminating sex trafficking in their country.[69] Tier two is comprised of those countries whose governments do not fully comply with government standards but that are "making significant efforts to bring themselves into compliance."[70] Tier three is reserved for those countries that are "not making significant efforts" to comply with the minimum governmental standards for reducing and eliminating sex trafficking.[71] When determining whether a particular country is bringing itself within the standards, the government considers certain factors, such as "(1) the extent of trafficking in the country; (2) the extent of governmental noncompliance... and (3) what measures are reasonable to bring the government into compliance with the minimum standards."[72]

B. The Prosecutorial Remedies and Tools Against the Exploitation of Children Today Act of 2003

In 2003, Congress passed the Prosecutorial Remedies and Tools Against the Exploitation of Children Today Act of 2003[73] ("PROTECT Act"). The PROTECT Act targets U.S. citizens entering other countries to exploit children and individuals exploiting children in the United States. The PROTECT Act amends a portion of Title 18 of the United States Code and imposes harsher sentences for American sex tourists and is the first initiative to make it illegal to travel abroad with the intent of taking pornographic images of children.[74] "Sex tourism" is the act of Americans traveling abroad, exploiting children, and then returning to the United States.[75] The PROTECT Act makes it a crime to commit an illegal act outside the United States. "Congress has the authority to enforce its laws beyond the territorial boundaries of the United States."[76] Therefore, a person who commits an illegal act outside of the United States can be prosecuted for the commission of that crime here in the United States. Committing heinous acts outside of U.S. borders does not allow a person to escape prosecution, thanks to the PROTECT Act.

III. A CRITICAL ANALYSIS: WHY THE TRAFFICKING VICTIMS PROTECTION ACT OF 2000 FAILS TO ADEQUATELY PROTECT THE VICTIMS OF HUMAN AND SEX TRAFFICKING

Despite what appears to be a strong legal framework within which to prosecute perpetrators and effectively assist victims, enforcement of anti-trafficking laws such as the Trafficking Victims Protection Act of 2000[77] ("TVPA") and the Prosecutorial Remedies and Tools Against the Exploitation of Children Today Act of 2003[78] ("PROTECT Act") has been apathetic. Given these laws have been passed by the United States Congress and remain on the books, it is questionable why these laws are not operating to effectively protect the targeted victims. Nine years after the initiation of the TVPA, only 1,300 trafficking victims had benefitted from the "T-Visa" status.[79] Compare this to the tens of thousands of victims that are still illegally transported into this country on a yearly basis and one will quickly realize that this is not an effective enforcement policy.

A. Key Provisions of the Trafficking Victims Protection Act of 2000

In October 2000, the United States government crafted a way to assist the victims of severe forms of human trafficking by allowing them to receive relief under United States immigration law via the "Victims of Trafficking in Persons (T) nonimmigrant visa." This visa status, if granted, allows a victim to be able to remain in the United States if he or she agrees to help the United States government investigate and prosecute the perpetrators of the crime. This visa, while assisting victims, is designed to strengthen the government's ability to investigate and prosecute those that traffic humans.

Some of the qualifications for the T-nonimmigrant visa are (1) according to the laws of the United States, the individual has to be defined as a "victim of sex trafficking;" (2) the individual must be in the United States or any other recognized country as defined by the law; (3) the individual, unless seventeen years old or younger (or physically incapable or if so traumatized psychologically), must agree to cooperate fully with law enforcement in regards to the inquiry and trial of the traffickers; and (4) the individual must be able to demonstrate that he or she would "suffer extreme hardship involving unusual and severe harm" if forced to return to her country of origin.

Another method created under the Trafficking Victims Protection Act of 2000[80] ("TVPA") to help trafficking victims was to allow them to also qualify for the "continued presence" visa.[81] This section of the TVPA provides relief in the form of allowing work authorization for individuals who are possible witnesses in the government's cases against the traffickers.[82] In 2010, "continued presence" visas were given to "186 potential victim-witnesses" and victims of sex trafficking received 447 "T-Visas."[83]

In order for a victim to receive assistance under the TVPA, the victim must first be certified as a "severe trafficking victim." Severe trafficking is defined under the TVPA as

(A) Sex trafficking in which a commercial sex act is induced by force, fraud, or coercion, or in which the person induced to perform such act has not attained 18 years of age; or

(B) the recruitment, harboring, transportation, provision, or obtaining of a person for labor or services, through the use of force, fraud, or coercion for the purpose of subjection to involuntary servitude, peonage, debt bondage, or slavery.[84]

In order to receive the offered benefits, a victim must first be given approval, or certification, by the Department of Health and Human Services ("DHHS"), that she meets the standard of a "severe trafficking victim."[85] Once a victim receives the "approval" from DHHS, she is then eligible for governmental assistance with food, legal assistance, shelter, in some situations visas, and restitution. Many problems arise in this process. One of the main issues in this "certification" process is being able to properly identify victims of the sex trafficking industry and then somehow figure out who is a victim of a severe form of sex trafficking.

B. The Trafficking Victims Protection Act of 2000's Classification of "Severe Victims" Fails to Account for the Victims' Reality

Perhaps the main problem with identifying victims is the subversive and hidden nature of the industry. Many, if not most, of the victims are transported into the host country illegally and it is this component — immigration status — that helps the trafficker hide the victim. Many victims do not speak the language of the host country and are not familiar with the laws or their rights in that country. Victims are kept isolated and in squalid conditions and have their movements completely controlled by the trafficker. Many do not realize that they are victims and are being exploited and come to rely on the trafficker because of these factors. Fear is a major factor that helps to keep the victims trapped and enslaved. The victim often legitimately fears the trafficker and anyone in authority, as well as fears that harm may be done to their families.

Some victims are trapped through fear relating to cultural beliefs and superstitions. Author David Batstone tells the story of a young lady who was being rescued by a government worker employed as an advocate for victims of crime.[86] The young lady's trafficker had been arrested and was no longer in the home where she was being held captive.[87] The young lady refused to leave the premises because the trafficker had taken a lock of her hair and, because of her superstitious beliefs, she believed that he could harm her and her family as long as he had the lock of her hair.[88] She would not leave the home until the government worker retrieved the hair from the trafficker.[89]

Another problem that makes identification of victims less feasible is a general lack of awareness of the scope of the problem of sex trafficking. This lack of knowledge and understanding exists within the ranks of governmental officials tasked with assisting these victims. Many have a stereotypical image of what a victim of sex trafficking looks like and often these preconceived notions are inaccurate. It is evident that even though awareness of sex trafficking has increased, there is still not a full and complete comprehension of what victims look like and who they are. This ignorance causes many victims to remain unidentified and prevents them from receiving help.

C. Victims' Failure to Self-Identify

Prostitution cannot be viewed as a "victimless" crime if we seriously intend to see changes for the good of those victimized. The main rationale for why victims contacted by agencies tasked with helping victims go unassisted is that first, the victims do not specify or identify themselves as victims and second, the agencies are unable to identify the victims as victims. Many victims do not perceive themselves as "victims" because many do not know that what they have been subjected to is a crime. The trafficker has convinced the victims that they, the victims, are the criminals and are somehow deserving of their situation. Simply put, victims do not know that they are victims. Many tasked with identifying the victims have a view in their minds of what a victim looks like. When an individual comes and they do not look like a sex trafficking victim, the helper is not able to assist because they have not recognized the individual as a victim. This only operates to reinforce in the minds of victims that the trafficker is right: that they are to blame for what has happened to them and that no one is going to help them. Many governmental officials see the victims as criminals (prostitutes) and find that the easiest thing to do is have the person arrested and charged with a crime (and where applicable, deported). These acts strengthen the traffickers' position.

Education and awareness are crucial for officials to be able to adequately assist victims of sex trafficking. Agencies assisting victims must know how to properly identify victims so that the victims will be provided the help that is mandated by law. The Trafficking Victims Protection Act of 2000[90] ("TVPA") provides funding for this kind of training, but the agencies must use the funding effectively. The way that victims and the sex industry are viewed must be a priority for officials seeking to make a dent in this field.

D. The False Dichotomy Between Voluntary and Involuntary Victims

Another issue with the certification process is the way the law was written. The certification process delineates between those victims that are subjected to a "severe" form of trafficking and those that are not. Only a certain number of victims will receive assistance. The law dichotomizes between victims that are brought into the sex industry through "force, fraud or coercion" and those who "voluntarily" come into the industry. Victims who are brought into the sex trafficking industry through "force, fraud or coercion" are considered victims of a severe form of trafficking and can receive assistance. Victims who are not brought into the industry via "force, fraud, or coercion," however, are not considered to be under a severe form of sex trafficking. These "voluntary" victims include victims who "knew" that they were going to be prostitutes but were unaware of the barbaric and slave-like conditions in which they would reside and to which they would be subjected. The Trafficking Victims Protection Act of 2000[91] ("TVPA") does not provide help or assistance to voluntary victims.

The problem is exacerbated by a victim (who may have been tortured, brutalized, and abused) having to explain to an official that they were brought into sex trafficking through "force, fraud or coercion." The determination as to whether a victim will receive the help afforded them via the TVPA is contingent upon the victim being able to convince an official that she meets the specified standards. The determination must be evaluated with the fact in mind that many victims have been taught not to trust government officials, and many do not speak the language or understand the culture of the host country. Many victims have been physically beaten and emotionally abused to the point of where they are unable to speak up for themselves. And without a voice, they go unheard and will be placed back into a system that is ill equipped to help them.

E. The Requirement to Assist in Prosecution

Perhaps one of the biggest impediments to the Trafficking Victims Protection Act of 2000[92] ("TVPA") actually assisting victims is the requirement that the victim assist in the prosecution of her trafficker. The law specifies that in order to receive the social benefits, a victim must be willing to cooperate with the state in the prosecution of the trafficker.[93] The treatment that these victims have endured cannot be understated. These women (not children as this requirement does not apply to those seventeen and younger) have been traumatized and brutalized to the point of what one author equates to post-traumatic stress disorder.[94] These same victims are then expected to assist, cooperate, and testify in a court of law against the perpetrators that have inflicted this atrocious harm on them. To say that we, as a civilized society, will not afford the victims the services they need to function in our society unless they face the individual that enslaved them is a re-victimization all unto itself.

One of the problems with the TVPA's requirements for receiving benefits is the unwillingness of the victim to testify. There are many reasons a victim may choose not to testify against her perpetrator. Fear of retaliation is perhaps the greatest reason a victim would not want to assist in the prosecution. The victim, in most cases, has been beaten and brutalized and is in real fear. This fear extends not only to herself but also to her family and friends.

Many victims of sex trafficking (as well as rape) feel that they are being re-raped by the criminal justice system in being forced to testify and speak out against the trafficker. Some victims have issues recalling the details of what transpired due to the trauma sustained, as well as long periods of forced drug use.

There are ways to get around the fact that a victim may be too terrified or unwilling to cooperate with the state in the prosecution of the perpetrator. In domestic violence and assault cases where a victim who once was willing to testify against her abuser has changed her mind, the state has other routes to proceed. In cases where the state has witnesses to the violence, the state can call these witnesses to testify to their version of the assault. A witness can testify to what the witness saw (a punch, a slap, a kick) and what the witness heard (a scream, a thud, breaking glass). A witness will be able to testify to anything he or she experienced with any one of the senses. This will assist the trier-of-fact in assessing what occurred during the crime even if the victim is unwilling to testify.

The state may also have physical evidence from the crime, photographs of the victim's bloody face, a bloody footprint on the floor, a broken beer bottle, or a knife with blood on it. The police officers might be able to collect an array of items that will assist in the prosecution of the defendant for assault. These items will then be entered into evidence to prove the guilt of the defendant for the crime of assault.

Often, the state will have the victim's own statements immediately after the crime when she is angry, hurt, embarrassed, and desirous of prosecution of the defendant. These very statements can then be used to illustrate the victim's state of mind at the time of the assault, helping to prove the defendant's guilt. Along these same lines, there may also be medical evidence showing what injuries the victim sustained as a result of the assault. The kind of items that would be helpful in establishing a victim's medical condition would be a rape test kit, x-rays, doctor's notes, and blood and urine tests. All of these items could be used to help prove the defendant's guilt. Finally, the state will have the testimony of the officer that was on the scene during or immediately after the assault. The officer will be able to testify to the victim's demeanor, her physical injuries, any comments she made to the officer, and what the officer saw in the location where the assault took place.

The hope is that we can create ways in which the state can prosecute cases of sex trafficking even when the victim is unable or unwilling to assist and cooperate. The evidence used in cases of domestic violence and assault can similarly be used in sex trafficking cases. The state can have witnesses testify and can introduce medical evidence and any statements made by the victim at the time of the arrest. Additionally, the arresting officers can testify as to what they witnessed at the scene of the crime and any evidence they gathered. There are ways to get around not having a victim testify.[2]

1. *See generally* U.S. DEP'T OF STATE, TRAFFICKING IN PERSONS REPORT (2011), *available at* http://www.state.gov/j/tip/rls/tiprpt/2011/.

2. Margaret A. Healy, Note, *Prosecuting Child Sex Tourists at Home: Do Laws in Sweden, Australia, and the United States Safeguard the Rights of Children as Mandated by International Law?*, 18 FORDHAM INT'L L.J. 1852, 1884–88 (1995).

3. Ratna Kapur, *Travel Plans: Border Crossings and the Rights of Transnational Migrants*, 18 HARV. HUM. RTS. J. 107, 116 (2005) (quoting Protocol to Prevent, Suppress and Punish Trafficking in Persons, Especially Women and Children, Supplementing the United Nations Convention Against Transnational Organized Crime, G.A. Res. 55/25, Annex II, U.N. Doc A/55/383 (Dec. 12, 2000)).

---

2. Cheryl George, *The Strong Arm of the Law is Weak: How the TVPA Fails to Effectively Assist Victims of the Sex Trade*, 45 CREIGHTON L. REV. 563 (2012), reprinted by permission of the Creighton Law Review.

4. Beverly Balos, *The Wrong Way to Equality: Privileging Consent in the Trafficking of Women for Sexual Exploitation*, 27 Harv. Women's L.J. 137, 164 (2004).

5. Katrin Corrigan, *Putting the Brakes on the Global Trafficking of Women for the Sex Trade: An Analysis of Existing Regulatory Schemes to Stop the Flow of Traffic*, 25 Fordham Int'l L.J. 151, 157 (2001).

6. Michelle R. Adelman, *International Sex Trafficking: Dismantling the Demand*, 13 S. Cal. Rev. L. & Women's Stud. 387, 391 (2004).

7. *See* Siddharth Ashok Kara, Sex Trafficking: Inside the Business of Modern Slavery (2009).

8. John Bowe, *The Economics of Sex Slavery*, Mod. Am. Slave Lab. & Dark Side Global Econ. (Jan. 22, 2009), http://johnbowe.wordpress.com/2009/01/22/the-economics-of-sex-slavery/.

9. Balos, *supra* note 4, at 165.

10. Norma Hotaling & Leslie Levitas-Martin, *Increased Demand Resulting in the Flourishing Recruitment and Trafficking of Women and Girls: Related Child Sexual Abuse and Violence Against Women*, 13 Hastings Women's L.J. 117, 119 (2002).

11. Corrigan, *supra* note 5, at 156. Many women come from the Far East with the idea of traveling to Britain in order to pay off a family debt. *Police Uncover Human Trafficking Misery*, Scotsman.com (Dec. 5, 2007), http://www.scotsman.com/news/scottish-news/topstories/police_uncover_human_trafficking_misery_1_702485. Unfortunately, the women end up in the "sex industry after becoming 'debt-bonded' to a relative living in the UK." *Id.*

12. Corrigan, *supra* note 5, at 157. The following statistics represent the high estimates of men that have purchased sex acts in various countries: United Kingdom — 8.8%; Spain — 39%; Finland — 13%; Norway — 12.9%; Sweden — 13.6%; Netherlands — 21.6%; Switzerland — 19%; Japan — 37%; Thailand — 75%. Percentage of Men (by Country) Who Paid for Sex at Least Once: The Johns Chart, ProCon.org, http://prostitution.procon.org/view.resource.php?resourceID=004119 (last updated Jan. 6, 2011).

13. Donna M. Hughes, The Demand for Victims of Sex Trafficking 7 (2005), *available at* http://www.uri.edu/artsci/wms/hughes/demand_for_victims.pdf.

14. *State Top Choice of Human Traffickers*, Associated Press, Dec. 5, 2007, http://articles.latimes.com/2007/dec/05/local/me-briefs5.s2.

15. *Id.*

16. Human Trafficking: The Facts, U.N. Global Initiative to Fight Hum. Trafficking, http://www.unglobalcompact.org/docs/issues_doc/labour/Forced_labour/HUMAN_TRAFFICKING_-_THE_FACTS_-_final.pdf (last visited Apr. 7, 2012).

17. Handout on Human Trafficking Statistics from the Polaris Project (2009) (on file with author); *see also* Ten Years of Impact, Polaris Project, http://www.polarisproject.org/about-us/10-years-of-impact (last visited Apr. 7, 2012).

18. Corrigan, *supra* note 5, at 152–53.

19. Victoria Zunitch, *Experts Now Focusing on Demand-Side of Sex Trade*, Women's eNews.org (Oct. 17, 2003), http://www.womensenews.org/story/the-world/031017/experts-now-focusing-demand-side-sex-trade.

20. *Id.*

21. Press Release, FBI Minneapolis Field Office, Minneapolis Man Sentenced on Human Trafficking Charges (Nov. 5, 2007) (available through U.S. Fed. News).

22. Peter Landesman, *The Girls Next Door*, N.Y. TIMES, Jan. 25 2004, http://www.nytimes.com/2004/01/25/magazine/25SEXTRAFFIC.html?pagewanted=all (quoting President George W. Bush, Address to the United Nations General Assembly (Sept. 23, 2003)).

23. 22 U.S.C. § 7101(b)(1) (2000); Mohamed Y. Mattar, *Trafficking in Persons, Especially Women and Children, in Countries of the Middle East: The Scope of the Problem and the Appropriate Legislative Responses*, 26 FORDHAM INT'L L.J. 721, 721 (2000).

24. Nat'l Coalition Against Domestic Violence, Human Trafficking Facts (2006), *available at* http://www.ncadv.org/files/HumanTrafficking.pdf.

25. Tara McKelvey, *Of Human Bondage*, AM. PROSPECT (Oct. 17, 2004), http://prospect.org/article/human-bondage.

26. Clare Ribando Seelke & Alison Siskin, Congressional Res. Serv., RL34317, Trafficking in Persons: U.S. Policy and Issues for Congress, at i (2008), *available at* http://fpc.state.gov/documents/organization/99499.pdf.

27. *See generally* U.S. DEP'T OF STATE, *supra* note 1.

28. *Id.*

29. *See* Press Release, *supra* note 21, at 11.

30. Donna M. Hughes, Address at the U.S. Embassy and the Holy See, Pontifical Gregorian University, Rome, The Demand: Where Sex Trafficking Begins, A Call to Action: Joining the Fight Against Trafficking in Persons (June 17, 2004). According to Gary Haugen, president of the International Justice Mission, "You can only carry out this trade at significant levels with the cooperation of local law enforcement. In the developing world the police are not seen as a solution for anything. You don't run to the police; you run from the police," and according to a Mexico City official, "[c]orruption is the most important reason these networks are so successful." Landesman, *supra* note 22.

31. *See* U.S. DEP'T OF STATE, *supra* note 1, at 7.

32. Daniel Edelson, Note, *The Prosecution of Persons Who Sexually Exploit Children in Countries Other than Their Own: A Model for Amending Existing Legislation*, 25 FORDHAM INT'L L.J. 483, 488–89 (2001).

33. Vitit Muntarbhorn, *Report of the Rapporteur-General* (1996), http://www.csecworldcongress.org/PDF/en/Stockholm/Reports/Stockholm%20Congress%C20General%C20Rapporteur%C27s%C20Final%C20Report%1#996_EN.pdf. Many times, a pimp/trafficker is able to provide false identification to the underage victim and hope that she will be able to get through the system as an "adult." This is done in hopes that the minor will not get sent to a juvenile facility. If she is sent to a juvenile justice center, she may be "held, investigated, traced, and placed in foster care, mental health facilities, or group homes where . . . [she may] respond to counseling and rehabilitation." *What Is Human Trafficking?*, THE FIFTH STANDARD, http://fifthstandard.com/What_is_Trafficking_.html (last visited Apr. 7, 2012).

34. Mohamed Y. Mattar, *Monitoring the Status of Severe Forms of Trafficking in Foreign Countries: Sanctions Mandated Under the U.S. Trafficking in Victims Protection Act*, 10 BROWN J. WORLD AFF. 159, 161 (2003).

35. *See* Susan Tiefenbrun, *The Saga of Susannah a U.S. Remedy for Sex Trafficking in Women: The Victims of Trafficking and Violence Protection Act of 2000*, 2002 UTAH L. REV. 107, 117 (2002).

36. Kathryn E. Nelson, Comment, *Sex Trafficking and Forced Prostitution: Comprehensive New Legal Approaches*, 24 HOUS. J. INT'L L. 551, 555 (2002).

37. *Id.* at 556–57.

38. Francis T. Miko & Grace (Jea-Hyun) Park, Congressional Res. Serv., RL30545, Trafficking in Women and Children: The U.S. and International Response 2 (2002), *available at* http://fpc.state.gov/documents/organization/9107.pdf.

39. Facts and Statistics, Coalition Against Trafficking Women-Asia Pac., http://catwap.wordpress.com/programs/researchdocumentation-publications/facts-and-statistics/ (last visited Apr. 7, 2012).

40. *Id.*

41. Japan, HumanTrafficking.org, http://www.humantrafficking.org/countries/japan (last visited Apr. 7, 2012).

42. Thailand, HumanTrafficking.org, http://www.humantrafficking.org/countries/thailand (last visited Apr. 7, 2012).

43. B.E. 2539 (1996), superseded by Anti-Trafficking in Persons Act, B.E. 2551 (2008).

44. Thailand, *supra* note 42.

45. *Id.*

46. Prostitution Prevention and Suppression Act, B.E. 2539 § 9 (1996), translation *available at* http://www.ilo.org/dyn/natlex/docs/WEBTEXT/46403/65063/E96THA01.htm.

47. Anti-Trafficking in Persons Act, B.E. 2551 § 52 (2008), translation *available at* http://www.ilo.org/dyn/natlex/docs/ELECTRONIC/81747/91028/F1711230791/THA81747.pdf.

48. *Id.*

49. Thailand, *supra* note 42.

50. *Id.*

51. U.S. Dep't of State, *supra* note 1, at 62.

52. *Id.*

53. *Id.* at 205.

54. *Id.* at 295.

55. *Id.*

56. *See* Corrigan, *supra* note 5, at 158 n.23.

57. *Id.* at 156.

58. *Factbook on Global Sexual Exploitation: Ukraine*, Univ. R.I., http://www.uri.edu/artsci/wms/hughes/ukraine.htm (last visited Apr. 7, 2012).

59. Pub. L. No. 106-386, 114 Stat. 1464.

60. Pub. L. No. 106-386, 114 Stat. 1464.

61. 22 U.S.C. § 7102(9) (2006).

62. Kara C. Ryf, *First Modern Anti-Slavery Law: The Trafficking Victims Protection Act of 2000*, 34 Case W. Res. J. Int'l L. 45 (2002).

63. LeRoy G. Potts, Jr., *Global Trafficking in Human Beings: Assessing the Success of the United Nations Protocol to Prevent Trafficking in Persons*, 35 Geo. Wash. Int'l L. Rev. 227, 239 (2003).

64. *See* 22 U.S.C. § 7107(b)(1) (inferring importance of reporting requirement).

65. Presidential Determination with Respect to Foreign Governments' Efforts Regarding Trafficking in Persons, 68 Fed. Reg. 53,871 (Sept. 9, 2003).

66. *See generally* U.S. Dep't of State, *supra* note 1, at 40–42.

67. Jim Lobe, *Exploited Girls in U.S. Seek Same Protection Afforded Foreign Women, Common Dreams* (Mar. 5, 2004), http://www.commondreams.org/headlines04/0305-07.htm.

68. U.S. Dep't of State, *supra* note 1, at 13.

69. *Id.*

70. *Id.*

71. *Id.* at 14.

72. 22 U.S.C. § 7107(b)(4).

73. Pub. L. No. 108-21, 117 Stat. 650.

74. 18 U.S.C. § 2251 (2006).

75. Meril Eugene Anthes, Jr., *Regarding Women & Children: Using International Trade Relations to Stem the Growing Tide of the Sexual Exploitation of Children*, 14 Currents: Int'l Trade L.J. 69, 73 (2004).

76. EEOC v. Arabian Am. Oil Co., 499 U.S. 244, 248 (1991).

77. Pub. L. No. 106-386, 114 Stat. 1464.

78. Pub. L. No. 108-21, 117 Stat. 650.

79. Joycelyn M. Pollock & Valerie Hollier, *T Visas: Prosecution Tool or Humanitarian Response?*, 20 Women & Crim. Just. 127, 127 (2010).

80. Pub. L. No. 106-386, 114 Stat. 1464.

81. Trafficking Victims Protection Act of 2000, Pub. L. No. 106-386, § 107(c)(3), 114 Stat. 1464, 1477 (codified at 22 U.S.C. § 7105(c)(3) (2006)).

82. 22 U.S.C. § 7105(c)(3)(A)(i).

83. U.S. Dep't of State, *supra* note 1, at 374.

84. 22 U.S.C. § 7102(8).

85. *Id.* § 7105(b)(1)(A). This certification process does not apply to children 17 and younger. *Id.* They are not required to go through this process in order to receive the offered benefits. *Id.*

86. David Batstone, Not For Sale: The Return of the Global Slave Trade — And How We Fight It 242 (2007).

87. *Id.*

88. *Id.*

89. *Id.*

90. Pub. L. No. 106-386, 114 Stat. 1464.

91. Pub. L. No. 106-386, 114 Stat. 1464.

92. Pub. L. No. 106-386, 114 Stat. 1464.

93. 22 U.S.C. § 7105(b)(1)(E) (2006).

94. Melissa Farley, Prostitution, Trafficking, and Traumatic Stress xi, xii (2003). The book is a compilation of essays. In the preface to the book, Ms. Farley opines "the internal ravages of prostitution" are not understood in psychology. She equates the psychological damage done to the victims of war and its effects to those undergone by those used as prostitutes. *Id.*

The article we have just examined was published by co-author Page in 2012. As noted in Chapter 2, Congress amended the TVPA in 2013 to include, among other things, an attempt to prevent child marriage and child forced labor. These important efforts have nonetheless failed to stop either problem, although future reports from the U.S. Department of State might offer some insight as to the extent, if any, that these acts have improved the situation, and what further legislation might be necessary.

B. Is There a Relationship between Pornography and Trafficking?

If there is a link between pornography and trafficking, could efforts to regulate or limit the spread of pornography reduce sex trafficking? Co-author Cheryl Taylor Page addressed these issues in her 2013 article, *Porn and Commercial Sexual Exploitation*:

> Human Trafficking is a violation against humanity and a contradiction to the notion that all people are born free and have rights that are equal.[1] This global crime is a part of practically every country in the world. No nation is immune from its reaches.[2] Every year thousands of women, men and children fall prey to human commercial exploitation and are trapped in a criminal enterprise that profits in the billions. Human trafficking is defined as, "recruitment, transportation, transfer, harbouring or receipt of persons, by means of the threat or use of force or other forms of coercion, of abduction, of fraud, of deception, of the abuse of power or of a position of vulnerability or of the giving or receiving of payments or benefits to achieve the consent of a person having control over another person, for the purpose of exploitation."[3]
>
> Slavery is a component of our society and is weaved into our daily lives as consumers of goods. We use slave labor when we purchase certain chocolates, diamonds, energy and produce. We may not be aware of the origins and production costs of the products that we purchase. Many times, slave labor has been used in the product's supply chain[4] (http://www.enoughproject.org/publications/taking-conflict-out-consumergadgets-

company-rankings-conflict-minerals-2012). Slave labor is used rampantly and companies make it a point to not disclose its use of slave labor in the making of consumer goods. Such notification would not be good for business. We are more comfortable, as consumers, not being aware of the forced labor that went into the making of the products we use and most of us would be surprised to know that slavery is not running rampant worlds away. "49% of the profit made from trafficked labor comes from industrialized countries like the United States of America."[5]

Slaves come in many different forms and can be males or females, adults or children. Slaves could be made to work in seamstress shops, or as agricultural workers, domestic workers who cleans homes and care for children, fisherman, child soldiers or even as sex slaves.[6] Though the jobs may differ, there is a common denominator and that is that the individual has been forced into this exploitive situation through force, fraud or coercion. A conservative estimation shows that approximately 12 million people around the world are in some form of forced servitude and serve as slaves.[7] Other estimates are as high as 27 million slaves globally. That number is more than twice the amount of slaves stolen from the continent of Africa during the entire duration of the trans-Atlantic slave trade.[8]

Slaves, in whatever industry or field in which we find them, are dehumanized, abused, mistreated and viewed as less than human. Many times, the labor of these individuals is unknown or overlooked as "as part of life." Slaves that make up a "part of our lives" could work as miners in Congo, brick carriers in Nepal, Himalayan children forced to tote stones from quarries, in the textile industry in India, in agriculture in fields picking the grapes we enjoy as a snack, in restaurants, as domestic servants, perhaps as your dentist's nanny. And of course a slave could come in the form of a child (boy or girl) as young as seven being forced to "entertain" a male client in whatever sexual manner the client sees fit.

One has to wonder what could drive a human being to be able to abuse and dehumanize another human being for pleasure or for gratification. Pornography has the ability to create in the minds of certain people, the baseness needed in order to exploit a person. Pornography is not easily defined and was once spoken of by one judge when he famously said "I can't define pornography, but I know it when I see it."[9] Pornography is unquestionably "exploitative and oppressive of women, treating them as objects of male control.'[10] Some have argued that laws should be enacted to protect the civil rights of women as pornography is a form of violence.[11] Still others have gone to great lengths to argue that the current definitions of pornography that exist fail to cover all forms of pornography.[12] For purposes of this article, I am going to employ and reference the definition of pornography as defined by Catherin McKinnon and co-authored by Andrea Dworkin. Some have called this type of definition, an "oppression' definition,[13] but it is one that most feminists agree with and use in this discourse.

Dworkin defined pornography as:

> women turned into sub-humans, beaver, pussy, body parts, genitals exposed, buttocks, breasts, mouths opened and throats penetrated, covered in semen, pissed on, shitted on, hung from light fixtures, tortured, maimed, bleeding, disemboweled, killed. It is scissors poised at the vagina and objects stuck in it, a smile on a woman's face, her tongue hanging out. It is a woman being fucked by dogs, horses, snakes. It is every torture in every prison cell in the world, done to women and sold as sexual entertainment. It is rape and gang rape and anal rape and throat rape: and it is the woman raped asking for more. It is the woman in the picture to whom it is really happening and the woman against whom the picture is used, to make them do what the woman in the picture is doing. It is the power men have over women turned into sexual acts men do to women. It sexualizes inequality and in doing so creates discrimination as a sex-based practice. It is women, kept as a sexual underclass, kept available for rape and battery and incest and prostitution. It is the heretofore hidden system of subordination that women have been

> told is just life. Under male supremacy, it is the synonym for what being a woman is.[14]

Prof. MacKinnon emphasizes that the characteristics of pornography give rise to violent sexual assault, prostitution, and numerous abuses of the female body[15] (*see* my *Jailing the Johns* article http://works.bepress.com/cgi/viewcontent.cgi? article=1007&context=cheryl_george). This school of thought looks at the complete brutalization of the human psyche as is illustrated in pornography. Pornography is, in a sense, rape and sodomy and a host of crimes that are being depicted and shown repeatedly in the privacy of one's home. Pornography glamorizes, legitimizes and authorizes violent sexual acts and makes the mistreatment and debasement of those victimized look as if the victim is desirous of such actions. This industry is a multi-billion dollar a year business and began with an idea by Hugh Hefner to bring a magazine for the upwardly mobile, Caucasian male.[16] The magazine began in the early 1950's and clearly "struck a nerve with American men."[17] The magazine marketed itself as anything but a magazine for families.[18] This publication was specifically marketed to introduce the white American male to the concept of being a "Playboy." It portrayed women as "cripplers of American masculinity" who were only trying to trap men into marriages that would thus end the man's days of freedom and independence. Women were seen as being conniving, ruthless, freeloaders. The lead off article in the first edition of *Playboy*, was entitled, "Miss Gold-Digger of 1953." That was the essence of how women were portrayed in Hefner's newly imagined world of powerful men dominating over-bearing women who needed to be taught to be submissive. During an age when many single men were seen as being sociopathic or homosexual, Hefner understood that he needed to craft an image that depicted the single man as a hard-working man, who was "actively heterosexual" and continuously surrounded by numerous, sexy women and attractive women.

Playboy was able to be as successful at the time due to the lack of competition. Most other publications at this period were focusing on war related issues (guns, fighting, and death). Hefner realized that the majority of "pin-up" magazines that were sold conspicuously were not the kinds of magazines that most men felt proud of or ones that they would easily display on their living room tables. He knew that most of the American public would shun a full blown pornographic magazine. He instead, offered a neatly packaged, literary publication that contained "articles, fiction, pictures, stories, cartoons, humor and special features...."[19] In this benign description, the "pictures" were simply included as a part of the magazine and not the centerpiece of the magazine. Hefner sold the magazine as a way for regular, ordinary, everyday "Joe's" to become a part of the cultural elite. He showed the reader, via this magazine, that they could be a part of the upper crust of society. It was just a matter of following the ways of Playboy's instructions. The message was to enjoy the literary pieces included in the magazine, feast on the culinary articles, laugh along with the cartoons and, also view and delight in the "soft core" pornographic images of the lovely ladies as well.

Hefner's photographs of the women depicted in Playboy would be considered docile by today's standards of what is pornographic. The images did not show genitals or pubic hair. They were "dreamy' images of women in sexually provocative poses but nowhere near the provocation shown in the photographs that were to come when Penthouse and Hustler entered the market. And while Playboy attempted to introduce certain taboo topics (such as rape as pleasant, stimulating activity) the advertisers were not ready to allow their names to be placed in magazines that showed rape as sexual entertainment.[20] Penthouse and Hustler ushered in a new era of pornography. These publications took what Playboy had started and went to another level. Penthouse entered the market and directly attempted to compete with the market enjoyed by Playboy. They knew that they had to make the photographs of the women in the magazine much more sexually explicit in order to grab that "niche" market. Penthouse boldly used photography that exposed pubic hair as well as genitals. These women were posed in sexually provocative ways and used in clearly subservient, and many times in clearly physically abusive roles than had been seen by Playboy. Penthouse's articles, too, were much more edgier and erotic than were the articles used in Playboy. Penthouse offered women in simulated sexual acts, group sex acts as well as sexual violence. In practically every way, Penthouse attempted to push the envelope on sexual content and consumer consumption.

Eventually the much more provocative Penthouse photos proved to be too much for Playboy to ignore and Playboy began to respond to the gauntlet being thrown down, by making their photos much more sexually explicit as well. Playboy dropped the façade of being a "soft-core" porn magazine and began to have images that were more erotic and raw than those previously offered. That gamble paid off as Playboy's circulation was three times the amount of Penthouse.[21]

Hustler soon came on the scene as the publication that promised to deliver true porn. This magazine pushed the boundaries of sexually explicit imagery farther than had ever been done before. Because of the foundation that had been laid by Playboy and Penthouse, the advent of Hustler came easier as consumers were now much more accustomed to porn as "normal." Hustler benefitted greatly from the work done by the two previous publications and made their entering the industry easier. Unlike Playboy and Penthouse, Hustler did not attempt to masquerade their sexually explicit photographs behind articles, cartoons, literature or other materials. Hustler was on the scene to show women in sexually provocative, demeaning, degrading, ways and they did not attempt to do anything other than that. Hustler's advertisers were even industries that focused mainly on sexual products and services.[22] Hustler made the bulk of its money not from advertisers but from the individuals that subscribed to the magazine (subscription financed revenue) and that bet paid off handsomely for Hustler. Of the three magazines, Hustler is the most financially successful. Hustler has been referred to as being "the most 'vulgar' of" all three sexual publications[23] and their choice of portraying women in sexually explicit and provocative ways that had never been seen before was a financially beneficial decision. The gist of what these publications were able to do was to sanitize and popularize material that had heretofore been socially inappropriate and made it "fun, edgy, sexy and hot."[24]

Given the evolution and vast expansion of pornography, it is not surprising to see how porn has become a part of the fabric of our society. Porn has become a component of pop culture in a myriad of ways. Pornography has infested practically every aspect of our lives. It is seen in numerous mainstream media outlets as safe, ordinary and a given. It is just another facet of everyday life. Porn stars are now considered mainstream idols and people to emulate. Many porn stars now star in movies that are considered mainstream. Many get their big break by having been known as porn stars.[25] Some stars employ social websites to gather a following of fans and then attempt to catapult themselves into the Hollywood spotlight.[26] These porn stars interact one-on-one with their followers and usually discuss innocuous things like hobbies, likes and dislikes. This shallow banter allows the porn star to display a side of them that is not often seen when acting in pornographic movie. Scholars believe that sites like Facebook and Twitter have the power to alter the way a person views a porn actor thereby allowing the porn star to recreate their image directly with fans. This renewing of their self-identification may allow porn to be even more accepted in our society.

Another way that porn has infiltrated our society is through a phenomenon known as "Girls Gone Wild." This industry began with a few men with cheap, plastic beads and t-shirts being given to young, intoxicated females away on spring break to show their breasts on camera. GGW is marketed as real, innocent young looking women who are not porn stars showing their breasts and having fun on camera. Many of the girls are paid a nominal fee to kiss and fondle other girls (most of whom are intoxicated) while being videotaped. They have signed a "release" for their images to be used in video production and dissemination thereby releasing GGW producers from any liability. Many students feel that women who appear in the GGW videos have chosen to do so. No one forces them to expose their body parts and no one twists their arms to make them do what they do. One student is quoted as saying: "I wouldn't say exploiting is the right word; I'd say it's disrespectful," a college junior said. "It's fine if women want to be in them, but after enough of that stuff happens, it does begin to objectify women. But I wouldn't look down upon a woman who wanted to do it or (women who) are part of it."[27] The producers of the show justify their actions by saying that they simply "look for women who are confident in their bodies and excited to be on camera."[28] The fact that young women would be willing to allow their breasts to be viewed publicly and recorded for posterity, is an indication of how certain standards of what is appropriate and what is inappropriate have evolved over time. The boundaries of what is socially acceptable sexually and what is not have changed as a result of the vast exposure and proliferation of sexually explicit material. Given the amount of full and partial nudity seen in prime time television, magazine publications as well as other media outlets, young impressionable women may think it appropriate to expose their breasts and see such activity as "just having fun and living life."

Porn has become an accepted way of life and that is discernible in the craze that accompanies the latest release of the Sport's Illustrated Swimsuit Edition. This magazine purports to show off the latest in swim suit wear, but the magazine is marketed to males. Many of the models of the swimsuit wear double as porn star actors as well. These same models also appear in the Victoria Secret's models. These women wear little clothing but these publications are sold as every day, acceptable, safe publications. Many men and women look forward each year to the Victoria's Secret Fashion Show and view it as women simply modeling lingerie. The lingerie is so skimpy and the women are so scantily clad that one could hardly call it a fashion show, but such productions are a part of our mainstream society. Before publications like Playboy, Penthouse and Hustler, some of the materials we are being exposed to as a society were unheard of and would not have been tolerated in our society. But because of the inundation of sexuality, promiscuity and sexualization of women, we have now grown accustomed to such instances of blatant sexual exploitation of women.

When one thinks of the commodification of women and girls, one may not think of television programming for children, but there is evidence that even in children's television programming, there is bias. Studies have been done that show 18% of female characters are "wearing sexy attire."[29] This is compared to a little more than 10% of male characters dressed in "sex attire."[30] When the study looked at characters "with exposed skin," the numbers showed that 17.2% for female characters and 12.4% for males. The disparity in numbers is greatest when one looks at characters being portrayed "with thin bodies." There the numbers are males at 18.7% and females at 37.4%.[31] In "family films" women are portrayed with a thin body 34.3% of the time whereas men are portrayed with thin bodies 10.7% of the time. The bottom line is that children are being exposed to certain sexualized images at a tender age where they are most impressionable and subject to their thoughts being molded for a lifetime.

A parent should never have to worry about their children watching pornographic images while watching a station dedicated to children's programming, but that is exactly what happened to one North Carolina family. A mother pre-recorded a cartoon for her children (ages 2, 3 and 5) to watch and while they were watching it, the show inadvertently switched to porn for six minutes.[32] The mother was in another room and heard the noise and assumed that the children had switched the television to another station. When she later went back to check the tape, after the children swore they had not turned the channel, the mother saw six minutes of pornography that had indeed been aired on live television. Neither Dish Network nor the Disney Channel have been able to explain the "mix up." But the children were traumatized by the incident as is shown in the fact that the 3 and 5 year old now, according to the mom, "mimic[ed] the action and sound of a couple having sex." This is an indication of the power of pornography on a developing mind.

This short introduction, six minutes worth, has infiltrated these children's minds and changed how they think and has reformatted what they think.

Officially what happened, when the children saw the six minutes of the pornographic movie, is called "signal bleed." Signal bleed is where a signal from a cable channel that a subscriber does not have authority to view "bleeds" through and becomes viewable to that subscriber.[33] Cable companies encrypt or scramble these particular channels and restrict access to them for customers that have not paid for the channel's content. In the case of this North Carolina family, they had no authority (because they had not requested and paid for the channel) to view the channel that "bled" through to their television and thus the "mix up." The Government has created laws that stipulate to cable companies that provide adult programming that they must restrict the adult programming to certain hours where, presumably, children are asleep. The hours are between 10:00 p.m. and 6:00 a.m. Between these hours, cable companies are restricted from playing the adult content movies.

It is estimated by government experts that twenty-nine million children are potentially exposed to a harmful phenomenon known as audio and video "signal bleed" from sexually explicit adult programming on cable television.[34] Some theorize that such exposure is not accidental or unintentional. Some believe that this kind of "teasing" plays a major role in opening the doors for juveniles to explore pornography and sexually charged images of sex.

The Psychology of Watching Porn

Experts believe that by watching porn, a chemical change begins to happen in the brain. That chemical change is akin to changes that occur when a person ingests an intoxicant. What has made this understanding of the changes that can occur when one watches pornography, is the vast availability and access to these sexually explicit materials. The largest consumers of pornography are men. Men are much more visual creatures than women. Men are no longer viewing rudimentary, basic figures on a wall in a cave but have access to a myriad of sexual images (still as well as video) in the comforts of their homes and at the push of a button. When a man has an encounter with pornography and the hormones that bring pleasure, these "encounters" create new wiring of the brain and each additional "encounter" re-affirms that wiring making it stronger and stronger.[35] This then causes the desire for more "encounters" to increase and for the individual to seek out and find more instances where they can view pornography. It is like a drug addict. The same thought process and pattern is formed in those addicted to drugs as those addicted to pornography. It is the same basic premise. Similar to drug addicts, enough never becomes enough. Just as with a person who is addicted to drugs gets to the point where the high is no longer sustainable nor sufficient enough, they will then resort to more drugs or a stronger kind of drug. Whatever action it takes to the next, better "high." Drug users have abused narcotics to the point that they lose spouses. Drug addictions more times than not lead to criminal activity, and so too with porn addictions. Marriages end because of porn addictions. People are murdered because of porn addictions.[36] Addictions to pornography can and have led to criminal activities.

In many pornographic movies, women are brutalized and subjected to inhumane treatment. Bondage and bestiality videos show women being treated in ways that an animal should not be treated. These kinds of images and videos are being viewed by men in many countries in the world. These same men are subjected to the same phenomenon just described as an addiction.

One of the aspects of pornography that is most damaging to the real world, is that it had the ability to make the viewer believe that what is being acted out on the screen can and should be acted out in real life. What the viewer sees on the screen, which is highly scripted and directed, is what the viewer begins to believe should happens in his life and with the women that he has sexual contact with. One of the things that prostitutes note is that a large percentage of the acts that they are requested to perform are some form of imitative act that the john has seen in a pornographic movie. Johns have seen certain acts performed on women, men and children so long that they now think that these acts can be replicated on people who are not employed in the adult film industry. They have a sort of "disconnect" with reality in that they want to have done to them what they have seen on camera and well as them doing to others acts that have been performed on actors.

Make Love Not Porn is a book where the author addresses depictions that take place in the world of pornography and how those acts are perceived to be what is expected to happen in the real world. The book details the account of a young man who has just ejaculated on his sexual partner's breasts. As she is wiping the ejaculation off of her chest, she quietly tells him that she did not like when he ejaculated on her in that way. He asked her why she had previously told him that he could and she said she only allowed it because it made him happy. The young man then took it upon himself to conduct an unscientific experiment by calling up a few prior sexual partners to see why they had allowed him to ejaculate on their faces, stomachs, buttocks or practically anywhere he chose. Every single one of the ladies said they allowed it because it made him happy. He then began an introspective look into himself to see why that particular act brought him happiness and he soon realized that it was because that is what he learned as a young boy watching pornography. When he watched it in pornographic movies, the ladies all enjoyed that act and seemed very happy. The viewing of that act while watching porn and seeing what he did not understand was a scripted, rehearsed and crafted depiction, created a desire in this young man to do exactly what he saw acted out on the screen. The pornography taught him a false reality.

But pornography has the same ability to set up a false sense of reality in women just as much as men. Pornography teaches women "how to act" during the sex acts. It shows women how to moan, when to moan, when to appear sad, and even when to scream for joyous pleasure. This and so much more are shown to women on what the appropriate way is to please the man. This is shown by the preceding example of the young women that allowed the young man to ejaculate on their body parts even though they were clearly uncomfortable and unhappy with that act. They allowed him to do it because the pornographic movies said that women enjoy it. So, they pretended to enjoy it, thus perpetuating the damage that can be done by pornographic movies.

A contrived reality is a by-product of living in a world filled and over flowing with pornography. These falsified realities rewire the brains understanding of what sex, love, attraction and sexual desire is supposed to be in a meaningful and lasting relationship. Pornography has a way of creating an "alternate sexual universe" in the minds of those that view on a regular, systematic basis. It then establishes a reality that makes it difficult for a person to function in a healthy sexual relationship because what is portrayed in the pornographic movie is very different from what happens in a real-life sexual relationship. This then makes those actors in the sex act more likely to behave in less satisfying, unnatural, non-genuine ways as a result of this pseudo reality....

Part of the manufactured reality fostered in pornographic movies is the degrading, dehumanizing and debased ways in which women are portrayed. Women are, many times, shown in ways that strip away all manner of humanity and shown to viewers as nothing more than a piece of meat.

How These Laws Came to Be

A. History

Trafficking

The first laws dealing with trafficking were put into effect in 1948. Some of the laws dealt with fraud and misuse of visas,[37] peonage,[38] sale into involuntary servitude,[39] and transportation of minors.[40] Fifty years later, the Trafficking Victims Protection Act of 2000 was passed. In the act, Congress found that slavery was continuing in the world today in the form trafficking. Around the world, at least 700,000 persons were trafficked annually with around 50,000 being trafficking into the United States, the majority being women and children.[41] According to the Polaris Project,[42] the law provided a three pronged approach:

a. Prevention through public awareness programs overseas and a State Department-led monitoring and sanctions program;
b. Protection through a new T-visa and services for foreign national victims; and
c. Prosecution through new federal crimes.

Since 2000, there have been several revisions of the Trafficking Victims Protection Act. In 2003, the act authorized more than $200 million over two years to combat human trafficking and it created a federal civil cause of action for trafficking victims to sue their traffickers.[43] A 2005 revision authorized $300 million over two years for combating trafficking, addressed sex tourism with prevention programs, and expanded federal criminal jurisdiction to trafficking offenses committed by U.S. government personnel and contractors while abroad.[44]

A 2008 revision created a database that integrated data on human trafficking from all federal agencies.[45] It also authorized a new program for providing services to U.S. citizen survivors of human trafficking.[46] The act also expanded criminal liability of financially benefiting from human trafficking crimes, as well as obstruction and conspiracy.[47] The law was also expanded to give federal criminal jurisdiction to U.S. citizens and permanent residents who travel abroad to commit, attempt, or conspire to commit human trafficking crimes.[48]

Pornography

Basic pornography law began with obscenity laws in the nineteenth century. Early efforts of prohibiting came through the work of Anthony Comstock. In 1873 he successfully lobbied Congress to pass an anti-obscenity statute known as the Comstock Act. The act made it a crime to distribute obscene material through the mail.[49] The law fell short in defining obscenity and courts were left with the burden of determining what was and was not obscenity.

Through the years, the Supreme Court adopted different tests for defining obscenity. The first was *Rosen v. United States*,[50] in which the Court adopted the same obscenity standard used in a British case, *Regina v. Hicklin*.[51] The *Hicklin* test defined material as obscene if it tended "to deprave or corrupt those whose minds are open to such immoral influences, and into whose hands a publication of this sort may fall."[52] The Court ruled in *Roth v. United States* that the Hicklin test was inappropriate and instead replaced it with obscenity as "whether to the average person, applying contemporary community standards, the dominant them of the material, taken as a whole, appeals to the prurient interest."[53] In *Jacobellis v. Ohio*, the Court expanded the community standards to mean national and not local standards.[54] It was also found that obscenity material would be "utterly without redeeming social importance."[55] It was until 1973 when the Supreme Court decided *Miller v. California* that the current test for obscenity was solidified.[56]

From the *Miller* test, pornography has been found to generally be protected speech with the exception of child pornography. The 1982 Supreme Court case of *New York v. Ferber* held that child pornography, even if not obscene, is not protected speech justifying this by the government's compelling interest in safeguarding the physical and psychological well-being of minors.[57] The first statutes involving child pornography were passed in 1978. These laws have been further tweaked by further laws and rulings by the Supreme Court.

B. How the Laws are Practiced

Trafficking

According to the Polaris Project, not all cases with trafficking victims are prosecuted using trafficking statutes.[58] Prosecutors, on a case by case basis, consider several factors in determining what charges to bring, including the specific situation, victim status, the condition of available witnesses, and applicable laws in order to get the most successful conviction.[59] Many times, even with a human trafficking offense, the defendant is prosecuted through other crimes committed.[60]

Pornography

When the *Miller* test became law, there were but few ways to view pornography: darkened movie theaters and magazines. Since *Miller*, pornography has since moved onto cable and hotel pay-per-view TV, home video players and especially onto the Internet.[61] The late 1980's saw the last of the aggressively pursued obscenity cases, in which seven of the nation's largest pornography distributors were put out of business.[62]

The mid-90's saw a change of focus for the DOJ from obscenity cases to child pornography cases.[63] It was also during this time period in which internet use exploded and with it internet pornography. Jason Krause puts things in perspective when he says, "... the Internet happened to arise at a time when the number of prosecutions for obscenity fell toward zero, which means a dearth of court guidance on what a community standard is on the Web."[64] Thus far, the case *United States v. Thomas*, has tested whether *Miller* can be applied to Internet businesses. The *Thomas* court determined that whether the material on the defendant's electronic bulletin board is harmful must be judged by the standards of each individual community where the disputed material was received, even if the standards in each of the recipient communities varied one from the next, and even if the material was acceptable in the community from which it was sent.[65]

There does not seem to have been any switch back from prosecuting child pornography to obscenity. And while prosecution of child pornography is a noble cause, lack of obscenity prosecutions are having an effect. Some statistics point out that ninety percent of children between the ages of eight and sixteen have been exposed to Internet pornography.[66] How many children were exposed to pornography before pornography was available at the click of a mouse? In the 1980's the mail was the primary means of supplying child pornography.[67] Over the past two decades, the dramatic increase in Internet availability has provided a relatively anonymous opportunity for immediate exchange of pornographic images that more easily thwart authorities.[68]

The Effectiveness of These Laws

A. Trafficking Prosecution Statistics

The data on trafficking prosecution comes from the Bureau of Justice Statistics data brief on Federal prosecution of human trafficking from 2001–2005.[69] Of the 555 human trafficking suspect in matters opened by U.S. attorneys between 2001 and 2005, peonage and involuntary servitude represented eleven percent, sale into involuntary servitude represented twenty-eight percent, transportation for slavery represented three percent, forced labor represented twenty-four percent, trafficking slaves represented nine percent, and twenty-three percent represented sex trafficking of children. Almost half of the human trafficking matters opened by U.S. attorneys were in Federal judicial districts in four states: California, Florida, Texas, and New York.[70] Thirty-seven percent of sex trafficking of children matters were referred by U.S. attorneys in California.[71] There were seventy-eight defendants adjudicated in Federal courts for a human trafficking offense.[72] Of those seventy-eight defendants, fifty-seven pleaded guilty and eighteen were found guilty at trial.[73] Those convicted defendants received prison sentences eighty-five percent of the time, probation seven percent of the time, and other sanctions eight percent of the time.[74] The median prison sentence was seventy months.[75]

Another report from the Bureau of Justice Statistics in 2008–2010 featured the characteristics from suspected human trafficking incidents.[76] Sixty-two percent of the confirmed labor trafficking victims were age twenty-five or older, compared to thirteen percent of confirmed sex trafficking victims.[77] Confirmed sex trafficking victims were more likely to be white (26%) or black (40%), compared to labor trafficking victims, who were more likely to be Hispanic (63%) or Asian (17%).[78] Eighty percent of victims in confirmed sex trafficking incidents were identified as U.S. citizens while most labor trafficking victims were identified as undocumented aliens (67%) or qualified aliens (28%).[79]

B. Pornography Prosecution Statistics

The data on child pornography prosecution comes from the Bureau of Justice Statistics bulletin on Federal prosecution of child sex exploitation offenders from 2006.[80] From 1994 to 2006, there was an eighty-two point one percent growth in suspects referred to U.S. attorneys for child pornography.[81] In 2006, of the 2,376 suspects of child pornography, fifty-eight point five percent of those were prosecuted.[82] Thirty-seven point eight percent of the 2,376 suspects were declined for prosecution with twenty-four percent of that number being declined because of weak evidence.[83]

The demographics of the defendants involved in child pornography are these.[84] Ninety-eight point seven percent were male with a median age of forty-two years old.[85] The main race of those defendants was white at eighty-eight point nine percent with the next highest category being Hispanics at six point six percent.[86] Most defendants (seventy-nine point nine percent) had no prior felony conviction.[87] Two in three child pornography defendants were sentenced for having ten or more items, such as books, magazines, or films.[88] Ninety-five percent were sentenced for materials depicting a minor under age 12, and ninety-seven percent were sentenced for the use of a computer in the offense.[89]

Pornography can have grave, negative impacts on those that watch it and on those that are affected by the detrimental behaviors of those that are addicted to it. Pornography has the ability to warp a person's mind to such a degree that they are more able to harm others in the process of acting out the pornographic acts that they have seen. This can easily translate into innocent victims being abused by those people whose minds have been warped by pornography. Those individuals that watch pornography and believe that they can act out what they see on unwitting victims, are predators and should be prosecuted to the fullest extent of the law, where appropriate. Pornography has the ability to create an environment (in the minds of those that do not have the capability to discern reality from a highly scripted act) that they can act out what they have seen. It also can make the viewer not see the victim as a human being with feelings, emotions and a voice (especially when many pornographic movies show the victim's mouth taped, covered or stuffed with items). Once a person is aware of the mental hold that pornography can have on the viewer, then that an individual can make a more intelligent and informed choice in watching (recognizing the potential for harm that can occur).

Parents also must recognize the fragile and impressionable states of mind their young child experiences at certain ages of their lives. They can then watch what they children are viewing on television, in print media as well as on computers. When a child is exposed to pornographic images at certain points in their growth, the exposure can taint and scar a child's mind for life. It is crucial that children's minds be guarded so as to not cause this kind of life-long permanent damage.

In addition to the damage that can occur in children, the damage is just as real for teenagers and adults. Pornography can cause a chemical imbalance in the brain and create an unstable mentality in the brain of the viewer. Pornography has the same effects on certain people as drugs on drug addicts. They lose their ability to curb or monitor their viewing. They, in effect, become addicted. It is these people that have a great opportunity to participate in the trafficking of women and children. Pornography's reach can be that wide reaching and pervasive.[3]

1. Declaration of the Rights of Man and of the Citizen, Art.1, Approved by the National Assembly of France, Aug. 26, 1789, http://www.hrcr.org/docs/frenchdec.html (last viewed Dec. 18, 2012).

2. John D. Sutter, *Slavery's Last Stronghold*, CNN (Mauritania did not officially end slavery until 1981 and create legal penalties for owning another human being until 2007), http://edition.cnn.com/interactive/2012/03/world/mauritania.slaverys.last.stronghold/index.html (last visited Dec. 18, 2012).

3. United Nations Office on Drugs and Crime, http://www.unodc.org/unodc/en/human-trafficking/what-is-human-trafficking.html (last visited Dec. 18, 2012).

---

3. Cheryl George, *Porn and Commercial Sexual Exploitation*, W. J. of Crim. Just. 5.1 (2013), http://works.bepress.com/cheryl_george/11, reprinted with permission of Western Journal of Criminal Justice.

4. Alexandra Hellmuth & Sasha Lezhnev, *Taking Conflict Out of Consumer Gadgets: Company Rankings on Conflict Minerals 2012*, EnoughProject.org (Aug. 16, 2012), http://www.enoughproject.org/publications/taking-conflict-out-consumer-gadgets-company-rankings-conflict-minerals-2012.

5. https://www.facebook.com/?ref=hp#!/photo.php?fbid=458267744223821&set=a.258664337517497.77906.235085629875368&type=1&theater; or http://slaveryfootprint.org/.

6. National Underground Railroad Freedom Center, http://freedomcenter.org/slavery-today/ (last visited Dec. 18, 2012).

7. *Id.*

8. Lisa Kristine, *Glimpses of Modern day Slavery*, TED (Aug. 2012), http://www.ted.com/talks/lisa_kristine_glimpses_of_modern_day_slavery.html.

9. Jacobellis v. Ohio, 378 US 184, 197 (1964) (Stewart, J., concurring).

10. David E. Guinn, *Pornography, Prostitution and International Sex Trafficking: Mapping the Terrain, in* Pornography: Driving the Demand in International Sex Trafficking 16 (David E. Guinn ed., Captive Daughters Media 2007).

11. *Id.*

12. Michael C. Rea, *What Is Pornography?*, 35 (1):118–145 (2001); or http://nd.edu/~mrea/papers/What%20is%20Pornography.pdf (Jon Huer defines pornography as "any object mass produced and distributed with the purpose of marketing it for profit by appealing to our sexual interests." This definition is lacking as it implies lingerie, vibrators, flavored condoms and other sex toys/aides as pornography while not including strip shows, peep shows, amateur stag videos. Fred Berger defines pornography as "art or literature which explicitly depicts sexual activity or arousal in a manner having little or no artistic or literary value." The problem with this definition is a lot of what actually counts as pornography is not at all art. Sex calls and peep shows are clearly not art but are widely accepted as pornographic. Margaret Smith and Barbara Waisberg define pornography as "sexual imagery which presents the human subjects as only sexual objects for the use of the viewer." This definition fails to give necessary conditions for something's being pornography, for example, there would be no way for a photo or a video to portray a human being as only or only as a sexual being. Catharine MacKinnon and Andrea Dworkin defined pornography as "the graphic sexually explicit subordination of women through pictures or words that also includes women dehumanized as sexual objects, things, or commodities." The main problem with this is something counts as pornography on this definition only if it is a depiction that subordinates somebody but it is not clear what it takes for a depiction to do this).

13. Rea, *supra* note 12, at 129.

14. Andrea Dworkin, *Against the Male Flood: Censorship, Pornography and Equality*, 8 Harv. Women's L.J. 19, 26–27 (1985).

15. *See* Cheryl George, *Jailing the Johns: The Issue of Demand in Human Sex Trafficking*, 13 Fla. Coastal L. Rev. 293, 321 (2012).

16. Gail Dines, Pornland: How Porn Has Hijacked Our Sexuality 2 (Beacon Press 2010).

17. *Id.*

18. *Id.* at 2–3.

19. Dines, *supra* note 16, at 7.

20. Dines, *supra* note 16, at 11–12 (Story in a July 1962 issue of Playboy that focuses on the rape of a seventeen year-old by an older man. Advertisers threatened to cancel contracts with Playboy and some newsstands refused to carry the issue.).

21. Dines, *supra* note 16, at 14 (Playboy had a circulation of 3.5 million and Penthouse had a circulation of a little more than 1 million.).

22. Dines, *supra* note 16, at 15 (industries that offered services and products like sex toys, sexual devices, sexual enhancers and even telephone sex).

23. Dines, *supra* note 16, at 19.

24. Beauty Redefined, *Porn and Pop Culture: A Deadly Combination*, Beauty Redefined Blog (Mar. 2, 2011), http://www.beautyredefined.net/porn-pop-culture-a-deadly-combination/.

25. Jim Spellman, *Porn Stars Use Twitter to Go Mainstream*, CNN (July 19, 2012, 9:29 AM), http://www.cnn.com/2012/07/19/showbiz/porn-stars-twitter/index.html.

26. *Id.* (estimated that 90% of porn actors use Twitter in an effort to build their Brand and establish a name for themselves in mainstream media).

27. Whitney Biber, *The Naked Truth About Girls Gone Wild*, Weekend (Mar. 5, 2008), http://www.idsnews.com/news/weekend/story.aspx?id=12016.

28. *Id.*

29. Stacy L. Smith, Marc Choueiti, Ashley Prescott & Katherine Pieper, *Gender Roles & Occupations: A Look at Character Attributes and Job-Related Aspirations in Film and Television*, SeeJane.org, http://seejane.org/downloads/KeyFindings_GenderRoles.pdf (last viewed Dec. 18, 2012).

30. *Id.*

31. *Id.*

32. Phil Vinter, *Six Minutes of Porn Interrupts Kids Program Lilo and Stitch*, Engineering Evil (Sept 19, 2012, 3:45 AM), http://engineeringevil.com/2012/09/19/six-minutes-of-porn-interrupts-kids-program-lilo-and-stitch/.

33. FCC, http://transition.fcc.gov/cgb/consumerfacts/objectionabletv.pdf, (last viewed Dec. 18, 2012).

34. U.S. v. Playboy Entertainment Group, Inc., 529 U.S. 803, 839 (2000).

35. William M. Struthers, Wired for Intimacy: How Pornography Hijacks the Male Brain 85 (InterVarsity Press 2009).

36. Michael Stone, *Necrophilia: Pastor Kills Fiance's Daughter in Sadistic Sex Fantasy*, Examiner (Nov. 2, 2012), http://www.examiner.com/article/necrophilia-pastor-kills-fiance-s-daughter-sadistic-sex-fantasy.

37. 18 U.S.C.A. 1546 (2012).

38. 18 U.S.C.A. 1581 (2012).

39. 18 U.S.C.A. 1584 (2012).

40. 18 U.S.C.A. 2423 (2012).

41. 22 U.S.C.A. 7101(b)(1) (2012).

42. Polaris Project—Trafficking Victims' Protection Act (TVPA)—Fact Sheet. Go to: http://www.polarisproject.org/resources/resources-by-topic/anti-trafficking-efforts Click on Trafficking Victims Protection Act Summary Resource Pack. Last viewed 3/7/13.

43. *Id.*

44. *Id.*
45. *Id.*
46. *Id.*
47. *Id.*
48. *Id.*
49. Michael J. Rosenfeld, The Age of Independence: Interracial Unions, Same-Sex Unions, and the Changing American Family 28 Harvard University Press (2007). Last viewed 3/8/13, http://books.google.com/books?id=dpSlkT2loyUC&pg=PA 28#v=onepage&q&f=false.
50. Rosen v. United States, 161 U.S. 29, 43 (1896).
51. Regina v. Hicklin, L.R. 3 Q.B. 360 (1868).
52. *Id.*
53. Roth v. United States, 354 U.S.476, 489 (1957).
54. Jacobellis v. Ohio, 378 U.S. 184 (1964).
55. *Id.*
56. Miller v. California, 413 U.S. 15, 24 (1973).
57. New York v. Ferber, 458 U.S. 747 (1982).
58. Polaris Project — Federal Labor Trafficking/Forced Labor and Sex Trafficking Cases in the United States 2000–2008, http://www.polarisproject.org/resources/resources-by-topic/human-trafficking, Click on either Federal Labor Trafficking/Forced Labor Cases in the United States 2000–2008 at the bottom of page (last visited Mar. 4, 2013).
59. *Id.*
60. *Id.*
61. Jason Krause, *The End of the Net Porn Wars*, ABA J. (Feb. 1, 2008, 10:01 AM), http://www.abajournal.com/magazine/article/the_end_of_the_net_porn_wars/.
62. *Id.*
63. *Id.*
64. *Id.*
65. United States v. Thomas, 74 F.3d 701, 711 (6th Cir., 1996).
66. Family Safe Media — Pornography Statistics, http://familysafemedia.com/pornography_statistics.html#anchor4 (last visited 3/5/13).
67. Mark Motivans & Tracey Kyckelhahn, *Federal Prosecution of Child Sex Exploitation Offenders, 2006*, Bureau of Just. Stat. Bulletin (Dec. 2007), http://bjs.ojp.usdoj.gov/content/pub/pdf/fpcseo06.pdf.
68. *Id.*
69. Mark Motivans & Tracey Kyckelhahn, *Federal Prosecution of Human Trafficking, 2001–2006*, Bureau of Just. Stat. Data Brief (Oct. 2006), http://bjs.ojp.usdoj.gov/content/pub/pdf/fpht05.pdf.
70. Motivans, *supra* note 30.
71. *Id.*
72. *Id.*
73. *Id.*
74. *Id.*
75. *Id.*

76. Duren Banks & Tracey Kyckelhahn, *Characteristics of Suspected Human Trafficking Incidents, 2008–2010*, Bureau of Just. Stat. Special Report (April 2011), http://bjs.ojp.usdoj.gov/content/pub/pdf/cshti0810.pdf.
77. *Id.*
78. *Id.*
79. *Id.*
80. Motivans, *supra* note 28.
81. Motivans, *supra* note 28.
82. *Id.*
83. *Id.*
84. *Id.*
85. *Id.*
86. *Id.*
87. *Id.*
88. *Id.*
89. *Id.*

C. First Amendment Limitations on Anti-Pornography Efforts

However, attempts to define and address "pornography" will encounter the necessity of considering the 1st Amendment implications. Consider the result when the City of Indianapolis enacted an anti-pornography ordinance:

771 F.2d 323 (7th Cir. 1985)

American Booksellers Association, Inc.

v.

Hudnut

Before Cudahy and Easterbrook, Circuit Judges, and Swygert, Senior Circuit Judge.

Indianapolis enacted an ordinance defining "pornography" as a practice that discriminates against women. "Pornography" is to be redressed through the administrative and judicial methods used for other discrimination. The City's definition of "pornography" is considerably different from "obscenity," which the Supreme Court has held is not protected by the First Amendment.

To be "obscene" under *Miller v. California*, 413 U.S. 15 (1973), "a publication must, taken as a whole, appeal to the prurient interest, must contain patently offensive depictions or descriptions of specified sexual conduct, and on the whole have no serious literary, artistic, political, or scientific value." ... Both offensiveness and an appeal to something other than "normal, healthy sexual desires" ... are essential elements of "obscenity."

"Pornography" under the ordinance is "the graphic sexually explicitly subordination of women, whether in pictures or in words, that also includes one or more of the following:

(1) Women are presented as sexual objects who enjoy pain or humiliation; or

(2) Women are presented as sexual objects who experience sexual pleasure in being raped; or

(3) Women are presented as sexual objects tied up or cut up or mutilated or bruised or physically hurt, or as dismembered or truncated or fragmented or severed into body parts; or

(4) Women are presented as being penetrated by objects or animals; or

(5) Women are presented in scenarios of degradation, injury, abasement, torture, shown as filthy or inferior, bleeding, bruised, or hurt in a context that makes these conditions sexual; or

(6) Women are presented as sexual objects for domination, conquest, violation, exploitation, possession, or use, or through postures or positions of servility or submission or display." ...

The statute provides that the "use of men, children, or transsexuals in the place of women in paragraphs (1) through (6) above shall also constitute pornography under this section." The ordinance as passed in April 1984 defined "sexually explicit" to mean actual or simulated intercourse or the uncovered exhibition of the genitals, buttocks or anus. An amendment in June 1984 deleted this provision, leaving the term undefined.

The Indianapolis ordinance does not refer to the prurient interest, to offensiveness, or to the standards of the community. It demands attention to particular depictions, not to the work judged as a whole. It is irrelevant under the ordinance whether the work has literary, artistic, political, or scientific value. The City and many amici point to these omissions as virtues. They alter the socialization of men and women rather than to vindicate community standards of offensiveness. And as one of the principal drafters of the ordinance has asserted, "if a woman is subjected, why should it matter that the work has other value?" Catherine A. MacKinnon, *Pornography, Civil Rights, and Speech*, 20 *Harv. Civ. Rts.-Civ. L. Rev.* 1, 21 (1985).

Civil rights groups and feminists have entered this case as amici on both sides. Those supporting the ordinance say that it will play an important role in reducing the tendency of men to view women as sexual objects, a tendency that leads to both unacceptable attitudes and discrimination in the workplace and violence away from it. Those opposing the ordinance point out that much radical feminist literature is explicit and depicts women in ways forbidden by the ordinance and that the ordinance would reopen old battles. It is unclear how Indianapolis would treat works from James Joyce's *Ulysses* to Homer's *Iliad*; both depict women as submissive objects for conquest and domination.

We do not try to balance the arguments for and against an ordinance such as this. The ordinance discriminates on the ground of the content of the speech. Speech treating women in the approved way—in sexual encounters "premised on equality" (MacKinnon, *supra*, at 22)—is lawful no matter how sexually explicit. Speech treating women in the disapproved way—as submissive in matters sexual or as enjoying humiliation—is unlawful no matter how significant the literary, artistic, or political qualities of the work taken as a whole. The state may not ordain preferred viewpoints in this way. The Constitution forbids the state to declare one perspective right and silence opponents.

III

"If there is any fixed star in our constitutional constellation, it is that no official, high or petty, can prescribe what shall be orthodox in politics, nationalism, religion, or other matters of opinion or force citizens to confess by word or act their faith therein." *West Virginia State Board of Education v. Barnette*, 319 U.S. 624, 642 (1943). Under the First Amendment the government must leave to the people the evaluation of ideas. Bald or subtle, an idea is as powerful as the audience allows it to be. A belief may be pernicious — the beliefs of Nazis led to the death of millions, those of the Klan to the repression of millions. A pernicious belief may prevail. Totalitarian governments today rule much of the planet, practicing suppression of billions and spreading dogma that may enslave others. One of the things that separates our society from theirs is our absolute right to propagate opinions that the government finds wrong or even hateful.

Under the ordinance graphic sexually explicit speech is "pornography" or not depending on the perspective the author adopts. Speech that "subordinates" women and also, for example, presents women as enjoying pain, humiliation, or rape, or even simply presents women in "positions of servility or submission or display" is forbidden, no matter how great the literary or political value of the work taken as a whole. Speech that portrays women in positions of equality is lawful, no matter how graphic the sexual content. This is thought control. It establishes an "approved" view of women, of how they may react to sexual encounters, of how the sexes may relate to each other. Those who espouse the approved view may use sexual images; those who do not, may not.

Governments that want stasis start by restricting speech. Culture is a powerful force of continuity; Indianapolis paints pornography as part of the culture of power. Change in any complex system ultimately depends on the ability of outsiders to challenge accepted views and the reigning institutions. Without a strong guarantee of freedom of speech, there is no effective right to challenge what is.

IV

The definition of "pornography" is unconstitutional. No construction or excision of particular terms could save it. The offense of trafficking in pornography necessarily fails with the definition....

> ... The district court came to the same conclusion. Its judgment is therefore
>
> Affirmed.[4]

The Supreme Court of the United States subsequently affirmed the 7th Circuit's decision without issuing an opinion. Three justices dissented, however, concluding that the Court should have set the case for argument. 475. U.S. 1001 (1986).

However, any constitutional questions regarding the validity of anti-pornography attempts do not preclude individuals from making better choices for themselves and their families. Even if pornography is constitutionally protected, that obviously does not mean that we are constitutionally compelled to view it or allow our children to view it. Just as the proponents of smut have the constitutional right to advocate for it, others have the constitutional right to speak out against it in an attempt to educate others of its evils and discourage its promotion.

D. Addressing Sex Trafficking on the Internet

Any attempts to reduce trafficking will also have to consider the role of the internet in its promotion. While First Amendment considerations will obviously play an important role in these discussions, consider the ways that human sex trafficking takes place constantly on the internet. Co-author Cheryl Taylor Page discussed these concerns in her article, *How the Internet is Used to Facilitate the Trafficking of Humans as Sex Slaves*:

> **How the Internet Is Used to Facilitate the Trafficking of Humans as Sex Slaves**
>
> Sex trafficking is so widespread, that "no country, no race, no religion, no class and no child is immune." (Nathan Wilson, Founder, Project Meridian Foundation, as cited in Neubauer, 2011)[1]

---

4. American Booksellers Association, Inc. v. Hudnut, 771 F.2d 323 (7th Cir. 1985).

Introduction

Human trafficking is, sadly, a part of the fabric of the 21st century global community, but it has different goals than those of sex trafficking. One expert defines human trafficking as "'an opportunistic response' to the tension between the economic necessity to migrate... and the politically motivated restrictions on migration" (Chuang, 2006, pp. 137, 140).

To give an idea of how widespread sex trafficking is, understand that it is now more profitable for criminals to sell women for sex than it is to sell drugs. Drugs are disposable and finite. Women can be resold over and over and over again. These "commodities" are not as expendable as drugs.

Sex trafficking is multifaceted but can be viewed from the basics of how the crime is defined. The definition of the *severe* form of sex trafficking is defined as being "severe" if force, fraud, or coercion is involved. The other definition is noted as not being "severe" if no such force, fraud, or coercion is present or if the victims cannot prove such ("Protocol to Prevent," 2000). This paper uses the two-tiered definition's portion that does not require a showing of force, fraud, or coercion because that definition examines the exploitive nature of this entire criminal activity. By distinguishing between victims of this heinous industry who are able to show force, fraud, or coercion and those who are not, we are essentially giving the traffickers an "out" in being able to argue that the victim somehow cooperated or agreed to be trafficked.[2]

When one contemplates the sheer volume of victims — from rural areas of Asia to bustling cities such as Brazil — it is astounding to realize we are considering the devastation of the lives of millions of innocent women and children (Corrigan, 2001; Parker, 2007).[3] One must recognize that America is a major importer of sex slaves, with conservative estimates fluctuating between 18,000 and 20,000 (*Opposing and Preventing*, 2012). Of those, nearly 80% are women and half are minors (Parker, 2007). Cases of human trafficking have been reported in all 50 states in the United States (Polaris Project, 2012).

In the document *Opposing and Preventing Global Sexual Trafficking* (2012), posted by the Salvation Army,

> Over the last 10 years, the numbers of women and children [who] have been trafficked have multiplied so that they are now on par with estimates of the numbers of Africans who were enslaved in the 16th and 17th centuries.[4]

Given the expansive growth of this industry and how it is a fluid, ever-changing business, the ways in which this is able to occur must be examined.

Analysis: The Use of the Internet and How It Facilitates Sex Trafficking

There are multiple ways in which "sexual exploitation, such as prostitution, sex tours, bride trafficking, pornography, live sex shows and rape videos for sexual entertainment" are encouraged and advertised (Hughes & Coalition Against Trafficking in Women [CATW], 1988). There once was a time in the not too distant past when individuals who wanted to have illegal sexual relations with a minor or with a stranger had to get up, get dressed, leave their home, and travel to a specific location. These predators would have to travel domestically or internationally to fulfill their perverted desires of molesting these victims. Those days are long gone. Men who desire to have sexual relationships with children and unconsenting women can do so at the push of a button. Finding victims is as easy as turning on a computer and searching online for unwilling individuals who are being used as sex slaves. The Internet has created a booming industry for sex slaves. Even though the majority of sex slaves are women, boys are targeted by predators as well.

One of the many avenues in which victims are taken advantage of and exploited is through the use of electronic media. Hughes and the Coalition Against Trafficking in Women (CATW) (1988) have called the Internet "the most unregulated communications network in the world." The Internet has increased in commercial activity exponentially with the onset of the commercial sex industry. Historically, pornography was available predominantly in "photographs, magazines and videos" (U.S. General Accounting Office [GAO], 2003). Today, pornographic websites, online classified services, and the Internet are large facilitators of sex trafficking (Kloer, 2009). The profits made from offline pornography is estimated to be approximately $8 billion in the United States alone (Regan, 2002). Other estimates show that figure to be even higher at $10 to $14 billion a year (Geisler, 2009). An indication of the vast amounts of money to be made in the porn industry is a court case that pitted a battle over the domain name www.sex.com. The ruling in this case found the domain name to be valued at $65 million (Samson, 2003).[5]

There can be no discounting the power of pornography online as the estimates are that Internet pornography is now believed to net more than $12 billion a year (The Third Way Culture Project, 2006). This is approximately the equivalent of ABC, NBC, and CBS's combined yearly revenue.

Individuals can stay seated in the comfort of their home and "bid" on potential victims for sex and even pay for them via the Internet ("Teen Sold as Sex Slave," 2010). This kind of transaction done in obscurity and anonymity has created an underworld that is fueling the sex trafficking industry. Men are able to hide behind screen names and firewalls and make identification much more difficult that when an officer could apprehend them on the streets.

Craigslist, which is used all over the country to sell anything from clothes to cars and everything in between, has also been used in offering for sale the sexual services of women and children. It has been estimated that Craigslist's profits in 2010 were $122 million with $436.3 million from adult ads alone (Stone, 2010).

Craigslist has been referred to as an "online pimp" due to the extensive volume of sexual services offered on their site. The site officials have responded to negative media attention on this issue by saying that they are policing their website and "looking for signs of exploitation"; however, as of February 2010, there had been more than 3.5 million adult services ads posted by Craigslist the previous calendar year (Kloer, 2010).

Craigslist insists they are changing their process of screening ads, but it must be noted that even if Craigslist had 100 employees whose sole job was to screen these ads, each of these 100 employees would have to review approximately 1,000 ads a day (Kloer, 2010). That is the sheer volume of the quantity of ads posted on this site.

On May 19, 2010, an ad was printed in the *San Francisco Chronicle* as well as listed on the popular website *Huffington Post*. The ad was authored by two young girls who were "sold" repeatedly on Craigslist by the men who exploited them. The girls, one as young as 11, were forced to have sex with strangers for "10 hours with 10 different men." The pimp, of course, pocketed the money and forced these girls to do this over and over and over again. The ad is basically imploring Craigslist to take down and discontinue the "Adult Services" section of Craigslist. The young ladies were being forced to post their own ads on Craigslist and respond personally to the calls generated from their ad. They were transported from city to city and were in fear of beatings or ice water baths.[6]

Cook County Sheriff Thomas J. Dart took a stand against Craigslist and filed a federal lawsuit against the online service for creating a public nuisance via the "erotic services" section of their page. The Sheriff called Craigslist "the single largest source of prostitution" in the U.S. Sheriff Dart's claim was based upon the volume of "human trafficking and juvenile prostitution arrests his vice officers" had made (Sheriff Thomas J. Dart, 2012).[7]

The Internet, as a conduit for sex trafficking, allows for cites like the Yellow Pages Online, mail-order bride sites, fraudulent employment opportunities, as well as numerous e-mail solicitations to be used as ways to trick, coerce, and entice unsuspecting victims into the web that is sex trafficking (*The Internet and Human Trafficking*, 2009).

Another form of exploitation via technology is online photo sharing. This process allows for large-scale production and dissemination of pornographic images of children, without the intrusive photo developer or postal worker uncovering the images (Kloer, 2009). Online photo galleries allow for the sexual deviant to choose victims to be sexually exploited from the comfort and privacy of his home. This also allows for the traffickers to have an even greater amount of flexibility to be mobile, all while sharing their pornographic images to their "clients." These men are now able to choose escorts, companions, or even wives, after viewing this online photo album.

This technology has revolutionalized the way traffickers and pimps exploit their victims, remain "hidden" from the public eye, avoid detection by authorities, and maximize profitability (Kloer, 2009).

One such case of how pornography has moved from printed material to the World Wide Web arose in New Brunswick, Canada. Douglas Stewart, 51, was apprehended for being in possession of "millions of images of child sexual abuse" (CBC News, 2011). The judge in the case admitted that he needed time to access a proper sentence in the case because there had never been such a large amount of child pornography in a single case with a single defendant. This defendant possessed almost six million images of children being abused or in sexual positions.[8] His stash of pornography "'completely overwhelmed'" law enforcement (The Royal Canadian Mounted Police) who had to employ additional servers to accommodate the evidence.[9]

In a similar case in Vancouver, the authorities arrested Warren Allen for being in possession of pornographic images of children (Fraser, 2011). This man was a part of a global community of sexual predators who participate in online trading of images involving children being sexually abused. This global sharing of graphic images of children being abused and abased included children as young as 4 years old. To indicate the global reach of this practice, law enforcement arrested 12 individuals in Canada, ten in the U.S., and three in Europe. Thankfully, 25 children were rescued.

There are numerous cases where men employ discretionary tactics in order to go undetected while sharing these illegal images. One such way is peer-to-peer file sharing programs (*Man Arrested*, 2011). These programs allow users to upload and/or download files to and from other users or groups of users. This is done in order to be surreptitious and to go undetected as they work directly with each other's files. These programs do not allow the content to be viewable to the general public, and the content is not shared on a global, open network (*P2P & File-Sharing Software*, 2012).

The U.S. General Accounting Office (2003) (hereinafter referred to as GAO) has done research on how readily accessible pornographic images of children are on peer-to-peer networks. GAO was able to determine when using specific terms associated with child porn online that 42% of the results netted child porn images, 34% was adult porn, and 24% was nonpornographic.[10] This same group also noted that juveniles are at greater risk of being unintentionally exposed to pornographic images if they use peer-to-peer networks. Predators have realized that if they embed these pornographic images in links that include search terms used by juveniles, these young people will "stumble" upon the images and land on these pornographic sites.[11] Figure 1 contains a classification of downloaded images as gathered through the Customs CyberSmuggling Center.[12]

With the advent of social media sites such as MySpace and Facebook, young people are bombarded with "friend" requests from individuals who could potentially be hundreds of thousands of miles away. These people, who are strangers, could have nefarious motives.

Figure 7.1. Classification of Images Downloaded Through Peer-to-Peer File-Sharing Programs

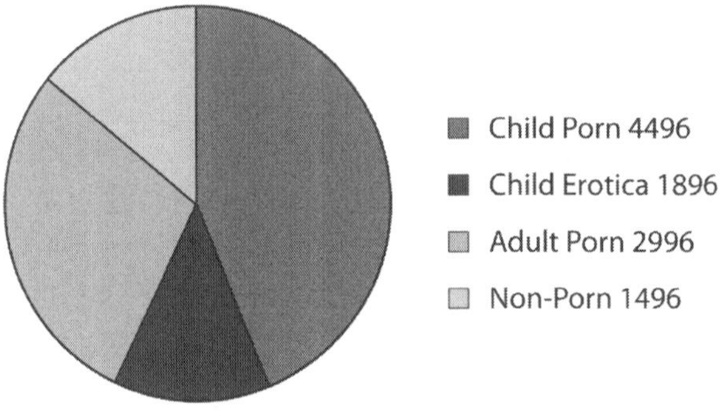

Real Stories of Sex Trafficking Victims

The general public may wonder how and why these victims are able to be sold and trafficked. These women and children are victimized, brutalized, and treated in inhumane ways that create a genuine fear for their lives. Traffickers take control of their victims by isolation, confinement, and holding them captive. These perpetrators use and threaten to use violence against the victims and/or their families. Many victims have been traumatized to the point that they believe that the abuse is their fault and that they deserved it. Another tactic by pimps is to make victims become dependent upon them. Some force drugs on these woman and children thereby creating an addiction. Some victims in this process actually "bond" with the trafficker. These victims are taught to distrust law enforcement and have been told that they will be deported if they attempt to contact the authorities. Many are not even aware that they have a right to go to the police and are duped into believing that they owe exorbitant amounts for fabricated debts (*Ways Traffickers Control Their Victims*, 2011).

There are countless stories of victims being exploited for sexual purposes via the Internet. One such story is of Katya,[13] a foreign exchange student, who came to America with a friend to work as a waitress in Virginia Beach, Virginia. Once she and the friend arrived at Dulles Airport, they were greeted by two men (Alex Maksimenko and Michael Aronov) holding signs with their names on them. These men told the young ladies that they had been reassigned to jobs in Detroit where they would work but also would have time to work on their English skills. They then were given bus tickets to Detroit and had no reason to suspect any illicit motives. When they arrived in Detroit, their identification was confiscated, and they were given "stripping" clothes and told that they would have to dance for men in a nightclub for 12-hour days. As is employed in many trafficking cases, the victims are told that they owe the traffickers an exorbitant amount of money for varying fees. These fees are often five to six times more than the actual travel expenses. These women were severely beaten and sexually abused by their captors. They, and other women and children caught up in this sex trafficking industry, are intimidated through the use of physical violence, mental torture, as well as food and sleep deprivation. Katya and her friend were fortunate enough to confide in a trustworthy customer who, after months of planning, was able to help the ladies escape from captivity. Maksimenko and Aronov were charged, convicted, and sentenced to time in federal prison for these offenses (Kahng, 2007).

As disturbing as this may seem, there is a website, www.slavefarm.com, that openly advertises for sale women who appear to have been beaten, abused, and tortured who are photographed bound, chained, and tied.[14] This site openly claims to be "the world's largest amateur BDSM site since 1998." Beneath a photograph of a woman, hands tied behind her back, lying on her stomach, with her anus appearing to be bruised and bleeding, is a caption that says, "securely cuffed, hogtied and waiting for her punishment. This new slave is learning fast." The photos are horrendous and brutal. They do not appear to be fabricated or staged. Another caption beneath a photograph of a naked lady with her nipples pierced by a chain that is attached, has a whip draped around her neck and has tape on her mouth as well as her eyes covered reads, "Can't see, can't talk… just waiting for pain and lust."[15] Other captions read, "our favorite slave Cathy tied hard and tormented," "beautiful slave babe tied in the pillory," "pet girl with rubber hood forced to drink like a dog," and "blonde bitch gagged and hanging by her feet" (Franzblau, 2007). One photograph shows a naked woman lying on a table on her stomach, her arms are tied to the legs at one side of the table and her legs are tied right below the knees to the other two legs on the table.[16] A member on the site leaves a post that reads, "Man does that look like fun. I would whip that ass til is (*sic*) was red and then fuck that right in the ass. Love her tied down like that."[17]

In addition to having access to graphic, violent, and brutal pornography, membership has its "privileges." Members have the ability to use the site to participate in auctions and rentals of victims, mainly women.[18] The author notes that these sections of the website are "essentially host sites for sex traffickers." When an NGO brought this website's actions and activities to the government's attention, no action was taken against the site, and it still is in operation up to the date of this publication.[19]

An obvious example of this Internet site being used as a means for sex trafficking was a posting that was shown last year in which there was an offer to sell women who were from Thailand and Ghana to men in Sweden, Norway, Denmark, Italy, France, Germany, the Netherlands, and the U.S.[20] These poor and desperate women were being sold at a set rate and were described as "willing to become a 'perverted man's slave, toy and housekeeper.'"[21] After the preference particulars were worked out, the buyer would be sent pictures of the slave and she would then be signed to a contractual slave agreement. The seller agreed to ensure that all entry documents for the slave would be provided as to her entry to the destination country.

One member, in response to an ad that stated, "I am very much interested in being auctioned off and am open to location," gave a warning to all those viewing the post:

> Bear in mind that slavery is illegal in North America, and most parts of the world, so a slave auction would not result in any legally enforceable ownership. While this is a relatively common fantasy, the reality differs a great deal. In my limited experience actual slave auctions can be split into two drastically different categories. First there are auctions held within a community where the buyers and "merchandise" are all well known. These tend to be of relatively short duration and clearly defined terms for how the slave can be used. Since communities engaging in this form of "play," because it is play, tend to police themselves these seem to be generally positive experiences for all involved. People who are not suitable and trusted are not likely to be invited to participate in an event like this. The other sort of slave auction is associated with human trafficking. Nobody in their right mind would want to be subjected to this sort of sale. To these buyers kink or fe-

> tish is irrelevant; the return on investment is the only thing that matters. The property might be put to work in a brothel but just as likely put to work making counterfeit Nikes or harvesting crops. If you disobey these people you're not going to be spanked or caned, but rather beaten within an inch of your life or killed. There is nothing wrong with having this fantasy but you should be EXTREMELY careful about making it real. Think really hard about what you are trying to accomplish and make sure you have considered all of potential consequences, not just the fun ones.[22]

The person who posted this is well aware of the fact that trafficking in humans is illegal and is not advising potential buyers to not pursue the course of action but, rather, to "consider all potential consequences." Many of these members appear to see this all as a "fantasy" life and as a sort of parallel universe. But this is very real to these women who are being dehumanized, humiliated, and tortured for anyone with a computer to see.

This website is in violation of numerous laws, including the federal mandate known as the Mann Act, the Trafficking Victims Protection Act, as well as "most states' laws concerning conspiracy, facilitation, promoting prostitution, rape, assault, battery, and unlawful imprisonment."[23] This website is clearly being used as a vehicle for those intending to traffic in humans and promote the crime of prostitution. This information proliferated on this website should no more be considered free speech than a man walking down the street offering his sister up for sale to be used in pornography or as a prostitute.[24] The government's response to this website has been abysmal.

The World Wide Web is just that: WORLD WIDE. A person could be in Tokyo, Japan, writing another individual in Houston, Texas, and their communications are instantaneous. No delay in call and response. This ability to communicate to individuals all over the world at such a fast pace and with virtual ease has allowed websites like www.Dexterhorn.com to flourish and grow.[25] This is a website that, in no uncertain terms, promotes sex in Asia with underage individuals and has the banner of "Where to Find Sex and Adventure WORLDWIDE."[26]

In order to access the information regarding the "naked photo galleries," reading books online and video clips of "Hot Latina" and "Hot Asian" chicks, one would have to sign up to become a member and pay $7.95 per month.[27] The site sells pornographic videos as well as offers some pornographic videos for free in an effort to promote the sex tourism business.

Some of the videos that are for sale on the site include *Thai Teens in Heat, Vol. 1*, *Thai Teens in Heat, Vol. 2*, *Thai Teens in Heat, Vol. 3*, *Thai Teens in Heat, Vol. 4*, as well as *Thai Teens in Heat, Vol. 5*. The store also sells *How to Get Laid in Thailand*, *Oriental Baby Dolls*, and *Sex Odyssey in Thailand* (Franzblau, 2007).

The site sells books and includes titles such as *A Gentleman's Guide: The Erotic Women of Southeast Asia*. The book encourages men with low self-esteem to not be discouraged by their looks by saying,

> Southeast Asia: there's more pussy out there than you ever dreamed possible. Best of all, it's readily available to anyone. If you don't believe me ask my old friend, "Wheelchair Tom," as we called him. He was the ugliest 55 year old son-of-a-bitch I've ever known. If that guy could score three underage girls a day, without even blinking, I have a feeling you'll do just fine (as quoted in Franzblau, 2007, pp. 2–3).

This website not only promotes sex tourism but encourages travelers to videotape their sexual encounters with the children and women with whom they will be having sex (Franzblau, 2007).[28] The books note that the traveler is free to have any photographs developed in Thailand and mailed back to the U.S. but ONLY if the victim is over 18 years of age. The site offers materials that speak of not only renting the victims but of buying them as well. One of the many factors that contribute to the proliferation of sex trafficking is the lack of financial and educational opportunities offered to so many poor people in this world. Traffickers take advantage of that fact and capitalize on their victims' vulnerabilities. The books speak of that fact by signifying to the traveler that they are free to negotiate with the families of these young people as their desperation may get the traveler a good deal. The Internet is currently being used to promote and facilitate "johns" travelling to foreign countries to have sex with children and being offered opportunities to buy them from parents. Many times, these families are in desperate straits, impoverished, or have been tricked or coerced into selling their children. The Internet is being used to allow this to happen seamlessly and with little to no effort on the part of the buyer.

Conclusion

Likewise, for those of us who are in position to do something to combat human slavery, however small our contribution, neutrality is a sin (Inspector General Joseph E. Schmitz, Department of Defense, 2011).

The Internet has the power to allow people to communicate in ways once never imagined. The amount of information accessible to people just by way of their fingers is amazing. We can talk to one another, see one another, and exchange ideas with one another from hundreds of thousands of miles apart. This incredible way of communicating with one another has the potential for good and the potential for evil. This same Internet can be used to facilitate harmful and devastating pain in the lives of many. The Internet has allowed our world to become a global village where borders are no longer limiting where individuals may travel. This can be a positive; but in the context of sex trafficking, this is a negative.

The Internet is currently being used to facilitate sex trafficking via websites that advertise women and children for sex, websites that host auctions for people for rental and sale, and websites that advertise and promote sex tourism as well as pornography. The Internet is an avenue that traffickers, pimps, and johns have figured out can promote their business to levels never seen prior to the Internet's wide expansion and use.

Traffickers have created a fantasy world for the demand that is evident for these victims. They feed into the basest desires of johns, supplying these predators with women and children who are helpless to defend themselves. This fantasy world is all too real for these victims as the laws and the governing authorities have yet to adequately respond to this situation.

Trafficking includes a link in the chain of components that allow the industry to operate. The hidden link in the chain that must be addressed is the demand link (George, in press). We must tackle the demand issue in order to make a dent in the problem.

The CATW offered some laudable goals in its recommendation to the United Nations Working Group on Contemporary Forms of Slavery:

> [It is recommended] that governments, as a matter of priority, review, amend, and enforce existing laws, to prevent the misuse of the internet for trafficking, prostitution, and the sexual exploitation of women and children; that governments and nongovernmental organizations undertake further investigation of the misuse of the internet for the purpose of promoting and/or carrying out trafficking, prostitution, and the sexual exploitation of women and children; urges governments to act more forcefully to eliminate the trafficking in persons, the exploitation of the prostitution of others, and sexual exploitation on the internet; urges governments, in cooperation with interested nongovernmental organizations, to develop educational programs and policies and laws addressing the use of the internet by prostitution customers for the purpose of engaging in sexual exploitation; recommends that governments investigate and use as evidence of crimes and acts of discrimination advertising, correspondence, and other communications over the internet to promote sex trafficking, prostitution, and sex tourism... calls for new levels of cooperation among governments and national and regional law enforcement bodies in order to

> combat the escalating trafficking and prostitution of women and children, the globalization of this industry, and the misuse of the internet to promote and carry out acts of sex trafficking, sex tourism, sexual violence, and sexual exploitation (Hughes & CATW, 1998).

The World Wide Web is being used in such a way that many victims are being caught in its web of violence, sexual deviation, and fetishes. We, as a global community, must rise to the challenge and seek to find ways to punish the perpetrators and free the victims from this life of slavery.[5]

1. Nathan Wilson is the founder of the Project Meridian Foundation in Arlington Virginia, which helps police identify traffickers and their victims.

2. We are in essence providing a ready-made defense for these perpetrators who will argue that a victim was not forced or induced via fraud or coercion and as such she understood and/or agreed to be trafficked. These are cases were a victim may not be able to prove force, fraud, or coercion but nevertheless that is how she was tricked into this industry.

3. Parker (2007) references the movies *Sold* and *Trade*, which both chronicle the stories of victims of the sex trade and how their lives have been impacted.

4. Quoting Dr. Laura Lederer, a senior state department advisor on trafficking. She has studied sexual trafficking for over 20 years at Harvard University.

5. The District Court further awarded plaintiffs $40 million compensatory and $25 million in punitive damages against Defendant Cohen.

6. *See* www.stopenslavement.org/archives/stop-traff806.pdf (as quoted from Saada Saar [2010]).

7. Quoting from the article: "Sheriff Dart demanded [Craigslist] either better monitor [the] postings or remove the category altogether." Just two months later, amid growing national pressure, Craigslist's administrators relented and made the very changes Dart demanded. Continuing that fight, Dart established a first-of-its-kind prostitution intervention team, which has drawn nationwide interest. Made up of former prostitutes and licensed supervisors, sheriff's staffers accompany vice officers on prostitution stings and perform on-site intervention, after an arrest, encouraging women to immediately go to a recovery house and proceed with life-changing choices.

8. Stewart had been collecting pornographic images since the 1980s and had in his possession 4.7 million pornographic images and 1.2 million depictions of children nude or in bathtubs.

---

5. Cheryl George, *How the Internet Is Used to Facilitate the Trafficking of Humans as Sex Slaves*, Law Enforcement Executive Forum 12.1 at 40–50 (2012), http://works.bepress.com/cheryl_george/3, reprinted with permission from the Law Enforcement Training and Standards Board.

9. It took approximately 700 hours to categorize the images.

10. Of the 1,286 titles, 543 were child porn, which equaled 42%. In another search (using three specific words), the analyst downloaded 341 images, 44% of which were pornographic images of children.

11. These "search terms" included names of cartoon characters and celebrities.

12. The GAO noted that because pornographic images of children cannot be accessed legally by people or institutions outside of law enforcement for legal purposes, GAO worked with the Customs CyberSmuggling Center to perform the requisite searches. Customs "downloaded and analyzed the files; GAO performed analyses based on keywords and file names only."

13. Katya is not her actual name. Her identity is being concealed for her protection and privacy.

14. *See* www.slavefarm.com. Please note that this site is very graphic and disturbing (last visited November 9, 2011).

15. *Id.*

16. *See* www.slavefarm.com. Please note that this site is very graphic and disturbing (last visited November 9, 2011).

17. *Id.* Member's identity is not revealed.

18. *Id.* The site is being used as a vehicle to sell, purchase, and rent human beings.

19. *Id.* Equality Now went to the FBI and to the Department of Justice with "auctions" that were being held on www.slavefarm.com, and the governmental agencies indicated that if the women were not participating against their will, then they would not launch an investigation into the matter. I last visited the site on November 11, 2011.

20. *Id.*

21. *Id.* The seller was required to give an e-mail address, state whether he wanted a woman from Ghana or Thailand, her age, and what kind of sex she would be performing for him.

22. *Id.*

23. *Id.*

24. There is really no difference in these.

25. This site is based out of California; http://dexterhorn.com (last visited November 11, 2011).

26. *Id.* The opening page of the website shows approximately 11 Asian girls all naked, some in sexually suggestive poses with one another. The females all appear to be very young, but the website has a disclaimer at the bottom of the web page that reads, "All images contained on the website of a sexual nature are of persons 18 years of age or older."

27. *Id.* The site offers differing plans at differing prices. The basic "Silver Plan" costs $7.95 per month with some limited access to certain features. It costs $35.69 for 180 days for the "Gold Plan," which allows greater access, or $59.69 for a year with full access to the site's features.

28. *Id.* at p. 268. The book encourages the traveler by saying, "'there's nothing more exciting than making your own private collection of nudity photos and XXX rated home videos. When you see yourself on TV doing it with 2 or 3 young girls at the same time, well-hey! You're a star! Yeah, you're fat, toothless and stupid, but sure, you're a star.'"

References

CBC News. (2011, August 19). *Sentencing adjourned in record child porn case.* Retrieved February 14, 2012, from www.cbc.ca/news/canada/new-brunswick/story/2011/08/19/nb-moncton-child-porn-sentencing.html.

Chuang, J. (2006). Beyond a snapshot: Preventing human trafficking in the global economy. *Indiana Journal of Global Legal Studies,* 13(1), 137–63.

Corrigan, K. (2001). Putting the Brakes on the global trafficking of women for the sex trade: An analysis of existing regulatory schemes to stop the flow of traffic. *Fordham International Law Journal,* 25, 151–214.

Franzblau, K. (2007). Slavefarm, sex tours and the pimp John T: Using pornography to advance trafficking, sex tourism, and prostitution. In D.E. Guinn & J. DiCaro (Eds.), *Pornography: Driving the demand in international sex trafficking.* Los Angeles: Captive Daughters Media.

Fraser, K. (2011, July 21). Vancouver man caught in global child porn ring released on bail. *The Province.* Retrieved November 9, 2011, from www.theprovince.come/news/vancouver+caught+global+child+porn+ring+released+bail/5140888/story.html.

Geisler, E. (2009). *Pornography: A mirror of American culture?* Shelflife@Texas website. Retrieved March 19, 2012, from www.utexas.edu/opa/blogs/shelflife/2009/02/11/pornography-a-mirror-of-american-culture.

George, C. (in press). Jailing the Johns: The issue of demand in human sex trafficking, *Florida Costal Law Review.* (Forthcoming Spring 2012).

Hughes, D. M., & Coalition Against Trafficking in Women (CATW). (1988, May). *Misuse of the Internet for the purposes of sexual exploitation*(Resolution drafted by Hughes submitted by CATW to the United Nations Working Group on Contemporary Forms of Slavery, Geneva, Switzerland). Retrieved February 9, 2012, from www.uri.edu/artsci/wms/hughes/ppr.htm.

The Internet and human trafficking. (2009, January). *Anti-Human Trafficking Newsletter,* 7(1). Retrieved February 9, 2012, from http://homepage.mac.com/srjeanschafersds/stop-traffic/archives/stoptraff701.pdf.

Kahng, G. (2007, December 3). *Sex slaves, human trafficking… in America?* Today People website. Retrieved February 14, 2012, from http://today.msnbc.msn.com/id/22083762/ns/today-today_people/t/sex-slaves-human-trafficking-america.

Kloer, A. (2009). *The internet's role in human trafficking.* Abolish-Liberate-Emancipate NOW website. Retrieved February 9, 2012, from http://mgjack.wordpress.com/2009/09/23/the-internets-role-in-human-trafficking.

Kloer, A. (2010, February 27). *Boycott online pimp Craigslist; use Kijiji instead.* Change.org website. Retrieved February 9, 2012, from http://humantrafficking.change.org/blog/view/boycott_online_pimp_craigslist_use_kijiji_instead.

Man arrested for sharing child porn. (2011, November 2). WTHITV.com website. Retrieved February 14, 2012, from www.wthitv.com/dpp/news/crime/man-arrested-for-sharing-child-porn.

Neubauer, C. (2011, April 23). Sex trafficking in the U.S. called "epidemic": No class and no child is immune. *The Washington Times.* Retrieved February 9, 2012, from www.washingtontimes/news/2011apr/23/sex-trafficking-us-called-epidemic/?page=all.

Opposing and preventing global sexual trafficking. (2012). The Salvation Army website. Retrieved February 9, 2012, from www1.salvationarmy.org/ihq/www_sa.nsf/vwdynamicarrays/B5DD72A243A1150B80256E49006C621E?opendocument.

P2P & file-sharing software. (2012). Retrieved February 14, 2012, from http://download.cnet.com/windows/p2p-file-sharing-software.

Parker, K. (2007, September 28). *Slavery by any other name.* Real Clear Politics website. Retrieved February 9, 2012, from www.realclearpolitics.com/articles/2007/09/slavery_by_another_name.html.

Polaris Project. (2012). *Human trafficking cheat sheet.* Retrieved February 9, 2012, from www.polarisproject.org/resources/reources-by-topic/human-trafficking.

Protocol to prevent, suppress and punish trafficking in persons, especially women and children, supplementing the United Nations Convention Against Transnational Organized Crime, Annex II. (2000, December 12). *General Assembly Resolution 55/25,* UN Doc A/55/383.

Regan, K. (2002, January 31). Online porn profits still lurk in shadows. *E-Commerce Times.* Retrieved February 9, 2012, from www.ecommercetimes.com/story/16088.html?wlc-1288315323.

Saada Saar, M. (2010, May 19). Craig, please listen to us. *The Huffington Press.* Retrieved February 9, 2012, from www.huffingtonpost.com/malika-saasa-saar/craig-please-listen-to-us_b_582237.html.

Samson, M. (2003). *Gary Kremen, et al. v Stephen Michael Cohen, et al.* Internet Library of Law and Court Decisions website. Retrieved March 19, 2012, from www.internetlibrary.com/cases/lib_case326.cfm.

Schmitz, J.E. (2011). *Initiative against sexual trafficking.* Notable Quotes website. Retrieved February 14, 2012, from www.iast.net/notablequotes.htm.

Sheriff Thomas J. Dart. (2012). Cook County Sheriff Thomas J. Dart website. Retrieved February 9, 2012, from http://news.change.org/stories/the-internet-role-in-human-trafficking.

Stone, B. (2010, April 29). More on Craigslist and its adult ads. *New York Times* (Bits section). Retrieved March 19, 2012 from http://bits.blogs.nytimes.com/2010/04/29/more-on-craigslist-and-its-adult-services-ads.

Teen sold as sex slave on Craigslist: Experts say 100,000 in the U.S. are sold for sex every day. (2010, May 11). *KTLA News.* Retrieved March 19, 2012, from www.ktla.com/news/extras/ktla-sex-slaves-sweeps,0,3561067.story.

The Third Way Culture Project. (2006, January). *Taking on the Internet porn industry: Fighting on the side of families with children.* Retrieved February 9, 2012, from http://content.thirdway.org/publications/19/Third_Way_Memo_-_Taking_On_The_Internet_Porn_Industry_fighting_On_The_Side_of_Families_With_Children.pdf.

U.S. General Accounting Office (GAO), Committee on Government Reform, House of Representatives. (2003, March 13). *Child pornography is readily accessible over peer-to-peer networks.* Retrieved February 9, 2012, from www.gao.gov/new.items/d03537t.pdf.

Ways traffickers control their victims. (2011, January). *Anti-Human Trafficking Newsletter,* 9(1). Retrieved February 14, 2012, from www.stopenslavement.org/archives/stoptraff901.pdf.

E. Lawsuits against Traffickers

As noted in previous chapters, many of the federal and state legislative efforts to reduce trafficking contain provisions which allow victims to bring civil lawsuits against their traffickers. While the costs and other practical considerations might make it difficult for individual victims who are isolated to ever be able to bring these claims, there is nonetheless hope that private attorneys and advocacy groups will pursue such litigation. For example, the Southern Poverty Law Center brought an action against shipping companies who were involved in trafficking. *See* http://www.usnews.com/news/articles/2013/08/08/more-human-trafficking-lawsuits-filed-again st-major-us-shipbuilder. Another advocacy group for sex trafficking victims, Shared Hope, reports of ongoing litigation attempts by trafficking victims against an Internet page promoting trafficking. *See* http://sharedhope.org/.

F. Forced Abortion

While there is deep disagreement between pro-life and pro-choice advocates regarding the issue of abortion, there is one issue on which people of good faith on all sides of the abortion issue can agree. That involves the horrific situation where a pregnant sex trafficking victim is coerced into having an abortion by her traffickers so that she can be returned to generating income once again for those traffickers. It is obvious that the victim is suffering a double assault on her physical integrity under the circumstances. When a minor trafficking victim is involved, it is even more obvious that she is not consenting to this compounded violation. Maria Tavano discusses issues regarding forced abortions in her article, *Trafficking in Persons: A Focus on preventing Forced Labor.*[6] Stephen Wagner, who served as the head of the anti-trafficking program in the Bush administration argued: "[I]f someone is being trafficked — which is to say, under the domination of a pimp/trafficker — she is by definition unable to provide informed consent to an

6. Maria Tavano, *Trafficking in Persons: A Focus on preventing Forced Labor*, 32 Women's Rts. L. Rep. 324, 350 (2011).

abortion or to a regime of contraception. The victim has no voice in this decision. Indeed, providing such services to a victim of sexual trafficking benefits only the trafficker by getting the victim back out on the street and making money sooner.... The mortality rate for someone in commercial sexual exploitation is 40 times higher than for a non-exploited person of the same age. Helping a victim returned to exploitation more quickly by terminating a pregnancy increases the odds of death."[7]

At a minimum, then abortion providers must exercise extreme sensitivity to the possibility that one of their patients is a trafficking victim. The woman or girl should be interviewed apart from her potential traffickers. The providers should be willing to refer the trafficking victim immediately to law enforcement and to agencies which can assist her in escaping. Entities and agencies which can help are discussed below.

G. Think before Patronizing Trafficking Industries

President Obama urges, in the 2015 Trafficking Persons Report of the U.S. State Department, "Every citizen can take action by speaking up and insisting that the clothes they wear, the food they eat, and the products they buy are made free of forced labor. Business and non-profit leaders can assure their supply chains do not exploit individuals in bondage."[8] What are some of the industries where forced labor might be involved? On page 23 of the 2015 report, eleven sectors are cited as those which involve the highest risk of trafficking:[9]

1. Agriculture
2. Construction
3. Electronics
4. Fishing and Aquaculture
5. Forestry
6. Healthcare
7. Hospitality
8. Housekeeping and Facilities Operations
9. Mining and Basic Metal Production
10. Textile and Apparel Manufacturing
11. Transportation and Warehousing

---

7. Elizabeth Bewley, *A New Form of Ideological Capture: Abortion Politics and the Trafficking Victims Protection Act*, 8 Harv. L. & Pol'y Rev. 229, 248, n.146 (Winter 2014).

8. U.S. Dep't of State, *2015 Trafficking In Persons Report*, July 2015 at 44, *available at* http://www.state.gov/documents/organization/245365.pdf (last accessed Sept. 14, 2015).

9. *Id.* at 23.

A number of specific commodities are also listed:

- Bamboo
- Bananas
- Beans
- Brass
- Bricks
- Cattle
- Charcoal
- Citrus
- Coal
- Cocoa
- Coffee
- Coltan, Tungsten, Tin
- Copper
- Corn
- Cotton
- Diamonds
- Fish
- Flowers
- Gold
- Granite and Other Stone
- Jewels
- Leather
- Melons
- Nuts
- Palm Oil
- Pineapple
- Rice
- Rubber
- Salt
- Shrimp
- Silk
- Silver
- Steel
- Strawberries
- Sugar
- Sunflowers
- Tea
- Tobacco
- Tomatoes
- Wheat
- Wool
- Zinc

Obviously it is not likely that any individual consumer could avoid purchasing all of the listed commodities or avoid services from all of the industries on the list. Any widespread boycott of all those listed would be counterproductive because non-traffickers would be harmed by such a boycott. However, at a minimum, maintaining awareness of the problem might help consumers make more intelligent choices by enquiring of the providers regarding the origin of their products.

H. Combat Sex Tourism

A critical component in efforts to eradicate sex trafficking will be the reduction of sex tourism, particularly as it involves child victims. Co-author Page addressed this issue in her article, *Where Has Their Innocence Gone? Addressing Child Sex Tourism.*[10] Following is another excerpt from that article:

> **Problems Combating Sex Tourism**
>
> There are three key areas which prevent the effective combat of sex tourism: (1) corruption, (2) prosecution setbacks, and (3) the victims themselves. Each of these three areas presents

10. Cheryl George, *Where Has Their Innocence Gone? Addressing Child Sex Tourism*, Law Enforcement Executive Forum 14.3 (2014): 98–111. Reprinted with permission

unique challenges in the prosecution and handling of these cases.

Corruption

Sex tourism is an industry ripe in corruption. What are the reasons for such rampant corruption? Many of these destination countries are what can be classified as third world or developing countries. As such, state resources are limited, and wages are not high, especially among officials such as judges, police, and others (Fredette, 2009, p. 15). This is particularly troublesome since laws are only as effective as those who enforce them. For example, in Honduras, police officers have an average income of only $1,000 a year (Beyer, 2000–2001, p. 321; Cotter, 2009, p. 496). Such wages make it extremely tempting to look the other way, remain silent, or make "mistakes" in regards to collecting evidence and investigation.

A State Department report on Cambodia made the statement that "it was widely believed that some law enforcement and other government officials received bribes that facilitated the sex trade" (Cotter, 2009, p. 497). There was one case of a particular Cambodian judge who found two suspects not guilty of sexually abusing children even though there were photographs of men having sex with young children and e-mails discussing what they had done to the children (Atwell, 2008–2009, p. 175). A sex offender in the Cambodian legal system only has to pay $10,000 to $30,000 to have the charges dropped (p. 175). On a side note, Cambodian judges are paid $15 a week (Fredette, 2009, p. 15), so it is easy to see why some judges are tempted to make such decisions. The victims also see these sex tourists escaping justice, so they are even less likely to report it in the future as they lose faith in the justice system.

Another factor that contributes to corruption is lack of training. One example of this is the adversarial questioning of child prostitutes. Instead of treating the child as a victim, the police are treating the child as the problem, leading to the child

---

from the Illinois Law Enforcement Training and Standards Board.

to being uncooperative and not returning to the authorities after subsequent abuse. (Fredette, 2009, p. 16).

Prosecution Setbacks

Prosecution within the U.S. can be hindered due to expense of the prosecution (Patterson, 2007, p. 18). Considerable expense is incurred with getting witnesses and victims available and ready for testimony. The victim must be brought over from the destination country for testimony and remain for several days. Of course, there are ways around this with the advance of technology in video or satellite links (Fredette, 2009, pp. 25–26). This keeps the victim in a more comfortable setting in his or her home country. Even with the expenses involved, many police departments lack a specialized unit to investigate child exploitation and abuse (Patterson, 2009, p. 18).

Another potential issue for prosecution is when the destination country does not have an extradition treaty with the U.S. There is a way around this if the destination country cooperates. The U.S. can accomplish this by revoking a suspect's passport (Atwell, 2000–2001, p. 182). A can be denied a passport if he or she is "subject to an outstanding Federal warrant of arrest for a felony" (p. 182). Once the passport is revoked, the U.S. shows the destination country that the suspect is without a valid passport, and the destination country expels the person. From here, the suspect is escorted by ICE agents. From there, the suspect may be brought to trial in one of three venues: (1) in the district where the offender is first brought, (2) in the district where the offender last lived, or, if the offender's previous residence is unknown, (3) in the District of Colombia. Of course, such a way around extradition is contingent upon the cooperation of the destination country (p. 182).

The Victims

Many victims do not trust the police, especially when they see the police turn a blind eye, as already discussed. Even when legal representatives get the victims to stick around for long prosecutions, their memory may have been dimmed with the passage of time (Fredette, 2009, p. 25). Then there are also those victims brought to the U.S. for prosecutions. They can be traumatized through coming to such culturally unfamiliar states resulting in a compromised testimony. Some Non-Governmental Organizations (NGOs) have solved this problem by working closely with both victims and police departments, recording statements (p. 25) and caring for the victim during trials when the victims are not needed in court (Atwell, 2008–2009, p. 183). Another problem as it pertains to victims, is trying to ascertain to child's age. This was a problem specific to a case of a child in Honduras who had no documentation to confirm the child's age. Generally, a medical examination is required to get legal proof of the child's age (Beyer, 2000–2001, p. 322).

Solutions and Conclusion

In this day and age of technology and innovation, there is no reason why things cannot be improved in combating sex tourism. The resources and the laws are in existence. The willpower is present. The vast majority of people in the world abhor the notion of a child being forced to engage in sex acts. Equally abhorrent are those children being forced into prostitution through debt bondage, kidnapping, or slavery. So what can be done to further this cause?

In assessing the situation, one has to realize that these criminal enterprises in the flesh trade need to be specifically targeted. One possibility here is establishing an agency or organization like the Drug Enforcement Administration (DEA) or the Bureau of Alcohol, Tobacco, Firearms, and Explosives (ATF) that specifically goes after trafficking. This organization could work both internationally and domestically at curtailing trafficking activities, including sex tourism. Such an organization could work in tandem with foreign governments, developing training programs to deal with sex tourism and coordinating with local law enforcement to go after the criminal organizations running the sex trade. This agency would focus specifically on eradication and the proper funding (state and federal) to be efficient and operate in an effective manner.

Another potential solution needs to be increased victim support. Counseling services should be made available to these victims as well as some kind of halfway house transition them into society. The local police in these areas, with increased training, need to find a way to gain the trust of these victims so that the victims will not be afraid of confiding in them. The fears of repercussion from the pimps, brothel owners, or the criminal elements keep the victims from reporting abuse. The police or government need to find a way to create a safe zone for victims of sex tourism.

There also needs to easier ways to get their involvement in prosecuting these crimes — for example, eliminating the need to have the victims physically present for trials. It is a great expense to fly them around the world for testifying, especially in this technological age. Australian courts allow testimony through video link for the purpose curbing "unreasonable expense, inconvenience, psychological harm, or intimidation" (Fredette, 2009, p. 126). If that option is unavailable for evidentiary reasons, one author suggests bringing all cases to trial in one district, or at least one district close to the geographical area close to the affected area. For example, in Southeast Asia, the district could be Guam. The advantages here include less travel, to testify, less time away from families, less time on airplanes, and less time on airplanes, and less time in strange hotel rooms (Atwell 2008–2009, p. 183). Also, have counselors who are trained in this area readily available to talk to survivors (King, 2008). These women and children have been through horrendous acts of brutality and having someone to talk to can mean the difference between testifying against the perpetrator or trial or not. It could also mean the difference between life or death.

We must also tighten and make less confusing our immigration laws. Individuals and groups who have a low social standing are most vulnerable. We need to clarify which laws are on the books that are designed to assist victims of sex trafficking. If we do not have any that are specifically designed to assist them, then we need to enact such measures and ensure that they are utilized. Traffickers take advantage of the numerous loopholes in the laws and exploit the situation even further given that knowledge. We must end discrimination against minorities, and the disparate treatment of women and girls ("UNICED," n.d.).

We have to also work to create better financial opportunities for the poor. Traffickers, via "force, fraud or coercion" (Polaris Project, 2014a), are able to get parents to surrender their children to this industry. Many parents are unaware of the exact situation that they are placing their children in, but some are aware and still make the same choice. If given a chance wherein they could afford to pay for their family's basic needs, many (if not all) parents would never agree to sell their child into a life as a sex slave. But without other financial avenues, it is either sell your child and use the money to feed your other children or let them all starve to death. That is a real situation that many impoverished, uneducated families face ("Children for Sale!," 2010).

The majority of sexual predators who travel around the globe to have sex with children are westerners (or from industrialized nations). They travel to countries that are much less developed, where the laws are either nonexistent or barely enforced and where children are cheap and in abundance ("Children for Sale!," 2010). Enforce the laws that are on the books. In countries that are slow in having such laws, use the UN to make them enact these kind of laws. And where the countries have the laws but are slow and not enforcing them, place economic sanctions on them in an effort to get them to prosecute these traffickers and johns (UN Security Sanctions Committee, n.d.). Where the john abuses the child from the comforts of his office, bedroom or car via mobile electronic device, use the laws on the books to prosecute him or her.

Another way to assist with the problem of children being commercially exploited is to help raise awareness about the need to educate children (especially girls) around the globe. Malala Yousafzai won the hearts of millions as she became the face and voice of homeless, uneducated, marginalized children around the world ("The Heroic Women of the Year 2013," 2014). She has lent her voice to the cry for children to be educated, especially girls. "One child, one teacher, one book and one pen can change the world" (Sagan, 2013). Where there is abundant poverty and a vast lack of education (or educational opportunities), there is rampant vulnerability and exploitation. We, as a global community must recognize that when one child is harmed, our global peace is threatened. When one child is sold online to a predator (virtually or otherwise), we are all at risk for the same violence occurring in our backyard. Until we abhor the predator's brutal disregard for the value of human life, we are all in jeopardy of turning a blind eye and a deaf ear to what has become the worst crime against children in the history of the world.

I. Continuing to Educate Ourselves

Co-author Cheryl Taylor Page's *Creighton Law Review* article offers some approaches:[11]

IV. SUGGESTIONS FOR INCREASING EFFECTIVENESS IN PREVENTION, PROSECUTION, PROTECTION, AND PARTNERSHIP

There are no easy answers to the problems presented in global sex trafficking. One school of thought believes that legalizing prostitution will help alleviate the undesirable demand for women and children who do not enter prostitution voluntarily. In fact, the result is the exact opposite. Decriminalizing prostitution has resulted in a greater explosion of "local, legalized prostitution industries, an increase in illegal activities in these areas, and stepped-up trafficking of women and children from other countries to meet the new demand."[95] For example, in

---

11. Shelly George, *The Strong Arm of the Law is Weak: How the Trafficking Victims Protection Act Fails to Assist Effectively Victims of the Sex Trade*, 45 Creighton L. Rev. 563, 578–79 (2012), reprinted with permission from the Creighton Law Review.

Victoria, Australia, as well as in Sydney, Australia, both places where prostitution has been legalized, the number of establishments with prostitutes has doubled (Victoria) and tripled (Sydney).[96] Legalizing prostitution is not (and should never be) the answer to resolving problems involving sex trafficking.

Perhaps the best way to get through the apparent issues surrounding identification of victims and the inherent flaws in "certifying" victims is education. Educate the personnel of law enforcement agencies, first responders, and government offices as to what sex trafficking entails. Teach them what sex trafficking looks like, what it does not look like, and how to properly and appropriately identify a victim of sex trafficking.

Trafficking thrives in the shadows. And it can be easy to dismiss it as something that happens to someone else, somewhere else. But that is not the case. Trafficking is a crime that involves every nation on earth, and that includes our own.[97] What must be done to educate and address these woeful inadequacies in our legal system?

There are numerous organizations that have honorably taken on the task of bringing awareness and education to this heinous industry. One such organization is The No Project. This organization is an "independent anti-slavery [and anti-human trafficking] public awareness initiative that focuses on the role of demand and specifically targets youth awareness through MUSIC, the ARTS, EDUCATION and SOCIAL MEDIA."[98] The group aims to present a realistic picture of the reality of human trafficking by way of visual media throughout the world.[99]

Another group that is doing a great job of educating the public is The Polaris Project. This organization is an advocate for stronger federal and state laws, and it operates a resource hotline for human trafficking.[100]

Not For Sale is a non-governmental organization ("NGO") that "equips and mobilizes smart activists to deploy innovative solutions to re-abolish slavery" globally.[101] Ending slavery around the world is the mission of another NGO, Free the Slaves. Free the Slaves believes in attacking the systems that allow slavery to flourish. Their goal is to see the eradication of slavery in our lifetime and to educate the public as to the atrocities of twenty-first century slavery.[102]

An additional resource for education involving human trafficking (including sex trafficking) is "Stop Trafficking! Anti-Human Trafficking Newsletter." This newsletter offers invaluable information regarding awareness, advocacy, and action. The group promotes awareness in regards to human trafficking and the exchange of best practices in advocacy. It also encourages the empowerment of human trafficking survivors in addition to recommending actions to counter human trafficking.[103]

Each of these organizations, and many more like them, is actively engaged in raising awareness and educating others about the aspects and characteristics of sex trafficking. The key to solving many of the dilemmas faced in the enforcement of the laws currently on the books is education. If we are able to raise awareness and educate those in positions to make a difference for those bound by the chains of slavery, we can make a dent in this multi-billion dollar industry. If we can educate, we can make a difference. If we can make a difference, we can end slavery. If we can end slavery, we can save lives.[12]

95. Jody Raphael, Listening to Olivia: Violence, Poverty, and Prostitution 203 (2004).

96. *Id.* at 203–04.

97. Press Conference, Hillary R. Clinton, U.S. Sec'y of State (June 16, 2009).

98. About the NO Project, NO Project, http://thenoproject.org/english/the-no-project/about-the-no-project-2/ (last visited Apr. 7, 2012). The founder of this non-governmental organization is a modern day abolitionist who fights trafficking and slavery in Greece and other parts of Europe.

99. *Id.*

100. Polaris Project, Polaris Project, http://www.polarisproject.org/about-us/introduction (last visited Apr. 7, 2012). The Polaris Project has been working to assist victims of human trafficking since 2002. *Id.* The hotline (1-888-3737-888) operates to assist Polaris' clients as well as victims of human trafficking. *Id.*

101. Vision, Not For Sale, http://www.notforsalecampaign.org/about/vision/ (last visited on Apr. 7, 2012).

102. About Us, Free the Slaves, https://www.freetheslaves.net/SSLPage.aspx?pid=285 (last visited Apr. 7, 2012).

---

12. *Id.*

103. *Id.*; *see also* Stop Trafficking Newsletter, *Stop Trafficking!*, http://stopenslavement.org/ (last visited Apr. 7, 2012).

J. "S.O.S.!"

There might be an emergency situation where someone comes in contact with a trafficking victim. Where can that victim turn for help? These situations are life and death emergencies which merit a 911 call to law enforcement. The Polaris Project also provides a toll-free emergency number: 1-888-373-7888. Someone needing assistance can also text "HELP" or "INFO" to BeFree (233733). The Project offers specific advice to someone who encounters a victim who needs to escape, and also provides some warning signs to alert people to the outward signs that victims of trafficking often demonstrate. These include the following, although the list is not exhaustive:

Common Work and Living Conditions: The Individual(s) in Question

- Is not free to leave or come and go as he/she wishes
- Is under 18 and is providing commercial sex acts
- Is in the commercial sex industry and has a pimp/manager
- Is unpaid, paid very little, or paid only through tips
- Works excessively long and/or unusual hours
- Is not allowed breaks or suffers under unusual restrictions at work
- Owes a large debt and is unable to pay it off
- Was recruited through false promises concerning the nature and conditions of his/her work
- High security measures exist in the work and/or living locations (e.g., opaque windows, boarded up windows, bars on windows, barbed wire, security cameras, etc.)

Poor Mental Health or Abnormal Behavior

- Is fearful, anxious, depressed, submissive, tense, or nervous/paranoid

- Exhibits unusually fearful or anxious behavior after bringing up law enforcement
- Avoids eye contact

Poor Physical Health

- Lacks health care
- Appears malnourished
- Shows signs of physical and/or sexual abuse, physical restraint, confinement, or torture

Lack of Control

- Has few or no personal possessions
- Is not in control of his/her own money, no financial records, or bank account
- Is not in control of his/her own identification documents (ID or passport)
- Is not allowed or able to speak for themselves (a third party may insist on being present and/or translating)

Other

- Claims of just visiting and inability to clarify where he/she is staying/address
- Lack of knowledge of whereabouts and/or do not know what city he/she is in
- Loss of sense of time
- Has numerous inconsistencies in his/her story.[13]

K. Other Organizations

There are other organizations which can provide help as well. Following is a description of just a few of them.

National Center for Missing and Exploited Children

"Established in 1984, the National Center for Missing & Exploited Children® (NCMEC) is the leading nonprofit organization in the U.S. working with law enforcement, families and

13. *Recognizing the Signs,* Polaris Project, http://www.polarisproject.org/human-trafficking/recognizing-the-signs (last accessed Sept. 21, 2015).

other professionals who serve them on issues related to missing and sexually exploited children. As part of its Congressional authorization, NCMEC has created a unique public and private partnership to build a coordinated, national response to the problem of missing and sexually exploited children, establish a missing children hotline and serve as the national clearinghouse for information related to these issues.

Over the last 31 years, the national toll-free hotline, 1-800-THE-LOST® (1-800-843-5678), has handled more than 4 million calls. With help from corporate partners, they have circulated billions of photos of missing children, and their employees have assisted law enforcement in the recovery of more than 208,000 missing children. The organization has trained more than 312,000 law enforcement officers, prosecutors and health care professionals at the Alexandria, Va. headquarters, branch offices and online.

As the Internet has become a primary tool for sexually exploiting children, NCMEC received Congressional authorization to establish the CyberTipline which provides a centralized mechanism for the public and electronic service providers to report suspected child sexual exploitation which can often involve multiple jurisdictions. Since 1998, the CyberTipline has received more than 4.3 million reports of suspected child sexual exploitation, and the Child Victim Identification Program has reviewed more than 139 million child pornography images. Since launching their first safety programs more than two decades ago, they have worked to put in place the policies, educational initiatives and public-private partnerships to prevent the victimization of children.

Among other services, they rapidly deploy members of Team Adam, all retired law enforcement professionals, when children are critically missing to assist in the search and offer free resources. They have access to many public databases and can help with case analysis and mapping. Their forensic artists create age-progressed photos and facial and skull reconstructions, and provide assistance to help the U.S. Marshals track more than 100,000 noncompliant sex offenders. A team of social services professionals provides emotional support to families and victims. Outreach teams work in communities to make child safety a daily concern."[14]

Through April 2015 NCMEC has:

- Received and made available to law enforcement more than 4.3 million reports of suspected child sexual exploitation through the CyberTipline®.
- Analyzed more than 139 million images and videos depicting apparent child pornography through the Child Victim Identification Program®.[15]

Shared Hope International

"Shared Hope International strives to prevent the conditions that foster sex trafficking, restore victims of sex slavery, and bring justice to vulnerable women and children.[16]

Shared Hope International was established to provide hope to the hopeless women Washington State Congresswoman Linda Smith found enslaved in the brothels of Mumbai in 1998. Early efforts targeted the international sex trafficking industry. As they became established leaders in the international movement to end slavery, eyes were opened to the scourge of sex trafficking in the U.S. today. Shared Hope International leads prevention strategies, restoration programs and justice initiatives to combat trafficking in the U.S. and abroad.

The vision is to coordinate a national U.S. network of protection to improve the response to victims of trafficking. The organization's vision is to create a world where every survivor is surrounded by trained professionals, an alert community, just law and policy, knowledgeable service providers and appropriate shelter options."

---

14. National Center for Missing and Exploited Children, http://www.missingkids.com/NCMEC (last visited September 22, 2015).

15. *Id.*

16. Shared Hope International, http://sharedhope.org/about-us/our-mission-and-values/ (last visited September 22, 2015).

Selah Freedom

"Selah Freedom actively confronts the issue of sex trafficking and is being upheld as the statewide model for how to effectively bring solutions to survivors of sex trafficking & exploitation. Selah is a Hebrew word which means to pause, rest, and reflect. Selah gives women in the programs an opportunity to dream again; to discover who it is they were created to be.[17]

In 2009, Selah Freedom's founders discovered the horrifying truth that local children were being bought and sold for sex right here in their own communities.... What began as the grassroots initiative of women from across the country to be a voice for the voiceless, has quickly transformed into a thriving organization with four foundational programs: Awareness, Prevention, Outreach, and Residential.[18] These are all programs designed to assist survivors of varying forms of trafficking.

Selah Freedom closely partners with law enforcement, legislators, and influential leaders to not only shed light on the staggering statistics, but they are working together to change those statistics by changing lives...[19]

Selah Freedom brings Awareness and Education to the community and organizations through their speakers bureau team, CSEC (Commercial Sexual Exploitation of Children) 101 Course, law enforcement training, Global Training & Organizational Development—over 20,000 people annually! The My Life, My Choice Prevention Programming for teen girls ages 12–17 years old, empowers them with the tools they need to avoid being manipulated by a pimp. This survivor-written, survivor-led curriculum has a 90% success rate of preventing girls from being commercially sold. Their Outreach Program is active in the jail system and on the street and provides support groups, case management, and referral services to women currently in 'the life.' Selah Freedom has partnered with law enforcement and

---

17. Selah Freedom, http://www.selahfreedom.com/#!about-selah-freedom/c15yt (last visited Sept. 22, 2015).

18. *Id.*

19. *Id.*

the State Attorney's Office to launch the TYLA Program, a diversionary program for sex trafficking survivors in the legal system. [They] provide Residential Programming for survivors of sex trafficking and education, that includes a personalized educational plan, job placement, trauma therapy, life skills, medical and legal assistance, and holistic restorative care."[20]

On Eagles Wings Ministries (OEWM)

OEWM began as an outreach to women in the adult entertainment industry in 2007. OEWM learned very early on that some of the women employed by the clubs were victims of sex trafficking and were not there by choice. The founder of OEWM, Emily Fitchpatrick, read a report in 2008 written by Shared Hope International about the commercial sexual exploitation of U.S. Children. This report documented evidence of child trafficking in the U.S. It indicated that the average entry age was 13 years old, and indicated 300,000 youth were either being trafficked or were at high risk. The report specified that there was a severe lack of shelter for these children and many of them were being held in juvenile detention centers and treated as criminals. OEWM felt compelled to respond to this need. In 2009, through partnerships with service providers, law enforcement, community members, and Shared Hope International; OEWM launched the OEW Hope House a holistic, residential care program for domestic minor victims of sex trafficking. It was the first faith based home in the U.S. for this population. Since then, the OEWM team has established an effective network of programs under the OEWM umbrella. In addition to the OEW Hope House, OEWM launched Youth 4 Abolition, SHINE, and Fields of Hope.[21]

Switch

"Switch was founded in 2012 after a year of prayer, training and research. 'Switch' signifies what happens when you turn on a light and the darkness flees.

---

20. *Id.*

21. On Eagles Wings Ministries, http://www.oneagleswingsministries.org/#!background/cee5 (last visited Sept. 22, 2015).

Switch was inspired by Isaiah 42:16, which says 'And I will bring the blind by a way that they know not; in paths that they know not will I lead them; I will make darkness light before them, and crooked places straight. These things will I do, and I will not forsake them' (ASV). Switch is run by a community of believers who want to see an end to sex trafficking and sexual exploitation. However, Switch does not discriminate on the basis of religion or position. Switch seeks to serve the trafficked and the exploited as well as the traffickers and the exploiters.

Switch is a ministry that seeks to combat human trafficking and sexual exploitation through awareness, prevention, demand, intervention and restoration. Switch seeks to raise awareness and educate the community about the local problem and its solutions. We do this by educating community agencies, churches, and schools, as well as focusing on decreasing the demand through education and leading community outreaches.

Switch's Mission Statement is: To end human trafficking and sexual exploitation through various community programs focusing on awareness, prevention, demand, intervention, and restoration."[22]

Free the Slaves (FTS) is a global leader in the modern abolition movement.[23] The group focuses on communities who are most susceptible to traffickers based on the lack of education, adequate income, health care, and housing. FTS educates these communities, as well as providing access to legal protection, organizing community groups, and providing basic needs for food, shelter, and safety.[24] In 2014, FTS, working alongside grassroots coalitions, non-governmental organizations, and international aid institutions, freed 2,265 people from slavery, educated over 82,000 villagers on "how to protect their families from traffickers," trained over 1,200 government officials on

22. Switch, http://switchsc.org/about/ (last visited Sept. 15, 2015).

23. Free The Slaves, http://www.freetheslaves.net/about-us/mission-vision-history/ (last visited Sept. 22, 2015).

24. Free The Slaves, http://www.freetheslaves.net/our-model-for-freedom/community-based-causal-model/ (last visited Sept. 22, 2015).

"how to more effectively stop slavery," and arrested 163 traffickers and slaveholders.[25] FTS has concentrated group efforts in countries such as India, Nepal, Congo, Ghana, Haiti, and Brazil. For more information on Free the Slaves, visit www.freetheslaves.net.

Thistle Farms

What began as a residential program has catapulted into a $1,000,000 business which includes a restaurant, bath and body care line, tea and coffee brands, and a studio that creates everything from hand-bound journals to purses. Thistle Farms houses women rescued from trafficking and prostitution in a 2-year program where education, medical care, therapy, and job skills are provided.[26] Located in an 11,000 square foot facility in Nashville, Tennessee, Thistle Farms' social enterprises include the Thistle Stop Café, the Studios Workshop, and Shared Trade Global Marketplace, in addition to their natural bath and body product line.[27] The operations employs 40–50 "residents and graduates of the residential program."[28] All proceeds of the Thistle Stop Café, the paper and sewing studios, and the bath and body care lines "support Thistle Farms and the residential program, Magdalene."[29] For more information, visit www.thistlefarms.org.

Truckers against Trafficking

The world of trafficking and prostitution have a life of their own in the "trucking industry." The women and girls are sadly referred to as "lot lizards." Truckers see the girls, young men and women going from truck to truck offering their "services" and have come to refer disrespectfully to them. In an effort to combat this problem and bring awareness to this issue Truckers

---

25. *Id.*

26. Thistle Farms, http://thistlefarms.org/pages/our-model (last visited Sept. 22, 2015).

27. *Id.*

28. *Id.*

29. Thistle Stop Cafe, http://www.thistlestopcafe.org/menu/ (last visited Sept. 22, 2015).

Against Trafficking came into being. Founded in 2009, Truckers Against Trafficking (TAT) is a group designed to "educate, equip, empower, and mobilize members of the trucking and travel plaza industry to combat domestic sex trafficking."[30] TAT partners with law enforcement to "facilitate" human trafficking investigations.[31] TAT's trucker education program has resulted in increased calls to the Nation Human Trafficking Hotline; over 1,100 calls have been made by truckers alone.[32] Moreover, "over 360 potential cases of human trafficking came from these calls," and law enforcement investigated over 60 percent of them. *Id.* In 2015, TAT also implemented the Freedom Drivers Project, a "first-of-its-kind mobile exhibit that is a premiere tool in educating members of the trucking industry and general public about the realities of domestic sex trafficking."[33] The tractor trailer includes a theatre station, artifacts from previous trafficking cases, and profiles of real truckers who work to combat trafficking.[34] Sponsors of TAT include Ryder, Bridgestone, Freightliner, Volvo, Cummins, and Waltco.[35] For more information on Truckers Against Trafficking, visit www.truckersagainst trafficking.org.

The Deborah House is a Christian faith-based, residential program that offers education and counseling in a post-trauma treatment environment for Romanian girls that have been rescued from human trafficking rings as well as girls who have come from extreme sexual and physical abuse environments.[36] The Deborah House was established in 2002, after founder Lo-

---

30. Truckers Against Trafficking, www.truckersagainsttrafficking.org (last visited Sept. 22, 2015).

31. *Id.*

32. Truckers Against Trafficking, www.truckersagainsttrafficking.org/making-an-impact/ (last visited Sept. 22, 2015).

33. Truckers Against Trafficking, www.truckersagainsttrafficking.org/freedom-drivers-project-homepage/ (last visited Sept. 22, 2015).

34. *Id.*

35. *Id.*

36. Deborah House Center, www.romanianchildrenatrisk.org/deborahhouse.htm (last visited Sept. 22, 2015).

rena Rusovan, happened upon a six-year-old orphaned girl who had been severely sexually and physically abused by strangers.[37] The rescue was exceptionally difficult, as the "lack of child abuse laws, cultural indifference, and disinterested village police" did little to aid in the effort.[38] Despite the efforts of Rusovan, the girl was classified as "retarded" and placed in a government home.[39] Only five full-time caregivers tended to over 250 children.[40] Thus, the Deborah House was founded with the aid of Mission Link International and its American partner, Missio International.[41] Girls at the house undergo intense therapy and social skills counseling, and, when ready, are integrated back into school.[42] For more information about the Deborah House, visit www.romanianchildrenatrisk.org/deborahhouse.htm.

L. Concluding Observations

We might also remember that while the majority of the victims of sex trafficking are women and girls, there are many male and transgender victims as well. We cannot overlook this reality in attempting to address the evils of human slavery.

It is likely that the reader of this work will, fortunately, not ever be subjected to being trafficked. Given the widespread nature of the problem, however, it is very possible that the reader will encounter a victim. In that instance we must remember that we are our brother's (and sister's) keeper. And should we be tempted to reach a moral judgment about the behavior of the prostitute, we need to remember that he or she is likely a victim. Even if the behavior of the prostitute appears to be voluntary, it might do well to recall the words of an authority who

---

37. *Id.*
38. *Id.*
39. *Id.*
40. *Id.*
41. *Id.*
42. *Id.*

addressed this subject two thousand years ago: "Let he who is without sin cast the first stone."[43]

M. For Further Thought

1. Assume that you are an attorney in private practice, and that you come in contact with a person who you suspect might be a trafficking victim. Outline what you might say and do in this circumstance. Would it make any difference in your approach if the person is a client or potential client, as opposed to a witness or someone with whom you casually come in contact? Consider your obligations of confidentiality under Rule 1.6 of the American Bar Association Model Rules of Professional Conduct. Consider exceptions which permit revealing information that otherwise would have to be kept confidential.
2. Assume that you are asked to speak before a group regarding human trafficking. What information and advice would you give to the members of the group? Would your presentation differ, if at all, to groups consisting of middle school students, high school students, college students, business leaders, other attorneys or law students, or church groups? In what way(s)? Why?
3. Now that you have completed this study of human trafficking, how has your understanding of human trafficking changed, if at all, from the time you began this study?
4. Were you surprised to learn of the extent and the legacy of Native American slavery in this country? Why do you think this aspect of slavery and trafficking has gone undernoticed?
5. Does addressing the horrors of human trafficking include addressing the lingering effects of Native slavery? How might this process begin?

43. The exact wording of this quote varies among the various editions of the Bible, *but see John* 8:8, *Holy Bible*, New International Version (2011).

Index